# Domestic Abuse Law in Scotland



**Andrew M Cubie**
The Hon Lord Cubie

**Shona Gilroy**
Sheriff of Glasgow and Strathkelvin in Glasgow

**Diana McConnell**
Summary Sheriff of Glasgow and Strathkelvin in Glasgow

Bloomsbury Professional

LONDON • DUBLIN • EDINBURGH • NEW YORK • NEW DELHI • SYDNEY

**BLOOMSBURY PROFESSIONAL**

**Bloomsbury Publishing Plc,** 50 Bedford Square, London, WC1B 3DP, UK
**Bloomsbury Publishing Inc,** 1359 Broadway, New York, 10018, USA
**Bloomsbury Publishing Ireland,** 29 Earlsfort Terrace, Dublin 2, D02 AY28, Ireland

BLOOMSBURY and the Diana logo are trademarks of Bloomsbury Publishing Plc

First published in Great Britain 2025

Reprinted 2026

1



**British Library Cataloguing-in-Publication Data**

A catalogue record for this book is available from the British Library.

| ISBN: | PB: | 978-1-52652-977-0 |
| --- | --- | --- |
| | Epdf: | 978-1-52652-979-4 |
| | Epub: | 978-1-52652-978-7 |

Typeset by Evolution Design and Digital Ltd (Kent)
Printed in Great Britain by TJ Books, Padstow, Cornwall

FSC www.fsc.org MIX Paper | Supporting responsible forestry FSC® C013056

For product safety related questions contact productsafety@bloomsbury.com

# Domestic Abuse Law in Scotland

# Preface

On 26 August 2025, the High Court of Justiciary dealt with a crown appeal against sentence in the case of *HM Advocate v Fletcher* ([2025] HCJAC 41); the accused had faced charges under s 38 of the Criminal Justice and Licensing (Scotland) Act 2010 and s 1 of the Domestic Abuse (Scotland) Act 2018 which the court described as 'various forms of domestic abuse'. In giving the opinion of the court, the Lord Justice Clerk (Beckett) said at paragraph [26]:

> 'It is important to consider the effect of domestic offending by examining it as a whole ... Violence may be the most obvious and visible form of domestic abuse, but it is not necessarily the most serious. There is a growing awareness of the harm domestic abuse causes, and it is well understood that it extends beyond physical injuries. There is some force in the Crown's submission that the introduction of DASA section 1 signals a recognition of the insidious, varied, sometimes subtle, but often very damaging, forms domestic abuse can take.'

This book had its origins well before the court's decision, but seeks to reflect the same growing awareness of the separate and distinct aspects of domestic offending in the Scottish criminal context, tracing the development of measures to deal with such behaviour, culminating in, but not limited to the Domestic Abuse (Scotland) Act 2018 and most recently reflected in the provisions of the Bail and Release from Custody (Scotland) Act 2023 where the distinct area of domestic abuse was addressed, in terms, in relation to bail considerations. We also aim to show how the 2018 Act has operated in practice and the development of the law and practice as it affects such offending, in terms of evidence, vulnerable witnesses and sentencing.

We have been assisted and supported by many people. Paula O'Connell at Bloomsbury was patient, supportive and constructive. Particular thanks are due to Paul Crick for the substantial task of final copy editing, achieved quickly and thoroughly. And we are grateful to family and colleagues alike for understanding when attention to the book precluded other activities. Any errors in the text are our responsibility. We have aimed to state the law as at 1 July 2025.

*Andrew M Cubie*
*Shona Gilroy*
*Diana McConnell*
*September 2025*

# Contents

# Table of Statutes

*[All references are to paragraph number]*

# Table of Statutory Instruments

[*All references are to paragraph numbers*]

# Table of Cases

*[All references are to paragraph number]*

**M**

**W**



**Y**

*Chapter 1*

# Domestic Abuse: The Modern Context

## THE MODERN CONTEXT

**1.01** In the last 30 years, work undertaken largely by grassroots third sector women's organisations in Scotland to raise awareness of the scope, scale and impact of domestic abuse has led to significant changes in policy and law. Recognition of domestic abuse as a serious, societal ill has led to policies being embedded across a range of sectors, including health, housing, social work and education, for example, 'Responding to Domestic Abuse – Guidelines for Health Workers in NHS Scotland'[1] to assist healthcare workers in all NHS settings to respond appropriately to victims of domestic abuse.

## PREVALENCE: THE SCALE OF THE PROBLEM

**1.02** The Scottish Government (the SG) and statutory partners gather a range of data to understand the prevalence and trends over time of domestic abuse in Scotland. The latest statistics are presented briefly below.

**1.03** In 2023/24, Police Scotland recorded 63,867 incidents of domestic abuse, an increase of 3 per cent on the previous year.[2] This figure has been fairly constant over the last decade or so, ranging from 58,104 in 2015/16, to a peak in 2020/21 (the first year of the Covid lockdown) of 65,251.

**1.04** Statistics published by the prosecution service, the Crown Office and Procurator Fiscal Scotland (COPFS), reveal a fairly constant picture of the charges reported to COPFS with a domestic abuse identifier. In 2023/24, 30,100 such charges were reported. The proportion of charges with a domestic abuse identifier being prosecuted has increased over recent years and remains consistently high. In the same period, an initial decision to proceed to court was made in 93 per cent of charges reported.[3]

1 www.gov.scot/publications/responding-domestic-abuse-guidelines-health-care-workers-nhsscotland/pages/0/ [accessed 28 July 2025].

2 Domestic abuse: statistics recorded by the police in Scotland, 2023 to 2024: available at www.gov.scot/publications/domestic-abuse-statistics-recorded-police-scotland-2023-24/pages/incidents-of-domestic-abuse/ [accessed 28 July 2025].

3 Domestic Abuse and Stalking charges in Scotland, 2023-24: available at www.copfs.gov.uk/about-copfs/news/domestic-abuse-and-stalking-charges-in-scotland-2023-24/ [accessed 28 July 2025].

**1.05** It should be borne in mind that the domestic abuse recorded by the police does not reveal the true incidence of all domestic abuse in Scotland, as not all incidents are reported to police. Accordingly, the true extent of the problem remains unknown.

## A GENDERED CRIME?

**1.06** In the 2023/24 domestic abuse statistics, where the sex of the victim was recorded by the police, 81 per cent of incidents involved a male perpetrator and female victim. (Again, this figure has remained constant in recent years.) Of the remaining incidents, 15 per cent involved a female perpetrator and a male victim; in 3 per cent of incidents, where it was recorded, the victim and suspected perpetrator were noted as being the same sex.

**1.07** Thus, while anyone can experience domestic abuse, women are much more likely to be victims, regardless of race, ethnicity or religion, sexuality, or disability, while men are statistically more likely to be the perpetrator.

**1.08** In 2023/24, 50 per cent of domestic abuse incidents – where the relationship between the victim and suspected perpetrator was known – were between ex-partners. Just under half of incidents (49 per cent) involved current partners, defined as spouse/civil partner, partner and cohabitee. For the remaining 1 per cent of incidents the relationship was recorded as 'other'.

**1.09** The statistics confirm that the scale and scope of domestic abuse is a significant problem in Scotland. It confirms, too, that domestic abuse is most often carried out by men against women. This is a salient fact underpinning a great deal of consequential work and resource allocation. Recognition of domestic abuse prevalence across and as between the sexes allows the development of services sensitive to the differing needs of the individuals affected by it.

> 'Understanding gender as the central factor in domestic abuse enables us to develop services which are sensitive to the different needs of individuals affected by domestic abuse. It highlights that as men and women have differing needs they require different services and service approaches … Approaches which do not recognise the influence of gender in everyday experiences fail both men and women. Assumptions that experiences of men and women are equivalent will not achieve equality of outcome. Failure to acknowledge the influence of gender in perpetration of abuse, as well as the experience of abuse, presents a barrier to eliminating or reducing domestic abuse in our society.'[4]

4 C McFeely, N Whiting, N Lombard, O Brooks, M Burman, M McGowan, 'Domestic Abuse and Gender Inequality:
An overview of the current debate' (Centre for Research on Families and Relationships, Briefing 69, August 2013, available at: https://era.ed.ac.uk/bitstream/handle/1842/8769/briefing-69.pdf?sequence=1&isAllowed=y [accessed 28 July 2025]).

## CRIMINAL JUSTICE – THE CURRENT STRATEGY

**1.10** The SG's commitment to addressing violence against women and girls (VAWG) is to be found in its Equally Safe strategy.[5] The strategy was developed in partnership with CoSLA and public sector non-governmental partners, including Scottish Women's Aid, Rape Crisis Scotland, Police Scotland, and NHS Health Scotland. The strategy and associated delivery plan is aimed at 'preventing and eradicating violence against women and girls and the underlying attitudes and systems that perpetuate it.' Initially published in 2014, its latest iteration was released in 2023. It outlines a collaborative approach, with a vision of 'a strong and flourishing Scotland where all individuals are equally safe and respected, and where women and girls live free from all forms of violence, abuse and exploitation – and the attitudes that help perpetuate it'. The ambition is 'to stop it occurring in the first place, build the capability and capacity of support services, and strengthen the justice response to victims and perpetrators.'

**1.11** The strategy is explicit that the definition of VAWG includes domestic abuse/coercive controlling behaviours, or the threat thereof.

## DOMESTIC ABUSE: WHAT CONDUCT IS ENGAGED?

**1.12** Domestic abuse can involve a range of behaviours. It is conduct which breaches the trust fundamental to intimate relationships. It often takes place behind closed doors, in the home, rendering what ought to be a safe and secure place into a place of terror and tyranny. Increasingly, it is conducted online using social media and electronic communications, or these media are used to reinforce the abuse and provide a further means of control of victims of abuse.[6]

**1.13** In recent times, there has been a growing awareness that domestic abuse can involve psychological as well as, or instead of, physical abuse. The concept of coercive control is now recognised in Scots law, whereby one partner can coercively control the other, whether emotionally or financially.

5 The 2023 Refresh of the strategy: available at www.gov.scot/policies/violence-against-women-and-girls/ [accessed 28 July 2025].

6 The use of technology 'to directly abuse, track or monitor covertly or propagate abusive content, including with advances in Artificial Intelligence (AI) and AI generated images and videos (often known as "deep fakes") is now widely accessible and available'. (Equally Safe (2023)).

## A BRIEF HISTORY: DEVELOPMENT OF THE MODERN SCOTTISH RESPONSE TO DOMESTIC ABUSE

**1.14** This book cannot document all of the influences and landmarks on the journey to develop the modern approach to domestic abuse in Scotland. However, there are some key events it is appropriate to recognise.

**1.15** The work in Scotland over this period to raise awareness of domestic abuse is exemplified by the Zero Tolerance campaign of the 1990s, devised to raise public and political awareness of domestic abuse and work to prevent all forms of violence against women and girls. This groundbreaking public campaign[7] of posters and adverts raised public awareness about domestic abuse against women and children, displaying images of women and children in ordinary, familiar settings, coupled with stark messages and statistics about violence against women.

**1.16** In 1998, the then Scottish Office formed the Scottish Partnership on Domestic Violence, chaired by The Right Honourable Lady Smith KC to identify measures to tackle domestic violence.

**1.17** Membership of the Scottish Partnership on Domestic Violence comprised the key criminal justice organisations and third sector partners. The Partnership quickly recognised the importance of terminology and that discussion of domestic *violence* did not adequately capture the wide-ranging nature of the abuse perpetrated. The Partnership reported to the then Scottish Executive in 2000, proposing:

- a National Strategy for Addressing Domestic Abuse in Scotland;[8]
- an agreed definition of domestic abuse to be adopted by criminal justice partners and relevant agencies to inform practice, policy and service development, and to raise awareness of the nature of domestic abuse;

**1.18** The publication in 2000 of the Strategy identified the following aims:

- prevention – active prevention of domestic abuse of both women and children;
- protection – appropriate legal protection for women or children who experience domestic abuse; and
- provision – adequate provision of support services for women/children.

7 www.zerotolerance.org.uk/about-our-prevention-campaign/ [accessed 28 July 2025].
8 Official Report, 2 September 1999:

**1.19** Momentum gathered, with increasing recognition of the impact of domestic abuse on individuals and society. This period saw development of steps to tackle domestic abuse both in a domestic context and via international instruments. It ran in conjunction with an increased understanding of the needs of victims generally and recognition that a more systemic approach was required to support vulnerable victims and witnesses.

**1.20** A programme of work was set in motion which led to a number of legislative changes, supported by policy developments to improve the investigation and prosecution of domestic abuse, and to develop protections for victims, together with improved access to justice. A brief description of key legislative aspects follows below, expanded upon in later chapters.

## DEVELOPMENT OF LEGISLATION ADDRESSING DOMESTIC ABUSE

**1.21** New laws have been introduced with the aim of boosting public confidence and encouraging reporting of domestic abuse:

- statutory aggravation of an offence as being motivated by domestic abuse (see **Chapter 6**).
- the Criminal Justice and Licensing (Scotland) Act 2010, which criminalised stalking (see **Chapter 5**);
- The Victims and Witnesses (Scotland) Act 2014 (building upon the Vulnerable Witnesses (Scotland) Act 2004), which introduced greater protective measures for victims giving evidence (see **Chapter 8**). It was amended in 2018 to provide that complainers in cases involving domestic abuse are entitled to special measures *by default*;
- increased use of evidence on commission following the recommendation of the Evidence and Procedure Review (see **Chapter 8**);
- the Abusive Behaviour and Sexual Harm (Scotland) Act 2016, which criminalised intimate image abuse or so-called 'revenge pornography' (see **Chapter 5**);
- a prohibition on accused persons personally conducting their defence in domestic abuse cases (see **Chapter 8**);
- non-harassment orders require to be considered at sentencing (see **Chapter 9**); and
- the Domestic Abuse (Scotland) Act 2018 (**Chapter 5**), which introduced a specific offence of domestic abuse, placing Scotland on the global map with a gold standard in tackling intimate, gendered abuse.

**1.22** As compared to common law offences, statutory aggravations and offences are capable of being tracked and measured within the criminal justice system, allowing better statistical analysis and identification of trends. Prosecutors will generally proceed with a statutory offence over a common law one, where either is applicable.

## DEVELOPMENT OF CRIMINAL JUSTICE POLICIES ADDRESSING DOMESTIC ABUSE

**1.23** A range of policy commitments and service responses have been established across criminal justice partners, for example:

- The joint protocol between police and prosecution, which is kept under review – the latest iteration is its sixth edition (May 2023).[9] The definition of domestic abuse used by Police Scotland, as per the Joint Protocol between Police Scotland and COPFS, is:

  > 'any form of physical, verbal, sexual, psychological or financial abuse which might amount to criminal conduct and which takes place within the context of a relationship. The relationship will be between partners (married, cohabiting, civil partnership or otherwise) or ex-partners. The abuse can be committed in the home or elsewhere, including online.'

- Police Scotland's ten-year policing strategy identifies domestic incidents as 'the most resource-intensive type of incident attended by local police officers' and notes that domestic crimes account for 26 per cent of all violent crime in Scotland.[10]
- Publication of the Victims' Code for Scotland.[11]
- Establishment of COPFS Victim Information and Advice service (VIA) (see **Chapter 2**).
- Commencement of the Summary Case Management Scheme (SCMS) by the Scottish Courts and Tribunal Service (SCTS), to encourage early disclosure of evidence and early engagement with the Crown to maximise system efficiency, with the benefit to victims and witnesses of early resolution of cases/agreement of evidence. The operation of the scheme is detailed in Practise Note No 1 2025.[12]

9 www.copfs.gov.uk/media/xjtd4i4p/joint-domestic-abuse-protocol.pdf [last accessed 28 July 2025].

10 https://consult.scotland.police.uk/consultation/2026/results/policing-2026---consultation-analysis-report.pdf [last accessed 28 July 2025].

11 www.copfs.gov.uk/publications/victims-code-for-scotland/ [last accessed 28 July 2025].

12 Practise Note – https://www.judicialhub.com/mod/resource/view.php?id=19338 [.

- Specialist domestic abuse training for prosecutors and the Scottish judiciary.
- Multi-Agency Risk Assessment Conferences (Marac) coordinate the multi-agency response to domestic abuse across Scotland, addressing risk for domestic abuse victims.[13]

## IMPACT OF LAW, POLICY AND PRACTICE ACROSS THE CRIMINAL JUSTICE SYSTEM

**1.24** Scotland's track record in tackling domestic abuse has been identified as an exemplar.[14] Following the publication of the national strategy to address domestic abuse in 2000 (above at **1.18**), the response subsequently extended to cover all aspects of violence against women and girls, leading to the SG's Equally Safe strategy and the introduction of the Domestic Abuse (Scotland) Act 2018 (DASA 2018).

**1.25** The Domestic Abuse (Scotland) Act 2018 (DASA 2018) came into force on 1 April 2019. This Act created a new statutory offence of engaging in a course of behaviour which is abusive of a partner or ex-partner. DASA 2018 creates a specific statutory offence of domestic abuse and makes a number of associated changes to criminal procedure, evidence and sentencing in domestic abuse cases.

**1.26** The Act is intended to improve how the justice system responds to domestic abuse. The offence of 'abuse of a partner or ex-partner' is intended to ensure that the criminal law reflects that domestic abuse can often be a course of conduct which takes place over a sustained period of time, and that a course of abusive behaviour can consist of both physical violence and threats which could have been prosecuted under previously existing laws and psychological and emotional abuse which were much more difficult to prosecute under previously existing laws. (See **Chapter 5**)

**1.27** By enabling abuse of various types which takes place over a period of time to be prosecuted as a single course of conduct within a new criminal offence of domestic abuse, the criminal law better reflects how victims actually experience such abuse. It ensures that a course of conduct of entirely non-physical abuse of a person's partner or ex-partner is criminalised.

13 https://safelives.org.uk/about-domestic-abuse/domestic-abuse-response-in-the-uk/what-is-a-marac/ [last accessed 15 September 2025].

14 N Lombard and N Whiting, 'What's in a name? The Scottish government, feminism and the gendered framing of domestic abuse', in Lombard and Whiting (Eds), *The Routledge Book of Gender and Violence* (Routledge, 2017).

**1.28** Along with the introduction of the new domestic abuse offence, the Act provided for a statutory sentencing aggravation intended to reflect the harm caused to children by domestic abuse. The aggravation can be applied where:

- the perpetrator uses a child in committing the offence;
- the perpetrator directs behaviour at a child in committing the offence;
- the child sees, hears or is present when the abuse is taking place; or
- a child is likely to be adversely affected by the perpetrator's behaviour.

Where the aggravation is proven, the court is required to take account of this in sentencing the offender and state how the sentence differed from that which the court would otherwise have imposed. This ensures that the harm caused to children by the abuse of their parent or carer is formally recognised and recorded.

**1.29** The Act also provides for a number of associated reforms to criminal procedure, evidence and sentencing. These reforms are intended to reduce the possibility of an accused person using the processes of the justice system to further exert control and influence over the complainer and help to minimise the trauma for the complainer while ensuring the proper administration of justice is achieved (as set out in the Policy Memorandum[15]). The reforms include prohibiting the accused from personally conducting their own defence or precognition of the complainer and providing for a presumption that the court shall impose a non-harassment order on a person convicted of domestic abuse unless, in the particular case, the court concludes such an order is not necessary to protect the victim.

**1.30** The Scottish Crime and Justice Survey (SCJS)[16] data from 2019/20 reveals that psychological abuse is more commonly experienced than physical abuse. The proportion of respondents who said they had experienced at least one incident of psychological abuse since the age of 16 (14.6%) was higher than those reporting having experienced at least one incident of physical abuse (10.7%). Both psychological and physical abuse was experienced by 8.8 per cent of respondents. Victims were also more likely to have experienced psychological abuse than physical abuse in the 12 months prior to interview (2.9% compared to 1.3%). Women were more likely to experience psychological abuse than men (3.4% and 2.4% respectively). However, the proportion who

15 www.parliament.scot/-/media/files/legislation/bills/previous-bills/domestic-abuse-bill/introduced/policy-memorandum-domestic-abuse-scotland-bill.pdf [last accessed 28 July 2025].

16 www.gov.scot/publications/scottish-crime-justice-survey-2019-20-main-findings/ [last accessed 28 July 2025].

experienced physical abuse did not vary between women and men (1.5% and 1.0% respectively).

**1.31** In terms of a course of behaviour, the SCJS shows that partner abuse is often experienced on multiple occasions. Around two-thirds (67%) of those who experienced an incident of partner abuse in the 12 months prior to interview also experienced at least one incident prior to this period. Excluding those who responded 'don't know/can't remember' or who did not wish to answer, around three in five respondents (59%) had experienced more than one incident.

**1.32** Another key aspect of the Act is its recognition of the harm caused to children by domestic abuse. The SCJS shows that children were living in the household when a partner abuse incident took place in around a third of incidents (32%). In the majority of these cases (71%) the child was present in the most recent incident.

**1.33** In the 2022 report by the Scottish Centre for Crime and Justice Research on DASA 2018 and the Criminal Justice System,[17] the authors recognised:

> 'Scotland has taken a proactive approach in striving to provide a victim centred criminal justice system evident in the introduction of special protective measures available for court appearances through the Victims and Witnesses (Scotland) Act 2014; and a positive policing and prosecution approach with an emphasis on arrest and enhanced evidence gathering, supporting prosecution. There has also been a growing focus on victims' rights and a recognition that the system, at the very least, needs to treat victims with respect (Edwards, 2020). The recently refreshed Victims' Code for Scotland states that 'victims' interests remain at the heart of our criminal justice system', that victims should feel confident 'their voices will be heard' and that they will be 'treated with dignity and respect' (Scottish Government, 2018b; modified 2020).

**1.34** The report was part of the Reporting Requirement (s 14) of the Domestic Abuse (Scotland) Act 2018 whereby an obligation was imposed for the three years subsequent to commencement of the Act to report on the experience of witnesses (including child witnesses) at court, with a view to identifying improvements to the justice system that could improve victims' experiences. A number of recommendations are listed in the report, which may be of interest to practitioners in this field. Emerging, broad themes identified needs around training for criminal justice partners and improved

17 www.sccjr.ac.uk/wp-content/uploads/2022/08/Domestic-Abuse-Scotland-Act-2018-and-the-Criminal-Justice-System.pdf [last accessed 28 July 2025].

communication with victims. The need for trauma-informed practices for professionals was emphasised, an area which has become a focus in the training of many practitioners and the Scottish judiciary.

**1.35** A further piece of research[18] reporting on the experiences of victims and witnesses since the introduction of DASA 2018 contributed to the programme of work to meet the ministerial three-year reporting requirement of DASA 2018. It concluded that whilst the new law better reflected how adult victims experienced domestic abuse, a number of those interviewed considered its provisions were under-utilised.

**1.36** In a report published by HM Inspectorate of Constabulary on 12 January 2023, the policing response to domestic abuse in Scotland was considered.[19] The most recent figures are reported above, but those for 2022/23 were similar. It was noted that homicide figures, from the same period, show that 56 per cent of women killed died at the hands of a partner or ex-partner. It is accepted that a victim of domestic abuse is most at danger at the point they leave or attempt to leave the relationship. Danger and fear can be a major factor. Of women killed by a partner or former partner in England, Wales and Northern Ireland, 41% per cent had left or taken steps to leave. Of these, 81 per cent were killed in their own home (or one shared with the perpetrator). [20]

**1.37** The HMICS report acknowledges that it is widely accepted that domestic abuse is under-reported, with significant social, economic and cultural barriers persisting. It made 14 recommendations including:

- the need to ensure there is an adequate cadre of suitably trained officers; and
- the prioritisation of a robust system for progressing domestic abuse inquiries which will improve the service to victims.

**1.38** Most recently, in addition to maintaining priority in the 'traditional' management of domestic abuse cases, the judiciary and the SCTS have also explored the potential for domestic abuse cases to be managed differently, enhancing efficiency whilst developing a more trauma-informed approach.

**1.39** Building on the piloting of new approaches to managing summary criminal cases, SCTS have now launched a nationwide roll-out of the Summary

18 Domestic Abuse Court Experiences Research: the perspectives of victims and witnesses in Scotland: available at www.gov.scot/publications/domestic-abuse-court-experiences-research-perspectives-victims-witnesses-scotland/ [last accessed 28 July 2025].

19 www.hmics.scot/publications/hmics-thematic-review-of-domestic-abuse-phase-1/ [last accessed 28 July 2025].

20 Femicide Census 2020; available at www.femicidecensus.org/wp-content/uploads/2022/02/010998-2020-Femicide-Report_V2.pdf [accessed 28 July 2025].

Case Management scheme [21] which seeks to reduce the number of unnecessary hearings through facilitating early disclosure of evidence and early judicial case management. Key evidence will be available to be released to the defence prior to or at the first calling in all domestic abuse cases. In all other cases, specified disclosure material can be requested where it is considered that such early disclosure may make a material difference to a plea or the early resolution of issues. The differentiation of domestic abuse cases has been maintained in recognition of their particular impact and the desire for them to be prioritised.

**1.40** The automatic provision of key evidence in domestic abuse cases should put the defence in a significantly different position from the early stage of the case. It will allow the defence to engage more meaningfully with the Crown on plea resolution, failing which, on the agreement of evidence. This should lead to system efficiencies and help reduce the delays at court which victims of domestic abuse describe as being so distressing.

## INTERNATIONAL INSTRUMENTS AND OBLIGATIONS

**1.41** It is appropriate to recognise that the work in Scotland is not in isolation, but has a foundation in wider, international standards and obligations relevant to both Scotland and the UK. There are a number of international treaties which underpin the response of the criminal justice system in Scotland and set standards as to how victims of, or witnesses to, domestic abuse – or indeed the perpetrator – must be treated to observe their rights. The following offers a brief overview of relevant treaty obligations. (See the Scottish Law Commission paper on civil remedies for domestic abuse[22] for further details.)

**1.42** The two key instruments which create obligations on States as to how they must tackle domestic abuse are:

- the European Convention on Human Rights[23] (ECHR); and
- the Council of Europe Convention on Preventing and Combating Violence Against Women and Domestic Violence (known as 'the Istanbul Convention')[24].

21 www.scotcourts.gov.uk/media/akeboe15/all-scotland-summary-case-management-pn.pdf [last accessed 15 SEptember 2025].

22 Discussion_Paper_on_Civil_Remedies_for_Domestic_Abuse_(DP_No.178) available at: www.scotlawcom.gov.uk/files/9017/2959/8708/Discussion_Paper_on_Civil_Remedies_for_Domestic_Abuse_DP_No._178.vvx.pdf [accessed 28 July 2025].

23 European Convention on Human Rights available at: /www.echr.coe.int/documents/d/echr/convention_ENG [accessed 28 July 2025].

24 Council of Europe Convention on preventing and combating violence against women and domestic violence (CETS No 210) www.coe.int/en/web/istanbul-convention/text-of-the-convention) [accessed 28 July 2025].

**1.43** In addition, two further treaties are relevant to how Scotland and the UK approach domestic abuse:

- the United Nations Convention on the Elimination of all forms of Discrimination Against Women[25] (CEDAW); and
- the United Nations Convention on the Rights of the Child[26] (UNCRC).

**1.44** Whilst the ECHR has been incorporated into UK domestic law, the Istanbul Convention and CEDAW have not. The Scottish Parliament and the Scottish Government must observe the obligations recognised under the ECHR and the courts must interpret issues in a way which affords those rights. However, where matters are devolved, the SG and Holyrood may elect to implement international obligations differently from the UK Government and Westminster. As international relations are a reserved matter in terms of the devolution settlements under the Scotland Act 1988, the SG cannot sign, ratify or amend international treaties.

**1.45** The Scottish Parliament recently approved legislation which partially incorporates the UNCRC into Scots law. The UNCRC (Incorporation (Scotland) Act 2024[27] came into force on 16 July 2024, and any legislation now passed by the Scottish Parliament must comply with it.

## European Convention on Human Rights

**1.46** The UK enacted the Human Rights Act 1998, which incorporates 'convention rights' in the ECHR into UK law. This requires public bodies, including the courts and the Scottish Parliament to act compatibly with the ECHR. Although the text of the ECHR contains no direct reference to domestic abuse, the decisions of the European Court of Human Rights (ECtHR) make clear that domestic abuse attracts human rights protections. Several articles of the ECHR are relevant to consideration of domestic abuse:

- *Articles 2 and 3*

  These articles concern physical and mental integrity, covering the right to life, and the prohibition of torture, and of inhuman and degrading treatment. Both Articles impose a duty on the State to refrain from killing

25 Convention on the Elimination of All Forms of Discrimination against Women New York available at: www.ohchr.org/en/instruments-mechanisms/instruments/convention-elimination-all-forms-discrimination-against-women [accessed 28 July 2025].

26 UN Convention On The Rights Of The Child available at: www.unicef.org.uk/what-we-do/un-convention-child-rights/ [accessed 28 July 2025].

27 www.legislation.gov.uk/asp/2024/1#:~:text=on%20this%20site.-,United%20Nations%20Convention%20on%20the%20Rights%20of%20the%20Child%20(Incorporation,child%20prostitution%20and%20child%20pornography [last accessed 15 September 2025].

(except in limited circumstances) and from inflicting torture or inhuman or degrading treatment in any circumstances. States also have a duty to prevent the killing or torture and inhuman and degrading treatment of citizens where this is done by a third party. Case law from ECtHR is clear that this encompasses domestic abuse.

- *Article 6*

  This article protects the right to a fair trial, ensuring the rights of an accused person in the criminal justice system. Many court orders, including conditions of bail, place restrictions on perpetrators – including barring them from their own homes. Such conditions must take account of the perpetrator's Article 6 rights.

- *Article 8*

  This article constitutes the right to a private and family life and so has wide implications in regard to domestic abuse. It encompasses the right to physical and mental integrity, to family life and the right to privacy of correspondence. Notably, Article 8 is a qualified right and the State can balance it against the public interest and the rights of others, meaning it may be legitimately interfered with if such interference is necessary and proportionate to the legitimate aim being pursued. That may of course involve securing and protecting the Article 8 rights of the complainer.

- *Article 1 of protocol 1*

  This article protects certain property rights and therefore has application in respect of consideration of special conditions of bail or non-harassment orders which may involve excluding a perpetrator from their home. Property rights are not absolute and can be interfered with where there is a public interest in doing so and it is necessary and proportionate to the legitimate aim being pursued. That may include securing the Article 2 and 3 rights of the complainer.[28]

**1.47** In an article in the European Human Rights Law Review,[29] Lena Retsina notes that the recent case of *AE v Bulgaria*[30] demonstrates that:

> 'the Court through its jurisprudence has managed to develop clear principles concerning the protection of the victims of domestic violence as victims of human rights violations. The Court reaffirmed that domestic violence is no longer a private matter and that States have a positive obligation to implement adequate and effective legislation in order to protect the victims.'

28 Re Articles 2 and 3 see *Osman v United Kingdom (23452/94)* (1998) (87/1997/871/1083), para 116; *Kontrova v Slovakia* (2007) (7510/04); *Talpis v Italy* (2017) (41237/14).

29 Lena Retsinia, 'AE v Bulgaria' (Case Comment) [2023] 5 EHRLR, 516–18.

30 *AE v Bulgaria* (53891/20) 23 May 2023.

## The Council of Europe Convention on Preventing and Combating Violence Against Women and Domestic Violence: the Istanbul Convention

**1.48** The Istanbul Convention sets out obligations on States designed to facilitate the eradication of violence against women. The UK signed the Convention in 2012 and ratified it in 2022 (subject to certain reservations) The treaty sets out responses to domestic abuse, covering both criminal and civil law, procedure, awareness raising and substantive policy requirements. However, the Istanbul Convention has not been incorporated into the domestic law of the UK. Therefore, individuals cannot bring claims based on the Convention in court, and public authorities do not have a specific statutory duty to comply with it. However, the UK's ratification of the treaty means that it has committed to compliance (subject to the reservations (see above)).

**1.49** The Istanbul Convention focuses on violence against women generally, and domestic violence specifically. It covers criminal law, the treatment of both witnesses and perpetrators, and the delivery of victim support services. The following general principles form the basis for action:

(a) '[To] protect women against all forms of violence and prevent, prosecute and eliminate violence against women and domestic violence.'

(b) '[To] contribute to the elimination of all forms of discrimination against women and promote substantive equality between women and men, including by empowering women.'

(c) '[To] design a comprehensive framework, policies, and measures for the protection of and assistance to all victims of violence against women and domestic violence.'

(d) '[To] promote international co-operation with a view to eliminating violence against women and domestic violence.

(e) '[To] provide support and assistance to organisations and law enforcement agencies to effectively co-operate in order to adopt an integrated approach to eliminating violence against women and domestic violence.

## The United Nations Convention on the Rights of the Child

**1.50** The United Nations Convention on the Rights of the Child ('UNCRC') was adopted by the General Assembly of the United Nations on 20 November 1989 and came into force on 2 September 1990. The UK signed the UNCRC in 1990 and ratified it in 1991, subject to certain reservations. The Scottish Parliament has partially enacted the UNCRC (insofar as it has legislative competence) in the UNCRC (Incorporation (Scotland) Act 2024. As at 16 July 2024 all legislation passed by the Scottish Parliament must comply with the UNCRC.

**1.51** The treaty sets out the civil, political, economic, social and cultural rights held by children. Several of the rights have relevance to domestic abuse:

- Article 3 requires that, in all actions concerning children, the best interests of the child must be a primary consideration.
- Article 12 obliges States to take into account the views of a child in matters concerning them.
- Article 16 provides that the child shall have a right to private and family life.
- Article 19 requires States to protect children from violence, abuse and neglect, including mental abuse or injury.

**1.52** Articles 3 and Article 16 reflect the duties under Article 8 of the ECHR. Notably, both the UNCRC and the ECHR consider that the best interests of the child can eclipse the rights of either parent, and may also override the views of the child, if the view expressed by them is held to be contrary to their best interests. Under the UNCRC, the best interests of the child is a primary consideration in any action or decision concerning that child. This would extend to decisions around special conditions of bail (effectively removing a perpetrator from the family home or preventing contact). It may extend to sentencing decisions. Accordingly, observance of this requirement may involve the court being provided with the views of a child at relevant stages of the criminal justice process. Detailed guidance on the background to the UNCRC Act and Statutory Guidance for public authorities on acting in accordance with its principles is published by the SG.[31]

**1.53** It is widely established that domestic abuse affects the whole family. As a consequence, responses to abuse will also affect the whole family, including children, especially where the response involves changes to living arrangements or child contact. It is recognised too that witnessing domestic abuse can have a harmful, traumatic effect on children meaning Article 19 could be engaged. [32]

31 www.legislation.gov.uk/asp/2024/1#:~:text=on%20this%20site.-,United%20Nations%20Convention%20on%20the%20Rights%20of%20the%20Child%20(Incorporation,child%20prostitution%20and%20child%20pornography [last accessed 15 September 2025].

32 F Morrison and C Houghton 'Children's human rights in the contexts of domestic abuse and COVID-19', (2023) 27(9-10), The International Journal of Human Rights 1353–1368 at 1355.

## The United Nations Convention on the Elimination of all forms of Discrimination Against Women

**1.54** The United Nations Convention on the Elimination of all forms of Discrimination Against Women (CEDAW), was adopted by the General Assembly of the United Nations on 18 December 1979, and entered into force on 3 September 1981, after ratification. The UK signed the Convention in 1981 and ratified it in 1986, with certain general reservations. As with ECHR, the text of the Convention does not explicitly address domestic abuse, but some articles are significant in respect of the State's response.

**1.55** First, Article 15 of CEDAW sets out that women should be accorded identical legal capacity to men. Both male and female victims of domestic abuse should have access to the same civil remedies and male and female victims of domestic abuse should be treated equally under the law. Article 16 notes that within family relations and marriage, all discrimination against women is to be eliminated. It is stated that men and women should have 'the same rights and responsibilities during marriage and at its dissolution' and 'the same rights and responsibilities as parents irrespective of marital status'. However, Article 4 of CEDAW notes that temporary measures for the purpose of increasing equality are not to be considered discrimination so long as they are removed once equality of opportunity and equal treatment are achieved.

**1.56** General recommendation No 35 of CEDAW is also relevant. It provides that governments must act with 'due diligence' to protect women from domestic abuse and other forms of gender-based violence:

> 'The failure of a State party to take all appropriate measures to prevent acts of gender-based violence against women in cases in which its authorities are aware or should be aware of the risk of such violence, or the failure to investigate, to prosecute and punish perpetrators and to provide reparations to victims/survivors of such acts, provides tacit permission or encouragement to perpetrate acts of gender-based violence against women. Such failures or omissions constitute human rights violation.'

## NEXT STEPS

**1.57** There has been and continues to be significant effort by the parliament, police, prosecution and the courts to tackle domestic abuse. Across society, there has been strong signalling of the unacceptable nature of domestic abuse, in all its forms. Considerable resource has been dedicated across the public sector to the prevention of abuse and protection of its victims. But it is equally clear that recorded levels of domestic abuse remain consistently high and the costs to victims, their families and wider society are undiminished. The authorities in Scotland have each recorded their commitment to continue to prioritise measures to tackle domestic abuse.

**1.58** Recognising, too, that important protections for victims of domestic abuse can extend beyond the criminal law, the Scottish Law Commission is conducting a review of the civil remedies available to victims. The Commission is an independent statutory body, whose role is to recommend reforms to improve, simplify and update the law of Scotland. It published its Discussion Paper on Civil Remedies for Domestic Abuse on 23 October 2024.[33]

**1.59** Finally, the Scottish Sentencing Council is currently engaged in a review of sentencing in domestic abuse cases, to develop a draft guideline for sentencers, which will of course form a resource for practitioners in assessing and advising on likely outcomes.

33 www.scotlawcom.gov.uk/files/9017/2959/8708/Discussion_Paper_on_Civil_Remedies_for_Domestic_Abuse_DP_No._178.pdf [accessed 28 July 2025].

*Chapter 2*

# Prosecution Approach and Resources

## DEFINITIONS – DOMESTIC ABUSE AND ITS VICTIMS

**2.01** In a joint protocol[1] that sets out how they will investigate, report and prosecute allegations of domestic abuse, COPFS and Police Scotland define domestic abuse as:

> 'Any form of physical, verbal, sexual, psychological or financial abuse which might amount to criminal conduct and which takes place within the context of a relationship. The relationship will be between partners (married, cohabiting, civil partnership or otherwise) or ex-partners. The abuse can be committed in the home or elsewhere including online.'

**2.02** The protocol notes that, as a form of gender-based violence, domestic abuse is predominantly perpetrated by men against women. However, the definition is intended to recognise and include,

> 'abuse of male victims by female perpetrators and includes abuse of lesbian, gay, bisexual, transgender and intersex people within relationships.'

**2.03** The protocol also notes that its definition of domestic abuse:

> 'encompasses the entire spectrum of behaviour by perpetrators where this amounts to criminal conduct. This includes cases which involve isolated incidents as well as cases involving a course of conduct and includes both violent and non-violent abusive behaviour. Some cases will involve elements and tactics of coercive control, which can involve a range of behaviours designed to control and harm a victim, while others will involve isolated incidents of conflict provoked by situational factors.'

**2.04** Terminology used in the discussion of domestic abuse can vary. In Scots law, the term 'complainer' is used to describe the person against whom it is alleged a crime has been committed. Those who have experienced domestic abuse often prefer to use the term 'survivor'. In this book, we use the term 'victim' where that is the terminology used in legislation or individual policies,

1 Joint protocol between Police Scotland and the Crown Office and Procurator Fiscal Service (6th edition) (May 2023), available at: www.copfs.gov.uk/media/xjtd4i4p/joint-domestic-abuse-protocol.pdf [last accessed 29 August 2025].

otherwise we use the general description of 'complainer'. In using this term no assumption is made about the veracity of any allegations.

**2.05** We use the term 'suspected perpetrators' to provide consistency with Police Service of Scotland published data for reported crime and those charged by the police. Where proceedings have been raised by the prosecution, we refer to the 'accused'.

**2.06** Upon a report of a crime or offence by the Police Service of Scotland, the decision whether or not to prosecute in the public interest lies with the Crown Office and Procurator Fiscal Service (COPFS). As with all prosecutorial decisions, there must be a sufficiency of evidence **and** prosecution is in the public interest.

## THE PROSECUTION CODE

**2.07** The Prosecution Code[2] sets out the criteria for decision-making by COPFS and the range of options available to prosecutors dealing with reports of crime. By publishing this information, COPFS aims to provide a general explanation of the various factors which may influence decisions regarding prosecution or alternative action. It is intended that the Prosecution Code will help improve understanding of the decision-making process as well as explain its complexity. In considering the action to be taken in relation to reports of crime the prosecutor must take account of both legal and public interest considerations. Legal impediments could arise, for example, in consideration of any delay that has arisen in the investigation and prosecution and any applicable statutory time bars and relevant case law.

**2.08** Assuming that the report discloses sufficient admissible, reliable and credible evidence of a crime committed by the accused, the prosecutor must consider what action is in the public interest. Assessment of the public interest often includes consideration of competing interests, including the interests of the victim, the accused and the wider community.

**2.09** Where the accused and/or the victim or witness is a child, the best interests of the child require to be treated as a primary consideration and to be given appropriate weight, along with other relevant considerations, in assessing the public interest.

2 Crown Office & Procurator Fiscal Service Prosecution Code (updated 14 July 2023): available at www.copfs.gov.uk/publications/prosecution-code/ [accessed 29 July 2025].

**2.10** The factors which require to be taken into account in assessing the public interest will vary according to the circumstances of each case. Broadly, they may include:

(i) the nature and gravity of the offence;

(ii) the impact of the offence on the victim and other witnesses;

(iii) the age, background and personal circumstances of the accused;

(iv) the age and personal circumstances of the victim and other witnesses;

(v) the attitude of the victim;

(vi) the motive for the crime;

(vii) the age of the offence;

(viii) mitigating circumstances;

(ix) the effect of prosecution on the accused;

(x) the risk of further offending;

(xi) the availability of a more appropriate civil remedy;

(xii) powers of the court; and

(xiii) public concern.

**2.11** The Code sets out, too, the alternatives to prosecution which COPFS may select and the basis for proceeding in that fashion, some of which are discussed below.

## PROSECUTING DOMESTIC ABUSE

**2.12** In recognition of the harmful nature of domestic abuse and its impact upon individuals, families and society, prosecutors adopt a presumption in favour of prosecution in reports of domestic abuse and stalking, where there is sufficient evidence. This includes cases where there is a sufficiency of evidence even where no evidence is to be led from the victim. Where the allegation discloses violence or the threat of violence, there is an additional presumption that any proceedings raised will be taken in the Sheriff Court or High Court. (See Joint Protocol, above, para 52).

**2.13** Tackling domestic abuse is a priority for COPFS, as reflected in its strategic plan for 2023–27.[3] It is noted that COPFS anticipates that cases

3 Crown Office & Procuratore Fiscal Service Strategic Plan 2023-27, available at: www.copfs.gov.uk/publications/strategic-plan-2023-27/ [accessed 29 July 2025].

involving violence against women and children, sexual offences and domestic abuse will form the bulk of its casework for years to come.

**2.14** In a statement[4] in September 2023, responding to the publication of annual statistics on domestic abuse and stalking charges, the Lord Advocate, Dorothy Bain KC stated:

> 'No one should have to live in fear of a partner or former partner. The trauma suffered by victims – and children who witness these crimes – is profound and distressing.
>
> At COPFS, we recognise domestic abuse as a scourge on our society, to be tackled with every means at our disposal.
>
> We know that crimes perpetrated behind closed doors are every bit as serious as those which may be witnessed by many. Perpetrators must be brought to justice.
>
> Scottish prosecutors understand that robust and effective prosecution is crucial, along with the work of our justice partners, to building safer lives for victims, their children and all in our communities.'

**2.15** Where there is insufficient evidence in law, no proceedings can be taken. If, however, the initial report by the police does not disclose a sufficiency of evidence but there are lines of enquiry which may yield additional information, the prosecution will instruct that the police carry out those further enquiries. The circumstances of an incident of domestic abuse should not be considered in isolation: the police must have regard to the history and nature of the relationship; and to any previous incidents between the victim and the accused.

**2.16** Supplementing the Prosecution Code, COPFS provides prosecutors with detailed internal guidance as to how cases should proceed and sets out the various factors to be considered. For obvious reasons this guidance is confidential.

**2.17** In April 2024 a review by HM Inspectorate of Prosecution in Scotland into the prosecution of domestic summary cases at sheriff summary level was published[5]. It examined practise and performance against internal policy, exploring some of the public commitments by COPFS. The report confirms that the vast majority of prosecutions involving domestic abuse take place at sheriff summary level.

4 Lord Advocate urges victims of domestic abuse to seek safety and justice, available at: www.copfs.gov.uk/about-copfs/news/lord-advocate-urges-victims-of-domestic-abuse-to-seek-safety-and-justice/ [accessed 29 July 2025].

5 www.prosecutioninspectorate.scot/publications/the-prosecution-of-domestic-abuse-cases-at-sheriff-summary-level/ [accessed 15 September 2025].

**2.18** The Inspectorate report noted that in 2022/23, the police reported 30,139 charges with a domestic abuse identifier. The vast majority of charges – 94 per cent – were prosecuted. The most common reason for taking no action was insufficient admissible evidence. Of the charges in which proceedings were taken, 79 per cent were prosecuted at summary level. The Inspectorate assessed COPFS management and prosecution of cases involving domestic abuse at sheriff summary level, making a number of recommendations, all accepted by COPFS.

**2.19** The report noted the benefits of the dedicated Domestic Abuse Court at Glasgow Sheriff Court and highlighted good practice in Dundee Sheriff Court, which at that time was piloting the Summary Case Management Scheme (SCMS). After a successful evaluation, that scheme is in the process of being rolled out across the country (see Practice Note No 1 of 2025[6]). Principal features of the SCMS include the early disclosure of key evidence to the defence and early, active judicial management. This allows much faster consideration by the defence of the strength of the prosecution case, encouraging agreement of evidence and early resolution of cases. The benefits to victims/complainers are evident: a trial may not be required, meaning they do not have to give evidence as a witness, and that can be resolved at an early stage. It means trials are not fixed unnecessarily and reduces the volume of late pleas of guilty, when witnesses are in attendance at court. In this way, the system avoids delays and permits earlier programming of those cases which do require to go to trial.

## SERIOUS CASES AND THE OVERLAP WITH SEXUAL OFFENDING

**2.20** While the vast majority of domestic abuse incidents are at summary level, in more serious cases experience shows that rape and sexual offending is an all-too-common feature of domestic abuse allegations. In investigations of serial and/or high risk perpetrators who are identified as presenting a great risk of harm, the police may identify and approach ex-partners of the perpetrator to ascertain whether they want to make any allegations. This approach is pursued by the police at national level by the Domestic Abuse Taskforce (DATF). Proactively searching for investigative opportunities to secure corroborative evidence from additional victims/witnesses has allowed prosecutions to take place using the doctrine of mutual corroboration (see **Chapter 7**). At solemn level, it is common to find prosecutions that involve multiple ex-partners, triggered by the allegations of a single, initial complainer.

**2.21** During 2021/22, Police Scotland's DATF undertook over 200 investigations into high risk, serial perpetrators of domestic abuse across

6 www.scotcourts.gov.uk/media/ravpx42w/all-scotland-scm-pn-4.pdf [accessed 29 July 2025].

Scotland. In total, they were charged with over 300 crimes. Between April and December 2022, 30 perpetrators received custodial sentences totalling 208 years, with cumulative imposition of 152 years of non-harassment orders (NHO) and seven lifelong non-harassment orders imposed.[7]

## STATUTORY DUTIES AND THE VICTIMS CODE FOR SCOTLAND

**2.22** There are statutory duties on the prosecution authorities (and the police) in relation to the investigation and prosecution of crime. The Victims and Witnesses (Scotland) Act 2014 (VWSA 2014)[8] introduced general principles to which the Lord Advocate, and thereby the prosecution service, must adhere. ('Victim' is used in the Act to mean someone who is or appears to be a victim: VWSA 2014, s 1(1)).

**2.23** The principles, as set out at VWSA 2014, s 1(3) are:

'(a) that a victim or witness should be able to obtain information about what is happening in the investigation or proceedings,

(b) that the safety of a victim or witness should be ensured during and after the investigation and proceedings,

(c) that a victim or witness should have access to appropriate support during and after the investigation and proceedings,

(d) that, in so far as it would be appropriate to do so, a victim or witness should be able to participate effectively in the investigation and proceedings.'

**2.24** Further general principles are established as follows at VWSA 2014, s 1A(2) and (3):

'(2)(a) that victims should be treated in a respectful, sensitive, tailored, professional and non-discriminatory manner,

(b) that victims should, as far as is reasonably practicable, be able to understand information they are given and be understood in any information they provide,

(c) that victims should have their needs taken into consideration,

7 HMICS Thematic Review of Domestic Abuse – Phase 1, available at: www.hmics.scot/publications/hmics-thematic-review-of-domestic-abuse-phase-1/ [accessed 29 July 2025].

8 www.legislation.gov.uk/asp/2014/1/contents [accessed 29 July 2025].

(d) that, when dealing with victims who are children, the best interests of the child should be considered, taking into account the child's age, maturity, views, needs and concerns, and

(e) that victims should be protected from—

 (i) secondary and repeat victimisation,

 (ii) intimidation, and

 (iii) retaliation.

(3) In this section, 'child' means a person under 18 years of age.'

**2.25** The Act established a Victims Code for Scotland[9] and set out a victims' right to receive information and communications in a clear and understandable format; to be informed they may request referral to providers of victim support services; and to provide a right of review[10] by a victim of a decision of the prosecutor not to prosecute.

**2.26** The right to receive information about criminal proceedings is set out in VWSA 2014, s 6(7):

'(7) Information falls within this subsection if it is—

 (a) a decision not to proceed with a criminal investigation and any reasons for it,

 (b) a decision to end a criminal investigation and any reasons for it,

 (c) a decision not to institute criminal proceedings against a person and any reasons for it,

 (d) the place in which a trial is to be held,

 (e) the date on which and time at which a trial is to be held,

 (f) the nature of charges libelled against a person,

 (g) the place in which the hearing of an appeal arising from a trial is to be held,

 (h) the date on which and time at which the hearing of an appeal arising from a trial is to be held,

 (i) the stage that criminal proceedings have reached,

 (j) the final decision of a court in a trial or any appeal arising from a trial, and any reasons for it.'

9 Victim's Code for Scotland, available at: www.mygov.scot/victims-code-for-scotland [accessed 29 July 2025].

10 https://www.legislation.gov.uk/asp/2014/1/section/4 [accessed 29 July 2025].

## COMMUNICATION WITH VICTIMS OF DOMESTIC ABUSE – VICTIM INFORMATION AND ADVICE

**2.27** Once a case is reported by the police to COPFS, the responsibility for providing information and support to a complainer passes from the police to COPFS. COPFS delivers many of its duties towards victims of domestic abuse though its Victim Information and Advice service, known as VIA. VIA provides a national service for COPFS in criminal prosecutions.[11] It was launched in 2002 with the aim of making the experience of a criminal prosecution less traumatic for victims, witnesses and next of kin by providing case-related information and signposting sources of support. It was recognised that COPFS is uniquely placed to provide information about individual case progress and decisions.

**2.28** An important aspect of the VIA service is that information is provided to eligible victims, witnesses and next of kin pro-actively, with information and updates being provided regardless of whether or not the victim maintains contact with VIA. Procurators Fiscal refer victims to VIA in appropriate cases and, thereafter, the service is provided unless, or until, a victim 'opts out'. The rationale behind this approach (as promoted by groups supporting victims) is to ensure that the most vulnerable victims do not lose out on the service as a result of a failure to understand or appreciate the offer being made, or as a result of a lack of stability in their personal circumstances, or simply a disinclination to engage with the process. In its communications with victims, VIA explains to the victim that they do not need to use the service, but it is available when needed.

**2.29** The current VIA remit ensures information is provided in the following circumstances to victims who are:

- under the age of 18;
- state pension age or over;
- a victim of domestic abuse, hate crime, sexual crime or stalking;
- involved in a trial with a jury;
- a family member (next of kin) in a death enquiry;or
- assessed as needing additional support.

**2.30** In all other cases, information can be provided on request. The VIA website explains that the COPFS Enquiry Point – contactable on 0300 020

11 www.copfs.gov.uk/services/victim-services/victim-information-and-advice-via-service/ [accessed 29 July 2025].

3000 – can provide information about case progress and advice on support organisations.

## THE VIA ROLE

**2.31** VIA communicates with complainers to help them understand how the Scottish criminal justice system works, explaining what to expect at each stage of the process. Key procedural information includes:

- hearing dates;
- outcomes of bail decisions;
- verdicts and sentences; and
- why no proceedings are being taken (if that is the case).

**2.32** VIA officers can organise extra support for victims and witnesses at court, should they have to give evidence, by:

- applying to the court for use of special measures;
- referring the victim to other agencies to assist in the preparation of a victim impact statement in solemn cases;
- taking the views of the victim regarding imposition of a non-harassment order, where that is under consideration by the court;
- arranging a courtroom visit, so that the victim knows what to expect if the case goes to trial.

**2.33** In many of those cases, VIA's introduction will have opened a line of communication between the victim and COPFS, allowing VIA staff to assess the particular victim's vulnerabilities and needs. VIA can signpost other sources of support, for example, linking in with the Witness Service and arranging pre-trial court visits. VIA prepares notices or applications to the Court for special measures to be permitted for witnesses at trial, having assessed their vulnerability and considered the particular measures which will allow them to give their best evidence. Where necessary, VIA may gather material which supports that conclusion.

**2.34** In serious cases, in which VIA officers engage closely with victims and other support organisations, they can play a pivotal role in coordinating court arrangements and agency relationships to ensure that victims' concerns are allayed and their needs met. This can mean planning the attendance of victims and their supporters, negotiating arrangements with the court for their reception and accommodation, including use of alternative entrances to avoid the accused and his/her supporters, or the media. VIA will frequently facilitate meetings with the prosecutor and will retain a victim focus, to ensure explanations are understood and concerns addressed, in so far as possible. The role is different and distinct from the role of the prosecutor – and deliberately so.

**2.35** A principal part of VIA's role is to refer the victim to other support services that offer practical and emotional support. VIA's role does not extend to the provision of advice about matters unrelated to the criminal prosecution. In the aftermath of a crime, a victim may need advice and assistance on many legal and practical matters, such as housing, benefits and potential civil law remedies. It is against this background that a significant aspect of the VIA role is to ensure that victims are referred, where appropriate, to other organisations which are available to provide emotional support or counselling or practical assistance in cases which are out with the sphere of the criminal justice system. The VIA website signposts a number of external sources of support[12].

## CHILDREN AFFECTED BY DOMESTIC ABUSE

**2.36** Children can be profoundly affected by domestic abuse, whether witnessing it in the home, living with an abused parent, or as direct victims of abuse themselves. Sometimes the abuser will use children of the relationship as a means to further exercise power and control over the adult victim. When children are present during domestic abuse incidents or ordinarily form part of the household the police will assess whether, in addition to highlighting the child's general wellbeing, the information suggests there may be a child protection concern.

**2.37** If officers assess a child is at immediate risk of significant harm and there is no alternative to protect them, the provisions outlined in ss 37–39, 55 and 56 of the Children's Hearing (Scotland) Act 2011[13] should be used. These provisions contain a range of emergency powers to apply for a child protection order and removal to a place of safety.

**2.38** Where it is suspected that a child has seen or heard domestic abuse during a domestic incident, the attending officers will make all efforts to speak with the child to establish if:

- they are a witness to a domestic incident;
- they feel safe; and
- there is anything that is upsetting them.

12 www.copfs.gov.uk/services/victim-services/resources-for-victims/victim-support-organisations/ [accessed 29 July 2025].
13 www.legislation.gov.uk/asp/2011/1/contents [accessed 29 July 2025].

**2.39** Those responding to domestic abuse must be aware of trauma and the impact of adverse childhood experiences, such as growing up in a household where there is domestic abuse.

**2.40** When there is a child protection concern this must be immediately brought to the attention of the relevant Public Protection Unit for officers to assess the information and determine whether child protection procedures should be instigated. If so, core agencies will share relevant information to inform decision-making. This will include whether the child should be subject of a Joint Investigative Interview (refreshed following the Evidence and Procedure Review (2015), to ensure the interview is child-centred, trauma-informed and minimises the risk of further traumatisation.)

**2.41** In cases where it is considered that a child is in need of protection, guidance, treatment or control and that it might be necessary for a compulsory supervision order to be made, the Children's Reporter (Scottish Children's Reporter Administration (SCRA)) will be informed. The police report to the Procurator Fiscal should highlight any previous or ongoing involvement by the Children's Reporter or social work department into the child's wellbeing.

**2.42** Section 5 of the Domestic Abuse (Scotland) Act 2018 directs that where behaviour captured by the legislation is committed in the presence of children this will be an aggravation of the offence. Thus, when a child has been present this has to be flagged up in any standard prosecution report (SPR) submitted to the Procurator Fiscal, so that the relevant aggravation is included in any charge prosecuted.

## CHILDREN AS WITNESSES TO DOMESTIC ABUSE

**2.43** In domestic abuse cases corroborative evidence may be provided by children who witnessed the abuse of a parent or another person or were themselves a victim of domestic abuse. Child witnesses are those who were under 18 years of age at the commencement of proceedings. In summary cases, this is the date the complaint is served on the accused.

**2.44** The joint protocol between COPFS and Police Scotland requires standard prosecution reports (SPRs) about domestic abuse to address a range of issues relating to children, including:

- whether there are any children from the relationship or whether either the victim or the accused has children and where they reside;
- whether there are any concerns about the safety of the children;
- whether children witnessed or were present during the incident;

- if the offence involves a contravention of s 1 of the Domestic Abuse (Scotland) Act 2018, whether the offence is aggravated by involving a child;
- the children's expressed views, and the views of their parents or carers (other than the accused), on giving evidence against the accused; and
- any expressed views of the children in relation to the need for a non-harassment order.

**2.45** The protocol directs[14] that where a child is an essential witness in a domestic abuse case, the Procurator Fiscal must give careful consideration to the best interests of the child as a primary consideration, and to the views of the child and the ability of the child to give evidence. In deciding whether to take proceedings in the case, the Procurator Fiscal must balance the seriousness of the offence and the risk which the accused poses with the best interests of the child, including consideration of the effect on the child of giving evidence. Any information received from a specialist domestic abuse support or advocacy service or other professional regarding the child's views or well-being will be given careful weight in that assessment. Where corroboration can come from another source, it may be unnecessary to cite a child as a witness.

**2.46** Where a child is required as a witness at court, the Procurator Fiscal must consider which special measures are required to ensure that the matter is dealt with sensitively and to minimise any distress to the child. Witnesses aged seventeen and under at the date of commencement of proceedings are entitled to use standard special measures to assist them in giving their evidence at trial. Children may also benefit from using non-standard special measures and this should be given consideration. The Procurator Fiscal will assess which measures are appropriate and will seek and take account of the views of the child and their parents/carers (other than the accused) when making a decision.

**2.47** Victims may feel under pressure to maintain contact with the perpetrator to facilitate contact with children of the relationship, even in the face of court-imposed preventative conditions or orders. The court can stipulate that any contact be facilitated using a third party, with bail conditions attached to that effect (see **Chapter 4**). Prosecutors seek to include children in special bail conditions when appropriate and proportionate to do so.

## CITING CHILD WITNESSES

**2.48** COPFS has internal guidance for staff on when it is appropriate to cite child witnesses. Whether to cite a child as a witness will ultimately be case-

14 Paragraphs 80 and 81.

and child-dependent. It will be apparent that it may be additionally daunting for a child to speak out against a parent.

**2.49** Witnesses under the age of 18 years are referred to VIA. VIA will send an initial letter to the child witness and/or their parent or guardian setting out the right of the child to special measures to support them to give evidence. Similar to the initial letter sent to victims in summary domestic abuse cases, VIA states that they would like to discuss the special measures available but that if the child or parent/guardian does not get in touch, then VIA will apply for the default special measures, which vary depending on the age of the child:

- for children aged under 12, the default special measures are a TV link and a supporter;
- for children aged 12 to 15, the default measures are a screen and a supporter; and
- for children aged 16 to 17, the default measure is a supporter.

**2.50** Currently, VIA's approach to communicating with child victims and witnesses is based on the child's age, taking the view that for younger children, a parent or guardian is best placed to explain matters.

- If a child is aged under 12 years, information is sent to the parent or guardian in a letter. There is no direct communication with the child.
- If a child is aged between 12 and 15, a letter is sent to the parent or guardian enclosing a letter to the child.
- If a child is aged 16 or 17, a letter is sent to the child directly, with no information sent to the parent or guardian.

## CHILD OFFENDERS

**2.51** In April 2025, COPFS published a Statement of Prosecution Policy and Referral to the Principal Reporter in rape and other solemn level sexual offences where the accused is a child.[15] This followed a review instructed by the Lord Advocate of the use of non-court disposals and diversion from the criminal justice system for child offenders in serious sexual offences. As has been noted earlier, there can be an overlap between sexual offending and domestic abuse. The statement addresses circumstances where the report against the child offender involves domestic abuse. In such cases, the presumption in favour of prosecution (and the presumption that proceedings will be taken in the

15 www.copfs.gov.uk/publications/statement-of-prosecution-policy-diversion-referral-to-the-reporter-in-solemn-sexual-offences-where-the-accused-is-a-child/ [accessed 29 July 2025].

Sheriff Court or High Court where the case involves violence or the threat of violence) set out in the Joint Protocol on domestic abuse applies. The statement explains that the presumption in favour of prosecution must be carefully balanced against the rebuttable presumption against prosecution in court for all individuals under 18 years of age. Where a reported individual is a child, the presumption in favour of prosecution may be rebutted, when balanced against the best interests of the individual as a primary consideration under the United Nations Convention on the Rights of the Child and/or consideration of the public interest. When considering whether the presumption in favour of prosecution should be rebutted in such a case prosecutors must give careful consideration to the surrounding circumstances of the offence, including the nature of the relationship between the child offender and victim, as well as the nature of the offence itself.

## NO PROCEEDING DECISIONS

**2.52** Where there is an insufficiency of evidence, as a matter of law, a prosecution cannot follow. In addition, there are situations where, in observance of the Prosecution Code, prosecutors do not take proceedings. It may be helpful here to set out those situations in which the Crown will decide *not* to prosecute, and the applicable law and policy considerations leading to that decision.

**2.53** There are essentially two scenarios: where there is a decision to 'divert' the accused from criminal proceedings into social work programmes; or where the complainer has difficulty in or is reluctant to engage with the prosecution service. These are considered in turn.

## DIVERSION FROM PROSECUTION

**2.54** Diversion from prosecution[16] is the decision by the Crown to refer an accused to justice social work (or another agency) to address the underlying causes of the alleged offending. It goes without saying that there must be a sufficiency of evidence to establish the offence before diversion can be considered. Albeit there is a presumption in favour of prosecution in cases involving domestic abuse, this is capable of rebuttal, subject to other internal COPFS guidance, and alternative action may be taken. This could include a warning letter, a personal warning or diversion from prosecution.

**2.55** Diversion may be considered when the report by the police discloses there is an identifiable need which has contributed to the offending and which

16 www.copfs.gov.uk/the-justice-process/alternatives-to-prosecution/diversion-from-prosecution/ [accessed 29 July 2025].

may be addressed through diversion from prosecution, so as to address the causes of offending and reduce further offending. The assessment is always whether diversion or prosecution is in the public interest. The aim of diversion is to reduce the risk of reoffending; diversion should provide assurance that the offending behaviour is being addressed.

**2.56** It is COPFS policy that diversion from prosecution should be considered for all accused persons reported to it where there is an identifiable need which has contributed to the offending which can best be met through diversion. COPFS policy further states that diversion is appropriate where all of the following requirements are met:

- there is a sufficiency of evidence against the accused person;
- it is assessed that in all the circumstances of the case, diversion is the appropriate outcome for the accused; and
- diversion is in the public interest taking into account the nature of the offending and the impact of the offence on the victim.

**2.57** Internal instructions note that no category of crime is automatically excluded from consideration of diversion. It is however noted that, as a general rule, the more serious the criminal conduct, the more likely it is that prosecution rather than diversion is the appropriate course of action.

**2.58** Even in cases where there is an identifiable need, policy is that an accused person can only be diverted from prosecution where diversion is the most appropriate outcome for the individual and in the public interest. There will be circumstances where diversion is either not permissible or is inappropriate, such as:

- the accused has been charged with a very serious offence;
- the accused has numerous or serious previous convictions;
- there has been significant injury to or impact on the complainer;
- special bail conditions are considered necessary for protection of the victim/witnesses;
- an ancillary order from the court may be an appropriate disposal/protection for the complainer, such as a non-harassment order; or
- the accused has been charged with a statutory offence subject to an impending time bar and there has already been a delay in the submission of the SPR, for example, while awaiting forensic analysis in a drug-related case.

**2.59** Where an accused agrees to take part in a diversion programme, the prosecutor has two options. They can:

- decide not to prosecute the accused for the alleged offence. This is the waived model of diversion and doesn't tend to be used where there is an identifiable victim; or
- wait to see how the accused has co-operated with the programme, before making a decision on whether to prosecute. This is known as deferred model of diversion. Most of the time the deferred model is used.

**2.60** In most cases, prosecutors will be content that justice social work (or other partner agency) can start the diversion programme as soon as the accused accepts the offer of diversion and is assessed as suitable.

**2.61** In other, potentially more serious, complex or sensitive cases (including allegations of domestic abuse, stalking or sexual offending) the prosecutor will want to know what social work (or other partner agency) can do by way of a diversion programme, before work is started. Most diversions will be completed within three to four months, but in some cases may last as long as a year.

**2.62** Approval from a senior prosecutor is required before an accused in a case involving a domestic abuse allegation can be referred to justice social work for diversion.

**2.63** A principal issue in respect of diversion is the availability of suitable social work programmes. Local authority provision varies across the country. However, there is no requirement that a specific social-work programme be available before there can be consideration of diversion, as the local authority may be requested to produce one, suitable for the circumstances of the individual accused and the particular allegations. There is an understandable reluctance to disclose the content of and criteria for diversion programmes. Largely their focus is on some characteristic of the offender which is amenable to intervention, education and support, such as their age or issues with addiction.

**2.64** A 2023 Joint Review of Diversion from Prosecution was conducted by HM Inspectorate of Prosecution, HM Inspectorate of Constabulary in Scotland, the Care Inspectorate and HM Inspectorate of Prisons in Scotland.[17] It found that individualised support and a range of justice social work interventions for people diverted from prosecution were available in every community justice partnership area in Scotland. In accordance with the national guidelines, diversion interventions were largely bespoke, person-centred, and tailored to the needs and circumstances of the person.

17 https://prisonsinspectoratescotland.gov.uk/news/joint-review-diversion-prosecution-2023 [accessed 29 July 2025].

**2.65** Diversion requires acceptance by and the cooperation of the accused person. If willing to accept diversion, the accused will be referred to and assessed by a justice social worker. If that assessment is favourable, the accused will undergo a suitable social work programme. Upon completion, social work will prepare a report for the prosecution. COPFS will take the final decision as to whether to discontinue the proceedings, if undertaking a deferred prosecution model. A positive report will usually result in a decision that no proceedings will be taken. The views of any complainer are also taken during this process.

**2.66** An accused who declined an offer to participate in a diversion programme would most likely be prosecuted. Authorities are, understandably, hesitant to publish information about the content, intended audience or criteria of diversion programmes. If there is any preliminary information that diversion is indicated, the prosecution will give careful thought to the seriousness of the offence, the age and circumstances of the offender – particularly issues around addiction, any views expressed by the victim and whether social work programmes are capable of addressing identified needs.

## VICTIM VIEWS ON DIVERSION

**2.67** The views of victims are important and are a factor which will be taken into consideration by the prosecutor when deciding whether it is appropriate to offer diversion.

**2.68** Where the victim is a child, the views of the child, where appropriate, should be sought and given due weight in accordance with the age and maturity of the child in accordance with Article 12 of the UNCRC, regardless of whether views are provided by a parent/carer.

**2.69** However, a victim's views will not be determinative as to whether diversion is appropriate in the circumstances of each case and the prosecutor's assessment of the public interest requires them to take into consideration a range of different factors.

## THE RELUCTANT COMPLAINER

**2.70** In cases involving domestic abuse, the complainer and accused are, or have been, in an intimate relationship. For the complainer this can mean wrestling with conflicting loyalties or deep-seated trauma. There may be children of the relationship or other social, cultural or family dynamics forming a source of pressure. The complainer may fear the accused, or repercussions from others. There can be myriad reasons a complainer struggles to engage with police and prosecution. In addition, there can be fear of what the criminal justice system itself entails, and apprehension at the prospect of giving evidence at trial.

**2.71** COPFS policy makes clear that the decision as to whether a case will be prosecuted is one to be taken by the Crown, in the public interest. As such, the policy requires prosecutors to attach significant weight to the views of the complainer whilst also considering the nature of the offending behaviour – including the dynamics of coercive control – together with the risk posed by the accused, and the Crown's obligations in domestic and international law to prosecute domestic abuse (see **Chapter 1**).

**2.72** Where reluctance on the part of the complainer is known, in more serious cases prosecutors will seek to explore the reasons for the reluctance, and whether there are sources of support which can reduce or remove the reasons for the reluctance, allowing the complainer to engage. This will involve consideration of special measures such as evidence by commission or by live link. The Crown must also ensure that the complainer's decision not to engage with a prosecution is properly informed, understanding of the full consequences of a decision to take no proceedings.

**2.73** Where the Crown decides to proceed with a case despite the complainer's reluctance or difficulty in engaging, the policy does not exclude that there may be cases where it might be necessary to seek a warrant from the court when a complainer refuses to attend to give evidence. The policy states the expectation that such cases will be exceptionally rare. They do, however, arise, particularly where a prosecution involves multiple complainers, to invoke the doctrine of mutual corroboration.

## THE DECISION NOT TO PROSECUTE: THE VICTIM'S RIGHT TO REVIEW SCHEME

**2.74** Section 4 of the Victims and Witnesses (Scotland) Act 2014 requires the Lord Advocate to make and publish rules about the process for reviewing, on the request of a person who is or appears to be a victim in relation to an offence or alleged offence, a decision of the prosecutor not to prosecute a person for that offence or alleged offence. The purpose of s 4, and the rules the Lord Advocate has made under it, are to give effect to the right to review of a decision not to prosecute that was created by Article 11 of Directive 2012/29/EU ('the Victims' Rights Directive').

**2.75** The Lord Advocate's Rules[18] took effect in July 2015 and are publicly available. The right to review applies to decisions to take no action

18 www.copfs.gov.uk/publications/lord-advocate-s-rules-review-of-a-decision-not-to-prosecute/html/ [accessed 29 July 2025].

in a case reported by Police Scotland (or other reporting agency), or to stop or discontinue a case once court proceedings have started (but not where the decision is taken mid-trial by withdrawing a charge). The Rules exclude certain decisions and situations from the right to review: decisions taken by the court; decisions where one charge is stopped or discontinued (or changed) but the court proceedings for other substantial and significant charges with the same victim continue; where a plea has been accepted; where the case has been dealt with by use of a direct measure (like a warning letter or fiscal fine); where the case has been referred to the Children's Reporter; or where the accused has been told that the proceedings have been stopped or discontinued.

**2.76** Any victim can apply for a review. The application for review should normally be made within one month of the date the victim learns of the decision. The review will be taken by a lawyer ('a reviewer') who was not involved in the original decision, and he or she will consider the case papers and obtain any further information which may be required to take the decision. The reviewer will consider if the decision not to prosecute was reasonable, having regard to all the circumstances and in line with the Prosecution Code and COPFS prosecution policies. The review will ordinarily be completed within 20 working days. The Rules also allow for a person to request and receive more information about a decision not to prosecute, instead of or before deciding whether to exercise their right to review.

**2.77** Cases involving historic allegations and multiple victims, where the Crown relies on the doctrine of mutual corroboration in order to achieve a sufficiency of evidence, can cause problems. It is a difficult dynamic if one complainer is cooperative but another, upon whom the prosecution relies, is reluctant. The reluctant complainer's cooperation with the trial may be pivotal in prosecution decision making.

## DISCONTINUATIONS

**2.78** Throughout the life of a case, the decision to prosecute should be kept under continuous review. The initial decision to raise proceedings may no longer be appropriate if new evidence emerges or circumstances change. As prosecutors manage and prepare cases, they should reassess whether there is a sufficiency of evidence and whether it remains in the public interest to prosecute. Where that is no longer so, a decision to discontinue proceedings may follow.

**2.79** COPFS provides extensive internal guidance to staff setting out the policy and process for discontinuing cases. In domestic abuse cases, there is a presumption against discontinuation. It is understood that any decision to discontinue proceedings where a sufficiency of evidence still exists must be approved by a senior prosecutor who has also completed the domestic abuse accredited prosecutor training. Reasons for discontinuations must be recorded. This is to be distinguished from cases where there is no longer available any admissible evidence to secure a conviction. No approval is required as it is not an exercise of prosecutorial discretion where no sufficiency of evidence is available in law.

*Chapter 3*

# Arrest, Police Bail and Undertakings

## HISTORICAL DEVELOPMENT OF POLICE BAIL

**3.01** Prior to the case of *Cadder*[1] in 2010, the position of persons detained by the police on suspicion of having committed a criminal offence punishable by imprisonment, was governed by ss 14 and 15 of the Criminal Procedure (Scotland) Act 1995. Police officers were allowed to detain an individual for up to six hours during which time that individual could be questioned by the police. During this period a detainee had no right of access to a solicitor. The Supreme Court ultimately decided that this process was in breach of an individual's right to a fair trial as recognised by Articles 6(1) and 6(3) of the European Convention on Human Rights. This decision had a profound effect upon the rights of accused persons being detained by the police, and emergency legislation in the form of the Criminal Procedure (Legal Assistance, Detention and Appeals) (Scotland) Act 2010 was enacted to afford suspects the right of access to a solicitor. Given the issues which had been identified, a review of criminal law and practice was undertaken, led by Lord Carloway,[2] which ultimately led to the law being consolidated in the Criminal Justice (Scotland) Act 2016.

**3.02** The Criminal Justice (Scotland) Act 2016 is in seven parts, dealing with:

- Part One – (Arrest and Custody);
- Part Two – (Police Procedures);
- Part Three – (Solemn Procedure);
- Part Four – (Sentencing);
- Part Five – (Appeals and the Scottish Criminal Cases Review Commission);
- Part Six – (Miscellaneous); and
- Part Seven – (General and Ancillary Provision).

1 *Cadder v HM Advocate* [2010] UKSC 43.
2 www.scotland.gov.uk/About/Review/CarlowayReview [accessed 29 July 2025].

**3.03** The terms of Parts 1 and 2 are of particular importance in proceedings involving domestic abuse in relation to the early stages of a police investigation.

## ARREST AND CUSTODY

**3.04** The powers of a police officer to arrest an individual without a warrant are now contained in s 1(1) of the Criminal Justice (Scotland) Act 2016 (CJ(S)A 2016) which states that:

> 'A constable may arrest a person without a warrant if the constable has reasonable grounds for suspecting that the person has committed or is committing an offence.'

**3.05** An important extension of this power in CJ(S)A 2016 is that a person may be arrested more than once in relation to the same offence,[3] although this is subject to the caveat that a person may not be arrested more than once where they have been officially accused of committing an offence or an offence arising from the same circumstances as that offence.[4]

**3.06** Where that person is arrested then the constable effecting that arrest must inform them of their arrest[5] and the general nature of the offence for which they are being arrested.[6] Further they must be advised that they need say nothing, and need not answer any questions,[7] other than provide their name, address, date of birth, place of birth (in such detail as a constable considers necessary or expedient for the purpose of establishing the person's identity), and nationality.[8] A suspect must also be advised that they have the right to have information about their arrest sent to a solicitor[9] and they must be afforded access to a solicitor.[10]

**3.07** An arrested person must also be taken to a police station as soon as is reasonably practicable,[11] and on arrival at the police station, as well as intimation to a solicitor the suspect also has the right to have another person informed that they are in custody,[12] as well as to a parent where the suspect is under the age of 18.[13]

3 CJ(S)A 2016, s 2(1).
4 CJ(S)A 2016, s 2(2).
5 CJ(S)A 2016, s 3(a).
6 CJ(S)A 2016, s 3(a) and (b).
7 CJ(S)A 2016, s 3(d).
8 CJ(S)A 2016, s 34(4).
9 CJ(S)A 2016, ss 3(e)(i) and 43.
10 CJ(S)A 2016, ss 3(e)(ii) and 44.
11 CJ(S)A 2016, s 4(1).
12 CJ(S)A 2016, ss 5(2)(b) and 38.
13 CJ(S)A 2016, ss 5(2)(b) and 40.

**3.08** Where an individual is arrested and in custody without a warrant and since having been arrested has not yet been charged with an offence, then authorisation to keep them in custody must be sought as soon as reasonably practicable.[14] Authorisation must be granted by a constable of the rank of sergeant or above who has not previously been involved in connection with the investigation,[15] Authorisation may only be given if that constable is satisfied that the test as set out in s 14 of CJ(S)A 2016 has been met, namely that:

'(1) [...]

(a) there are reasonable grounds for suspecting that the person has committed an offence, and

(b) keeping the person in custody is necessary and proportionate for the purposes of bringing the person before a court or otherwise dealing with the person in accordance with the law.

(2) Without prejudice to the generality of subsection (1)(b), in considering what is necessary and proportionate for the purpose mentioned in that subsection regard may be had to—

(a) whether the person's presence is reasonably required to enable the offence to be investigated fully,

(b) whether the person (if liberated) would be likely to interfere with witnesses or evidence, or otherwise obstruct the course of justice,

(c) the nature and seriousness of the offence.'

**3.09** The general rule for the period in respect of which an individual may be kept in custody is set out in s 9 of CJ(S)A 2016, which provides that that a person who has been held in custody for a continuous period of 12 hours beginning from the time when authorisation was given for them to be held in custody in terms of CJ(S)A 2016, s 7, may only be held further if they are charged with an offence, authorisation to keep them in custody longer has been given in terms of CJ(S)A 2016, s 11 or they are detained under s 28(1A) of the Criminal Procedure (Scotland) Act 1995 in connection with a breach of bail conditions.[16] Where a suspect has previously been held in police custody in respect of the same offence or same circumstances, then the 12-hour period is reduced by the previous period in respect of which they were previously held in police custody.[17]

14 CJ(S)A 2016, s 7(2).
15 CJ(S)A 2016, s 7(3).
16 CJ(S)A 2016, s 9(2).
17 CJ(S)A 2016, s 10(2).

**3.10** The current Lord Advocate's Guidelines[18] provide in Section One that:

> 'At all times that a person is in police custody, police officers must have regard to that person's right to liberty under Article 5 of the European Convention on Human Rights (ECHR) and must consider whether it is reasonable and necessary to keep that person in custody.'

**3.11** It is also specifically recorded that there is a duty in terms of s 50 of the Criminal Justice (Scotland) Act 2016 to take every precaution to ensure that a person is not unreasonably or unnecessarily held in police custody. This must be considered in every case, and for a police officer to decide to keep an individual in police custody there must be reasonable grounds for suspecting that:

- they committed an offence; and
- that keeping them in custody is necessary and proportionate for the purposes of bringing the person before a court or otherwise dealing with the person in accordance with the law.

**3.12** When considering whether it is necessary and proportionate to keep an individual in custody, a police officer may have regard to:

- whether the person's presence in custody is reasonably required to enable the offence to be investigated fully;
- whether the person (if liberated) would be likely to interfere with witnesses or evidence, or otherwise obstruct the course of justice; and
- the nature and seriousness of the offence (CJ(S)A 2016, s 14(2)).

## POLICE BAIL AND UNDERTAKINGS

**3.13** Any person charged on summary complaint or on petition will be brought before a court and having been provided with an opportunity to make representations the court will decide whether to grant or refuse bail, with such conditions attached as the court deems fit in the event that bail is granted. In most cases involving domestic abuse, this application will be made on the next court date following the person being charged by the police, a position now consolidated in s 21 of the Criminal Justice (Scotland) Act 2016.

**3.14** Police bail was originally introduced in the Bail (Scotland) Act 1980 (which inserted the relevant conditions into the Criminal Procedure (Scotland) Act 1975. At that time however, the only conditions available to the police were the ability to require an accused not to commit further offences and to appear

18 www.copfs.gov.uk/publications/lord-advocate-s-guidelines-liberation-by-the-police/html/ [accessed 29 July 2025].

at court at a specified date and time. There was no provision for additional conditions. The power to admit an accused to bail was granted only to the officer in charge of a police station.

**3.15** The current position in relation to police bail and undertakings is now set out in CJ(S)A 2016, ss 16–19 (in relation to investigative liberation) and CJ(S)A 2016, ss 25–30 (in relation to Police Liberation).

**3.16** By virtue of the CJ(S)A 2016, a number of options are now available to police offers in relation to releasing persons from their custody. The form that any such liberation takes will depend on the status of the individual concerned. Broadly, there are two categories of liberation, namely:

(1) investigative liberation as covered by ss 16–19 of CJ(S)A 2016: and

(2). police liberation as set out in ss 25–30 of CJ(S)A 2016.

**3.17** Prima facie, both categories appear very similar and indeed they share many similar characteristics, however their rationales and operation are quite separate and distinct. Further there are within these categories a number of different options available to police officers when determining whether a person in their custody is to be held pending an appearance in court on the next lawful day or whether they are to be liberated pending further inquiries or released subject to an undertaking to appear at court on a future specified time.

**3.18** In cases involving allegations of domestic abuse police officers must take into account the prevailing guidelines of the Lord Advocate and must follow the procedures and practices detailed in the current joint protocol between Police Scotland and The Crown Office and Procurator Fiscal Service (COPFS) in determining whether an individual should be held in custody pending a court appearance or released subject to one of the statutory forms of liberation.

## INVESTIGATIVE LIBERATION

**3.19** The current statutory basis for investigative liberation is found in ss 16–19 of CJ(S)A 2016. This form of liberation applies to those circumstances where police officers have reasonable grounds for suspecting that an individual has committed an offence but are not yet at the stage where they are able to proffer a charge against that individual. The terms of s 9 of CJ(S)A 2016 set out a general rule that an individual can only be held in custody for a period of 12 hours, prior to being charged or released unless authorisation is provided by a constable of the rank of inspector or above to extend this period by a further 12 hours.[19]

19 CJ(S)A 2016, s 11.

**3.20** This can place significant pressure on police resources in situations where they are investigating particularly complex cases, even when an extension of the 12-hour period has been granted. In such cases where it is clear that the police might require to pursue further lines of inquiry, a process of investigative liberation has been formulated which allows police officers to liberate that person pending further inquiries. It also allows them to impose conditions on the person prohibiting them from interfering with the proper conduct of the investigation into the relevant offence, for example by interfering with witnesses or evidence.

**3.21** Specifically, the terms of s 16 of CJ(S)A 2016 refer to release on conditions and provides:

**Section 16 Release on conditions**

'(1) Subsection (2) applies where—

(a) a person is being held in police custody by virtue of authorisation given under section 7,

(b) a constable has reasonable grounds for suspecting that the person has committed a relevant offence, and

(c) either—

(i) the person has not been subject to a condition imposed under subsection (2) in connection with a relevant offence, or

(ii) it has not been more than 28 days since the first occasion on which a condition was imposed on the person under subsection (2) in connection with a relevant offence.

(2) If releasing the person from custody, a constable may impose any condition that an appropriate constable considers necessary and proportionate for the purpose of ensuring the proper conduct of the investigation into a relevant offence (including, for example, a condition aimed at securing that the person does not interfere with witnesses or evidence).

(3) A condition under subsection (2)—

(a) may not require the person to be in a specified place at a specified time,

(b) may require the person—

(i) not to be in a specified place, or category of place, at a specified time, and

(ii) to remain outwith that place, or any place falling within the specified category (if any), for a specified period.

(4) A condition imposed under subsection (2) is a liberation condition for the purposes of schedule 1.

(5) In subsection (2), 'an appropriate constable' means a constable of the rank of sergeant or above.

(6) In this section, 'a relevant offence' means—

(a) the offence in connection with which the authorisation under section 7 has been given, or

(b) an offence arising from the same circumstances as that offence.'

**3.22** It is apparent from these provisions that prior to the release of an individual on an undertaking in terms of s 16 of CJ(S)A 2016, a number of conditions must apply, and that a person must fall into one of two categories before the terms of the section can apply.

**3.23** The first category refers to individuals who are held in police custody by virtue of authorisation given under s 7 of CJ(S)A 2016.[20] This section refers to persons in police custody, who have been arrested in respect of an offence without a warrant, and who since being arrested have not yet been charged with an offence by a constable.[21] In such cases, authority to keep the person in custody must have been provided as soon as reasonably practicable[22] by a police officer who is of the rank of sergeant or above and has not been previously involved in the investigation of the offence.[23]

**3.24** Authorisation can only be given if the relevant officer is satisfied that the test as set out in s 14 of CJ(S)A 2016 is met, which requires that:

'(1) [...]

(a) there are reasonable grounds for suspecting that the person has committed an offence, and

(b) keeping the person in custody is necessary and proportionate for the purposes of bringing the person before a court or otherwise dealing with the person in accordance with the law.

(2) Without prejudice to the generality of subsection (1)(b), in considering what is necessary and proportionate for the purpose mentioned in that subsection regard may be had to—

20 CJ(S)A 2016, s 16(1) (a).
21 CJ(S)A 2016, s 7(1).
22 CJ(S)A 2016, s 7(2).
23 CJ(S)A 2016, s 7(3).

(a) whether the person's presence is reasonably required to enable the offence to be investigated fully,

(b) whether the person (if liberated) would be likely to interfere with witnesses or evidence, or otherwise obstruct the course of justice,

(c) the nature and seriousness of the offence.'[24]

**3.25** If authorisation is refused by a relevant officer, then the individual concerned can only be held in custody if they are charged with an offence, or if they are detained under s 28(1A) of the Criminal Procedure (Scotland) Act 2016, which allows for detention in connection with a breach of bail conditions.[25]

**3.26** The second category of persons who can be released on investigative liberation are persons whom the police have reasonable grounds for suspecting have committed a relevant offence[26] and either they have not been released subject to a condition as imposed under s 16(2) of the 2016 Act, or more than 28 days have elapsed since the first occasion on which such a condition was imposed on that person in connection with a relevant offence.

**3.27** A relevant offence is defined in s 16(6) of CJ(S)A 2016 as being any offence in connection with which authorisation has been given in terms of s 7 of CJ(S)A 2016 or an offence arising from the same circumstances as that offence.

## LIBERATION CONDITIONS

**3.28** If an individual falls within one of the above categories, then a constable may release that person from custody subject to such conditions as that officer deems necessary and proportionate for the purposes of ensuring the proper conduct of further investigation into a relevant offence.[27] The section specifies (as an example) the condition that the individual concerned must not interfere with witnesses or evidence.

**3.29** The Act further provides that a number of other conditions may or may not apply. It specifically states that a condition cannot be imposed that requires that a person should be in a specified place at a specified time,[28] thereby excluding the possibility of a 'curfew' condition. However, an imposed

24 CJ(S)A 2016, s 14.
25 CJ(S)A 2016, s 7(5).
26 CJ(S)A 2016, s 16(1)(b).
27 CJ(S)A 2016, s 16(2).
28 CJ(S)A 2016, s 16 (3)(a).

condition may require that a person must not be in a specified place or category of place at a specified time or that they must remain outwith that place.[29]

**3.30** Any conditions imposed, are to be treated as 'liberation conditions' for the purposes of breach proceedings in terms of CJ(S)A 2016, Sched 1.[30]

**3.31** Section 17 of CJ(S)A 2016 also provides that a condition imposed in terms of s 16(2) automatically ceases to have effect at the end of 28 days after the first occasion on which conditions were imposed.[31]

**3.32** Conditions may also cease to have effect before the expiry of that 28-day time period in the following circumstances, namely

(i) the condition has been removed under CJ(S)A 2016, s 18;

(ii) the person has been arrested in connection with a relevant offence;

(iii) the person has been officially accused of committing a relevant offence; or

(iv) the condition has been removed by a sheriff under CJ(S)A 2016, s 19.

**3.33** For the foregoing purposes, a 'relevant offence' is again defined as being an offence which is in connection with the condition which was imposed or an offence which has arisen out of the same circumstances as that offence.[32]

## MODIFICATION OF CONDITIONS

**3.34** It is competent for a police constable to seek the modification or removal of a condition or conditions in terms of s 18 of CJ(S)A 2016, which provides that a constable may modify by a notice given in writing to the person subject to that condition, that they have so modified or removed a condition imposed under CJ(S)A 2016, s 16(2). [33] Such a notice must specify the time from which the condition is modified or removed.

**3.35** In addition, a constable of the rank of inspector or above must keep under review whether there are reasonable grounds to suspect that a person subject to a s 16(2) condition has committed a relevant offence, and whether the condition imposed remains necessary and proportionate for the purposes of ensuring the proper conduct of the investigation into a relevant offence. [34] If the

29 CJ(S)A 2016, s 16(3)(b).
30 CJ(S)A 2016, s 16(4).
31 CJ(S)A 2016, s 17(1) (a).
32 CJ(S)A 2016, s 17(2).
33 CJ(S)A 2016, s 18(1) and (2).
34 CJ(S)A 2016, s 18(3).

reviewing officer is no longer satisfied that the condition or conditions remain necessary and proportionate then the constable must give notice to that person advising them that the condition has been removed or modified.[35] Notice to this effect must be given to the relevant person in writing as soon as is reasonably practicable.[36] Any such modification requires the authority of a constable of the rank of inspector or above, and the notice provided must also specify the time from which the condition ceases to have effect.[37]

## REVIEW OF CONDITIONS

**3.36** Provision also exists for a review of conditions by the court in terms of CJ(S)A 2016, s 19. By this process a person subject to a condition may apply to a Sheriff to have that condition reviewed.[38] Prior to determining any such application, the court must provide the Procurator Fiscal with an opportunity to be heard in relation to that application.[39] In the event that a Sheriff considers that a condition is no longer necessary or proportionate, then they have the power to either remove that condition altogether or alternatively to impose another condition that the Sheriff considers to be necessary and proportionate.[40] In the event that the Sheriff does impose a new condition, then this new condition imposed by the Sheriff is to be taken as having been imposed in terms of CJ(S)A 2016, s 16(2).

**3.37** The current position of the Crown in relation to investigative liberation is set out in Section 4 of the Lord Advocate's Guidelines: Liberation by the Police, and provides that persons arrested but not officially accused should only be kept in custody if it is not appropriate to release the person unconditionally, or to release the person on investigative liberation (see below) subject to appropriate conditions in terms of CJ(S)A 2016, s 16.

**3.38** Officers are required in terms of the Guidelines to take the following factors into account when considering whether it is appropriate to keep a person in custody, where there are ongoing enquiries, namely:

- the nature of the offence – if the investigation is not likely to result in solemn proceedings and/or does not involve vulnerable victims or witnesses then it is unlikely to be appropriate to keep an individual in custody whilst enquiries are ongoing;

35 CJ(S)A 2016, s 18(5).
36 CJ(S)A 2016, s 18(6)(a).
37 CJ(S)A 2016, s 18(6)(b).
38 CJ(S)A 2016, s 19(1).
39 CJ(S)A 2016, s 19(2).
40 CJ(S)A 2016, s 19(3).

- any significant risk posed to victims, witnesses or the public if the person is liberated; and
- the nature of the further enquiries required and the realistic timescales for completion of those enquiries.

**3.39** The Lord Advocate's Guidelines emphasise that there are no restrictions on the types of offences for which investigative liberation may be used, stressing instead that each case must be considered entirely on its own merits and assess the necessity and proportionality of imposing conditions.

## THE LORD ADVOCATE'S GUIDELINES AND THE JOINT DOMESTIC ABUSE PROTOCOL

**3.40** The Guidelines specifically address the question of domestic offending which involves a course of conduct, including offences in terms of s 1 of the Domestic Abuse (Scotland) Act 2018, which require to be fully investigated prior to any report being submitted to the Procurator Fiscal. This is to ensure that the full extent of the offending behaviour can be considered. Accordingly, police officers are instructed to apply the terms of the Joint Domestic Abuse Protocol[41] when considering whether investigative liberation is appropriate in respect of persons arrested for domestic abuse offences. Ultimately, and while it is stated that there is a general presumption of liberty, the Protocol sets out the criteria to be considered in each case, which include:

- the nature and circumstances of the offence, including the severity of the conduct;
- the likelihood of reoffending;
- the ongoing risk posed to the safety of the victim, children or any other member of the public;
- any relevant previous convictions or behaviour suggesting non-compliance with conditions or orders; and
- whether the incident is part of a course of conduct.

**3.41** The Guidelines recognise that there are particular risks associated with cases involving domestic abuse which mean that in some cases it will be both reasonable and necessary to keep a person in custody whilst relevant enquiries are completed. If however it is proposed to release a suspect on investigative liberation, a full assessment of any risk that the suspect may pose to any victim, witness, or the investigation is to be undertaken, which will take account of the

41 www.copfs.gov.uk/media/xjtd4i4p/joint-domestic-abuse-protocol.pdf [accessed 29 July 2025].

views of the victim. This will include any views regarding conditions which might be appropriate. Steps will be taken to ensure that victims are advised of a person's imminent release from custody, together with any conditions of release. All of this must be carefully explained to the victim.

## POLICE LIBERATION AND UNDERTAKING TO APPEAR IN COURT

**3.42** Perhaps of more common application, particularly in relation to cases involving domestic abuse, are the provisions contained within the Criminal Justice (Scotland) Act 2016 relating to police liberation.[42] These provisions set out the procedures whereby an individual can be released from police custody prior to a court appearance, subject to a requirement that they appear in court on a specified date and time. They can also be made subject to certain conditions. In terms of s 21 of CJ(S)A 2016, a person who is in police custody having been arrested under a warrant, or is in police custody and who having been arrested has been charged by a constable with an offence, shall, unless released from police custody in terms of s 25 of CJ(S)A 2016, be brought before a court to consider the question of bail before the end of the first day on which the court is sitting after the day on which the foregoing applied to that individual, or as soon as practicable thereafter.[43] Individuals charged with domestically aggravated offences will often be held by the police in custody in terms of this provision pending a court appearance the following day, or as soon as possible thereafter. In practice, use is now made of the procedure whereby persons who have been charged in custody are liberated to appear at a later date in court subject to a number of conditions. This includes of course the requirement to attend a specified court on a specified date and at a specified time.

**3.43** The specific provisions dealing with this procedure are set out in section 25 and 26 of the 2016 Act which provides:

**Section 25 Liberation by police**

'(1) Subsection (2) applies when—

(a) a person is in police custody having been arrested under a warrant (other than a warrant granted under section 37(1)), or

(b) a person—

(i) is in police custody having been arrested without a warrant, and

42 CJ(S)A 2016, ss 25–30.
43 CJ(S)A 2016, s 21(2).

(ii) since being arrested, the person has been charged with an offence by a constable.

(2) A constable may—

(a) if the person gives an undertaking in accordance with section 26, release the person from custody,

(b) release the person from custody without such an undertaking,

(c) refuse to release the person from custody.

(3) Where a person is in custody as mentioned in subsection (1)(a), the person may not be released from custody under subsection (2)(b).

(4) A constable is not to be subject to any claim whatsoever by reason of having refused to release a person from custody under subsection (2)(c).'

**3.44** The terms of this provision mean that persons charged can therefore be released on an undertaking providing that they accept a number of conditions as set out in the succeeding section, which states:

**Section 26 Release on undertaking**

'(1) A person may be released from police custody on an undertaking given under section 25(2)(a) only if the person signs the undertaking.

(2) The terms of an undertaking are that the person undertakes to—

(a) appear at a specified court at a specified time, and

(b) comply with any conditions imposed under subsection (3) while subject to the undertaking.

(3) The conditions which may be imposed under this subsection are—

(a) that the person does not—

(i) commit an offence,

(ii) interfere with witnesses or evidence, or otherwise obstruct the course of justice,

(iii) behave in a manner which causes, or is likely to cause, alarm or distress to witnesses,

(b) any further condition that a constable considers necessary and proportionate for the purpose of ensuring that any conditions imposed under paragraph (a) are observed.

(4) Conditions which may be imposed under subsection (3)(b) include—

(a) a condition requiring the person—

(i) to be in a specified place at a specified time, and

(ii) to remain there for a specified period,

(b) a condition requiring the person—

(i) not to be in a specified place, or category of place, at a specified time, and

(ii) to remain outwith that place, or any place falling within the specified category (if any), for a specified period.

(5) For the imposition of a condition under subsection (3)(b)—

(a) if it is of the kind described in subsection (4)(a), the authority of a constable of the rank of inspector or above is required,

(b) if it is of any other kind, the authority of a constable of the rank of sergeant or above is required.

(6) The requirements imposed by an undertaking to attend at a court and comply with conditions are liberation conditions for the purposes of schedule 1.'

**3.45** The first essential pre-requisite of this procedure is for the individual concerned to sign the undertaking form.[44] Thereafter the first requirement of the undertaking itself is that the individual concerned must attend at a specified court on a specified date and time.[45] This is a mandatory requirement,[46] and thereafter a number of conditions *may* be imposed in terms of subsection (3)(a). It is noticeable that these conditions largely mirror a number of the standard conditions of bail as contained in s 24(5) of the Criminal Procedure (Scotland) Act 1995.

**3.46** A police constable also has the power to impose any further condition or conditions they consider necessary and proportionate for the purpose of ensuring that the foregoing conditions are complied with.[47] Accordingly any such conditions imposed should not be punitive in nature but rather they must be justified as being conditions which will ensure compliance with the principal conditions.

44 CJ(S)A 2016, s 26(1).
45 CJ(S)A 2016, s 26(2).
46 CJ(S)A 2016, s 26(2)(a).
47 CJ(S)A 2016, s 26 (3)(b).

**3.47** The Act goes on to specify that, unlike conditions which can be imposed in relation to investigative liberation, the conditions imposed under CJ(S)A 2016, s 3(b) may include conditions that the person must be in a specified place at a specified time and must remain there for a specified time, thereby allowing for *inter alia* the imposition of a 'curfew'.[48] However as previously indicated, a condition of curfew cannot be imposed simply as a punitive measure. Any such conditions of curfew can only be imposed by a constable of the rank of inspector or above.[49] Another condition may also require that an individual must not be in a specified place or category of place at a specified time as well as a condition that they remain outwith that place for a specified period,[50] and such conditions can be imposed by a constable of the rank of sergeant or above.[51]

**3.48** In terms of s 26(6) of CJ(S)A 2016, any conditions imposed are to be treated as 'liberation conditions' in terms of Sched 1 to CJ(S)A 2016 in relation to the offence of breach of such liberation conditions.

**3.49** In the context of domestic abuse proceedings, the use of conditions in terms of CJ(S)A 2016, s 26(3)(b) are often utilised by the police, usually in providing that an accused person does not approach contact or communicate or attempt to approach contact or communicate with named individuals pending the appearance of the accused person in court. In practice this will usually be the complainer, and if there are children involved, those children. It is also a common requirement that an accused person does not enter or approach a specified locus, often the home address of the complainer or any other significant witness in the case. This again closely mirrors the type of bail conditions which are regularly imposed by the courts.

## MODIFICATION OF UNDERTAKING

**3.50** Where an individual has been released subject to police liberation, steps can be taken to modify the terms of that undertaking by the Procurator Fiscal who can, by notice:

(a) change the court at which the person must appear;

(b) change the time at which they must appear; and/or

(c) remove or alter any conditions imposed.[52]

48 CJ(S)A 2016, s 26(4)(a).
49 CJ(S)A 2016, s 26(5)(a).
50 CJ(S)A 2016, s 26 (4)(b).
51 CJ(S)A 2016, s 26(5)(b).
52 CJ(S)A 2016, s 27(1).

**3.51** Any notice issued which has the effect of modifying the terms of an undertaking must be in writing and served on the individual in accordance with the requirements of s 141 of the Criminal Procedure (Scotland) Act 1995, which sets out the lawful methods of citation.[53] The Procurator Fiscal is restricted in relation to the nature and extent of any modification.[54]

## POWER TO RESCIND AN UNDERTAKING

**3.52** The Procurator Fiscal does have the power to rescind an undertaking given in terms of CJ(S)A 2016, s 25(2)(a), irrespective of whether that person is to be prosecuted or not. [55] Again, this is done by a notice served in accordance with s 141 of the Criminal Procedure (Scotland) Act 1995,[56] and any rescission will take effect at the end of the day on which that notice is served.[57]

**3.53** A police constable is empowered to arrest a person without warrant if they have reasonable grounds to believe that a person subject to an undertaking condition is likely to fail to comply with the terms of that undertaking.[58] Where this occurs the original undertaking is treated as having been rescinded. [59] This situation also applies in the situation where, since being most recently arrested that individual has been charged with the offence in connection with which they were in police custody when the undertaking was given.[60] It also applies where a person subject to an undertaking is in custody on a separate matter and the constable has reasonable grounds to believe that the person has failed, or if liberated is likely to fail, to comply with the terms of the undertaking.[61]

## EXPIRY OF UNDERTAKING

**3.54** Any undertaking given under CJ(S)A 2016, s 25(2)(a) automatically expires at the end of the day on which the person had been required to appear at court, or on the day on which they have been brought to court having been arrested on a warrant issued at court as a result of that individual having failed to appear at court on the appointed date.[62] It is perhaps worthy of note at this stage that in relation to police liberation, as opposed to investigative liberation that there is no equivalent provision to that contained within CJ(S)A 2016,

53 CJ(S)A 2016, s 27.
54 CJ(S)A 2016, s 27(2).
55 CJ(S)A 2016, s 28(1).
56 CJ(S)A 2016, s 28(3).
57 CJ(S)A 2016, s 28(2).
58 CJ(S)A 2016, s 28(4).
59 CJ(S)A 2016, s 28(5)(a).
60 CJ(S)A 2016, s 28(5)(b).
61 CJ(S)A 2016, s 28(6).
62 CJ(S)A 2016, s 29(1)(a).

s 17(1)(a) whereby the conditions imposed automatically fall after 28 days, there being no such specific time limit mentioned in relation to police liberation.

**3.55** As well as the Procurator Fiscal's right to have any condition contained within an undertaking reviewed, an accused person also has the right to request that a condition or conditions are removed or to have an alternative condition imposed.[63] Such applications are made to the court and are determined by a Sheriff. As is the case with the similar process relating to investigative liberation, before disposing of any such application, the Sheriff must provide the Procurator Fiscal with an opportunity to make representations on the application. [64] If the Sheriff, having heard representations considers that the condition being reviewed is no longer necessary or proportionate, then they may modify the requirements of the undertaking by either removing the condition or imposing an alternative condition that the Sheriff does consider to be necessary and proportionate for that purpose. [65]

## BREACH OF LIBERATION CONDITIONS

**3.56** Provisions for breaches of undertakings are contained in Schedule 1 to the 2016 Act;

> '1 (1) A person commits an offence if, without reasonable excuse, the person breaches a liberation condition by reason of—
>
> (a) failing to comply with an investigative liberation condition,
>
> (b) failing to appear at court as required by the terms of an undertaking, or
>
> (c) failing to comply with the terms of an undertaking, other than the requirement to appear at court.
>
> (2) Sub-paragraph (1) does not apply where (and to the extent that) a person breaches a liberation condition by reason of committing an offence (in which case see paragraph 3).
>
> (3) It is competent to amend a complaint to include an additional charge of an offence under sub-paragraph (1) at any time before the trial of a person in summary proceedings for—
>
> (a) the original offence, or
>
> (b) an offence arising from the same circumstances as the original offence.

63 CJ(S)A 2016, s 30(1).
64 CJ(S)A 2016, s 30(2).
65 CJ(S)A 2016, s 30(3).

(4) In sub-paragraph (3), 'the original offence' is the offence in connection with which—

(a) an investigative liberation condition was imposed, or

(b) an undertaking was given.'

## PENALTY FOR BREACH OF LIBERATION CONDITIONS

**3.57** A breach of the terms of CJ(S)A 2016, Sched 1, s 1(1) renders that person liable on summary complaint to a fine not exceeding level 3 on the standard scale, or imprisonment for a period not exceeding 60 days where the conviction is in the District Court or imprisonment not exceeding 12 months where that conviction is in the JP Court. [66]

**3.58** Any penalty imposed in terms of CJ(S)A 2016, Sched 1, s 1(1) can be imposed in addition to any other competent sentence which that Court can impose.

**3.59** Where a person is to be sentenced in relation to an offence under CJ(S) A 2016, Sched 1, s 1(1) the Court may remit that individual to a court which is dealing with the original offence,[67] where the original offence is defined as being the offence in relation to which either the investigative condition was imposed, or the undertaking was given.[68]

**3.60** Again, the Lord Advocate's Guidelines stress that police officers must consider the terms of the Domestic Abuse Protocol when considering liberation on undertaking for persons charged with offences involving domestic abuse, and the general presumption of liberty is to be considered having regard to the particular risks associated with domestic abuse cases. Reference is to be made to the Joint Domestic Abuse Protocol and consideration given to imposing appropriate further conditions of undertaking, having regard to risk and safety considerations. Account is to be taken of the views of the victim or witness, and the best interests of any child witness or victim must be a primary consideration. Victims should be advised when a suspect is to be released before they are in fact released, and the conditions of that undertaking are to be carefully explained to that victim.

66 CJ(S)A 2016, Sched 1, s 2(1).
67 CJ(S)A 2016, Sched 1, s 2(5).
68 CJ(S)A 2016, Sched 1, s 2(6).

## APPLICATION OF THE EXISTING LAW

**3.61** Police Scotland and COPFS have developed a Joint Protocol which sets out their joint current positions in relation to the detection, investigation and prosecution of cases involving allegations of domestic abuse.[69] This protocol sets out the priorities of the police in attending at incidents of domestic violence and thereafter the steps to be taken in relation to the investigation of such incidents and their subsequent prosecution, and deals with the considerations of the appropriate authorities in considering the status of an accused person at different stages during this process. These guidelines should also be read in conjunction with the provisions of the Lord Advocate's guidelines: liberation by the police.[70]

**3.62** In relation to investigative liberation the protocol acknowledges that there may well be situations where the police require and should be afforded more time to undertake their investigations. This will be considered appropriate where the police believe that there are further enquiries to be carried out and the officers concerned are satisfied that these enquiries may be conducted whilst that person is at liberty and subject to conditions. They also require to be satisfied that where these further enquiries cannot be completed immediately that there is a reasonable prospect they will be completed within 28 days.

**3.63** The protocol highlights the fact that given the particular risks associated with cases involving domestic abuse, before a suspect can be released, police officers must give careful consideration to ascertaining what conditions should be attached to the release of the suspect. This will include a full assessment of any risk posed to the victim, witnesses, or the investigation itself. In this decision-making process the police will consider the views of the victim, particularly with regard to any conditions which might be appropriate.

**3.64** The protocol also provides that any identified victim will be advised of the fact of the release of the alleged perpetrator and advised about the conditions of release attached to such an undertaking. In the event that these conditions are modified or removed by the Court, then the police are instructed to notify the victim of any such modifications or removals.

69 www.copfs.gov.uk/media/xjtd4i4p/joint-domestic-abuse-protocol.pdf [accessed 29 July 2025].

70 www.copfs.gov.uk/publications/lord-advocate-s-guidelines-liberation-by-the-police/html/#:~:text=in%20each%20case.-,General%20principles,keep%20that%20person%20in%20custody [accessed 29 July 2025].

## POLICE LIBERATION OR CUSTODY?

**3.65** The protocol acknowledges that when there exists a sufficiency of evidence, an accused person will either be released on an undertaking to appear at court at an early diet in terms of CJ(S)A 2016, s 26 or, in appropriate circumstances, that person will be held in custody pending an appearance in court on the next lawful date.

**3.66** Police officers are specifically instructed that they must take every precaution to ensure that no person is unreasonably or unnecessarily held in police custody, although given the particular risks associated with domestic abuse cases, which include the risk of victims being pressurised to change/withdraw their statements, it is recognised that it may be reasonable and necessary to hold such accused persons in custody pending an appearance in Court.

**3.67** In determining whether an accused should be released on an undertaking or held in custody, police officers are directed that they must have regard to the following factors:

- Any ongoing risk posed to the safety of the victim, children, witness, or any other member of the public. In this connection, regard should be had to any risk assessment which has been conducted.
- The nature and circumstances of the offence including the severity of the conduct and likely forum for prosecution. It is worthy of note however that undertakings are available in both summary and solemn cases.
- The likelihood of the accused reoffending having regard to the frequency of repeat victimisation in domestic abuse cases.
- The police will also take account of any previous convictions, pending cases, previous investigative liberation or undertaking conditions, and previous bail orders or other court orders in place. This consideration will involve having regard to any history of non-compliance with previous investigative liberation, or undertakings, bail, or other court orders.
- Regard will also be had as to whether the incident which has been reported is part of a course of conduct or pattern of behaviour, which involves a consideration of any previous history of domestic abuse, including incidents not previously brought to the attention of the police.
- The police will also consider whether there are any further lines of enquiry which have been identified and which may establish sufficient corroborative evidence for additional offences. Given that these might take some time, consideration must be given to the risk posed to the victim, although it may be considered more appropriate to release an

accused on undertaking pending full investigation instead of reporting the present circumstances immediately.[71]

- Regard must also be had to the terms of the Lord Advocate's Guidelines on Liberation by the Police.

**3.68** The guidance provides that where there is a likelihood of the accused reoffending, of failing to comply with undertaking conditions, or where there is a significant risk to the safety of the victim, any child, a witness or any other member of the public and it is not considered that these risks could appropriately be managed by the imposition of proportionate conditions of undertaking, then the accused should be detained in custody pending their appearance at court.[72]

**3.69** The protocol also provides that where an accused person is released on an undertaking, that the reasons for release must be recorded in the police report with reference to the factors noted above.

**3.70** While the general rule in relation to undertakings is that an accused person should appear at court no later than 28 days after the date of liberation, the Lord Advocate's guidelines provide that in cases involving domestic abuse the date of that court appearance should be not later than 14 days after the date of liberation.[73]

**3.71** If the decision is made to liberate an accused person subject to an undertaking, consideration will be given to any appropriate further conditions which should be applied to that undertaking. This process is undertaken on a case-by-case basis and will take account of the individual circumstances as they pertain to each case.

## FAILING TO APPEAR AT COURT IN ACCORDANCE WITH AN UNDERTAKING

**3.72** The police also have instructions that where an accused, without reasonable excuse, fails to appear as required at court or to comply with an imposed condition, then the terms of the undertaking will be deemed to have been breached, and where sufficient evidence exists, then this is to be treated as a serious matter which must be reported to the Procurator Fiscal. Where a person is arrested for such a breach of undertaking conditions, instructions are

71 Joint Protocol between Police Scotland and the Crown Office and Procurator Fiscal Service (6th edition) (May 2023), paras 38 and 39.

72 Joint Protocol between Police Scotland and the Crown Office and Procurator Fiscal Service, para 40.

73 Lord Advocate Guidelines: Liberation by the Police, Section 6.

given that that accused person will not be a suitable candidate for a further undertaking unless exceptional circumstances exist. Accordingly, the default position in these circumstances will be detention in custody to appear at court on the next lawful day.

**3.73** If a constable has reasonable grounds to suspect that a person released subject to an undertaking has or is likely to break the conditions of the undertaking then notwithstanding that there is insufficient corroborative evidence to report them for a separate and distinct charge of breach of undertaking, that person can be arrested, and if so arrested the original undertaking is to be treated as having been rescinded and they will be dealt with as simply having been charged with the original offence which will be reported to the Procurator Fiscal. Again, in these circumstances they will, in the absence of exceptional circumstances, be detained in custody to appear at court on the next lawful day.

**3.74** If an accused person is not traced at the time of the incident and where there is sufficient available evidence, then the police will report the original circumstances to the Procurator Fiscal within the same accelerated timescales as if the accused were detained in custody and, if appropriate, a warrant will be sought for the apprehension of the accused.[74]

74 Joint Protocol between Police Scotland and the Crown Office and Procurator Fiscal Service, para 47.

# Chapter 4

# Bail

## OVERVIEW

**4.01** The currently applicable bail provisions are to be found in the Criminal Procedure (Scotland) Act 1995 (CP(S)A 1995) as varied most recently by the Bail and Release from Custody (Scotland) Act 2023 (BRC(S)A 2023), which brought particular domestic abuse considerations into the bail. The BRC(S) A 2023 amended Part 3 of CP(S)A 1995 to limit the circumstances in which the court may refuse bail, enable the court to receive information from justice social work or prosecutors to help inform its decisions on bail, and require the court, when it refuses or grants bail, to state and record particular reasons for its decision. The interests of public safety are explicitly stated to include the protection of the complainer from a risk of harm. In this context, 'harm' means physical or psychological harm and 'psychological harm' includes fear, alarm and distress.[1]

**4.02** The bail provisions in Scotland have their origins in the common law,[2] taking into account the requirement of Article 5 of the ECHR. Bail is to be granted unless there is a good reason for refusing to do so in the public interest [3]. The grounds upon which the court may determine that there is a good reason for refusing bail are narrated in CP(S)A 1995, s 23C(1)(b) and (c). In assessing those grounds or any of them the court is required to have regard to all relevant considerations, including whether the person was already on bail, and any previous convictions ( CP(S)A 1995, s 23C(2)). Whenever the court grants or refuses bail, it must state its reasons. (CP(S)A 1995, s 24(2A). There is a strong presumption in favour of bail. In determining whether there is a good reason to refuse bail the court must consider whether the imposition of special conditions (which includes electronic monitoring), displaces the necessity of a remand (CP(S)A 1995, s 23B(2)). Refusal arises from the existence of a good reason to refuse as well as the necessity of such refusal.

**4.03** Both parties (crown and defence) must be given the opportunity to be heard on the question of bail (CP(S)A 1995, s 23B(4)) but the decision is one for the court, and the attitude of the Crown does not determine the matter

1 (see CP(S)A 1995, s 23B(8), added by BRC(S)A 2023, s 2(2)(c)).
2 *Mackintosh v McGlinchy* 1921 JC 75
3 CP(S)A 1995, s 23B.

(CP(S)A 1995, s 23B(5)). Section 23B(7) of CP(S)A 1995 allows the court to request the prosecutor, the accused person's solicitor or counsel or an officer of a local authority to provide it with information relevant to the question of bail. The prosecutor may provide a conduit to domestic abuse advocacy services or Victim Information and Advice.

**4.04** Where the court considers that there may be good reason to refuse it despite the lack of opposition from the crown, the court is entitled to be provided with information, such as a record of any previous convictions, for the purposes of making a decision (CP(S)A 1995, s 23B(6)).

## ROLE OF THE COMPLAINER

**4.05** There is no right for a complainer to be represented or have a right of audience. Neither domestic law or European jurisprudence provide that it is necessary to grant a right of audience to a complainer in the circumstances of domestic abuse cases. The complainer is entitled to have their right to family life respected in terms of Article 8, but the procedures which exist are convention compliant.[4]

**4.06** The complainer has no right to be represented in court or to address the court in the circumstances; machinery exists for their views to be drawn to the attention of the court.[5] The route by which information on complainer safety should be obtained is from the prosecutor.[6]

## FACTORS WHICH BEAR ON BAIL

**4.07** As was recognised in *Porch*, one of the main problems in domestic cases relates to the potential for victim retraction due to the close and often intimate relationship between the accused and victim. It was similarly recognised that the reason why particular special conditions were often added in domestic abuse cases was that the nature of the relationship created an

4 *HM Advocate v Porch* [2015] HCJAC 111. This was discussed in the Scottish Parliament where the minister said: 'Domestic abuse involves complex dynamics in which it can be important that information about concerns that may lead to a partner or an ex-partner being placed on remand is not attributed to information that is provided by the complainer, so as not to compromise safety or make complainers fearful to engage.' (SP Official Report, 10 May 2023.)

5 In *Porch* the complainer was represented and made submissions to the court but the court held that she was not a party see paras 34–36 quote; See also *RR v HM Advocate* 2021 J.C. 167 paras 46 and 51 to show why complainer has no right to be convened as a party.

6 As was discussed at stage 2: 'It is clearly important in many cases, such as those involving domestic abuse, that information on potential harm is made known to the court, but that should be done via the prosecutor, and amendment 15 helps to strengthen the law in that regard.' (SP Official Report, 21 June 2023.)

increased risk that the standard conditions may not be obtempered, standing the relationship and the vulnerable position of victims of domestic violence.

**4.08** In many cases, the complainer will be anxious not to have contact with the accused in any way, and may be vulnerable to pressure or influence from the accused were such contact to take place. The imposition of special conditions may be considered necessary in an attempt to ensure the observance of the standard conditions that the accused should not interfere with witnesses, obstruct the course of justice or commit further offences against the complainer.

**4.09** Alternatively the complainer may make representations through the crown or through his or her own solicitor asking that there be no special conditions, or no bail order at all; while the complainer's view about such conditions may be a relevant consideration, it is not determinative. It may not coincide with the court's assessment of the wider public interest, or of the particular risk to the complainer. It is very common for such conditions to be imposed in domestic abuse cases, even against the wishes of the complainer. It may be that the risk of further offending, or of the accused pressurising the complainer to withdraw their complaint, justifies additional measures in a domestic abuse case which might not be required in a different context. In such cases it is usually argued that special conditions are necessary to ensure compliance with the standard conditions: not to offend, not to interfere with witnesses, and not cause alarm or distress to witnesses. In the absence of such a condition, the accused and complainer may continue to live together, or spend time together, while the accused awaits trial. In those circumstances it may be concluded that the risk of further offending, or of the accused seeking to discourage the complainer from engaging, is particularly high thereby necessitating additional conditions to ensure observance with the standard conditions.

**4.10** In *Porch,*[7] Lady Dorrian said:

> ' 40. … The imposition of special conditions of the kind which were imposed in the present case may be considered necessary in an attempt to ensure the observance of the standard conditions that the accused should not interfere with witnesses, obstruct the course of justice or commit further offences against the complainer. In circumstances where the complainer has indicated that she does not wish conditions imposed, or where she would rather they were removed, the court has to consider the situation in the context of the obligations in relation to the protection of victims of domestic violence. Victims of domestic violence are of a particular vulnerability and the need for active

7 [2015] HCJAC 111.

> state involvement in their protection has been emphasised in a number of international instruments, for example those referred to in *Opuz v Turkey* [2010] 50 EHRR 28. The steps which should be taken may include ensuring that the public prosecutor can continue a case even in the face of a retraction by the alleged victim (see *Wilson v UK* paragraph 49). In the case of *Criminal Proceedings v Gueye and others* [2012] 1 WLR 2672 …the European Court of Human Rights considered that the duty to enable victims properly to take part in criminal proceedings did not preclude a mandatory injunction in domestic violence cases preventing the accused from being in contact with the complainer for a specified period of time, even when the complainer sought a reconciliation.'

## CHILDREN

**4.11** Care should be taken in preventing contact with children, especially if they are not named complainers. The impact which contact arrangements with children may have on a vulnerable complainer will require to be considered carefully. It may be that conditions will require to be framed in consultation with domestic abuse advocacy services, where available. Each case must be considered on its own facts and circumstances. There is the opportunity to seek further information from the Crown and the Justice Social Work department, both on the impact on the complainer and wider issues such as children and family set up. Domestic abuse advocacy services, where available, can assist in providing fuller views from the complainer and a professional input as to risk. A condition keeping an accused away from the family home may have significant implications for family budgets, for division of childcare or other domestic responsibilities, for contact between parties. Consideration might be given to prohibiting contact between complainer and accused other than for pre-arranged and agreed contact between the accused and the children of the relationship.

## STANDARD CONDITIONS

**4.12** In granting bail, the court requires to impose certain 'standard' conditions. These are specified[8] as follows, that the accused:

> '(a) appears at the appointed time at every diet relating to the offence with which he is charged of which he is given due notice; or at which he is required by this Act to appear;
>
> (b) does not commit an offence while on bail;

8 CP(S)A 1995, s 24(5).

(c) does not interfere with witnesses or otherwise obstruct the course of justice whether in relation to himself or any other person;

(ca) does not behave in a manner which causes, or is likely to cause, alarm or distress to witnesses;

[...]

(d) makes himself available for the purpose of enabling enquiries or a report to be made to assist the court in dealing with him for the offence with which he is charged; and

(e) where the (or an) offence in respect of which he is admitted to bail is one listed in subsection (7A)(b), does not seek to obtain, otherwise than by way of a solicitor, any precognition of or statement by the complainer in relation to the subject matter of the offence.'

**4.13** If bail is granted, the sheriff should explain to an accused, if present, the effect of:

the standard conditions of bail;

- any special conditions of bail;
- the requirement to apply to the court, within seven days of the change, if their domicile of citation ceases to be their normal place of residence; and
- the consequences of breach thereof.[9]

Also, in all cases (whether or not the accused is present), the accused must be given a written explanation of the conditions, again in ordinary language.[10]

**4.14** A complainer in CP(S)A 1995, s 24(7A) is defined as the person against whom the offence is alleged to have been committed, including certain sexual offending, and an offence to which CP(S)A 1995, s 288DC applies (domestic abuse cases), meaning:

- an offence under s 1(1) of the Domestic Abuse (Scotland) Act 2018; or
- an offence that is aggravated as described in s 1(1)(a) of the Abusive Behaviour and Sexual Harm (Scotland) Act 2016.

9 CP(S)A 1995, s 25(A1).

10 CP(S)A 1995, s 25(B1). The enforceability of the bail order is not dependent upon the accused signing the bail order.

## BAIL – GENERAL CONSIDERATIONS

**4.15** Section 23B(1) of CP(S)A 1995 provides the grounds for determining that there is a good reason for refusing bail. The first task to the court is to identify if a ground for refusing bail exists. The grounds introduced by BRC(S) A 2023 remain as they were in CP(S)A 1995, s 23C, with a restriction added in respect of consideration of absconding or failing to appear in summary cases.

**4.16** CP(S)A 1995, s 23C provides:

> '(1) In any proceedings in which a person is accused of an offence, the following are grounds on which it may be determined that there is good reason for refusing bail—
>
> (a) subject to subsection (1A) any substantial risk that the person might if granted bail—
>
> (i) abscond; or
>
> (ii) fail to appear at a diet of the court as required;
>
> (b) any substantial risk of the person committing further offences if granted bail;
>
> (c) any substantial risk that the person might if granted bail—
>
> (i) interfere with witnesses; or
>
> (ii) otherwise obstruct the course of justice, in relation to himself or any other person;
>
> (d) any other substantial factor which appears to the court to justify keeping the person in custody.'

**4.17** The statute provides that if the court determines that there are good reasons for refusing bail, in any case where bail is refused, the reasons must be stated in court and recorded in the minutes of the proceedings assessment. Material will require to be placed before the decision maker ,such as a record of previous convictions, details about the allegations or information/intelligence about behaviour. There must be something upon which reliance can be placed to justify a finding that a ground is established. This chapter looks briefly at the various grounds.

### Substantial risk that accused might abscond

**4.18** A person may be remanded in custody pending trial, consistently with Article 5(3), where there is a justified fear that, if released on bail, they would fail to surrender. It is not enough, however, that it will be possible (or even easy) for an accused to abscond. What is required is' a whole set of circumstances … which give reason to suppose that the consequences and hazards of flight will seem to him to be a lesser evil than continued imprisonment'.[11] In *Monterroso v HM Advocate,*[12] a Guatemalan national was detained under the Immigration Act 1971. He was also charged with being concerned in the importation of cocaine. He was granted bail in respect of the criminal charge. The Crown appealed the grant of bail and the accused was remanded in custody. Bail was refused, on appeal, in view, *inter alia*, of the gravity of the offence. The accused petitioned the High Court for review of the refusal of bail on appeal. The court noted that the gravity of the offence and the consequent risk of a heavy sentence were plainly matters which might increase an accused person's wish to avoid trial and sentence. The risk of an accused absconding is one of the major considerations in deciding whether bail should be refused, and the nature and gravity of the alleged offence can clearly bear upon that question. In assessing the likelihood of the prisoner absconding, the gravity of the offence was not the only consideration to be taken into account.[13] The court concluded that there was a substantial risk of the accused absconding because of the gravity of the alleged offence, taken together with the absence of any pre-existing connection between the petitioner and Scotland; and the possibility that the alleged offence bore some of the marks of organised crime, and thus the possible availability of assistance in absconding.

## Substantial risk that accused will fail to appear at a diet as required

**4.19** A substantial risk that an accused will fail to appear will justify the refusal of bail, informed by whether the accused has previously failed to appear in the case or has previous convictions for failure to appear under CP(S) A 1995, ss 150(8), 27(1)(a) or s 27(7). Additionally, the notice of previous convictions will disclose if there have been previous failures to appear (even if these have not given rise to a conviction).This ground will, of course, be particularly relevant when dealing with an accused who is appearing to answer a warrant in respect of an earlier failure to appear. However, note that in summary proceedings bail can be refused on the sole basis of failing to appear or absconding only if the accuse has previously failed to appear in the current proceedings, or if the complaint includes a charge of failing to appear. Again the reason must be stated

11 *Stogmuller v Austria* (1979–80) 1 EHRR 155 at para 15. Particular circumstances cited by the court included the prospect of a significant sentence, the accused's particular distaste for detention, or the lack of well-established ties in the country in which he or she is seeking bail.

12 2000 SCCR 974.

13 *Letellier v France* (1992) 14 EHRR 83; Series A, No 207.

## Substantial risk of the commission of further offence

**4.20** A substantial risk of the accused committing further offences will justify the refusal of bail. In assessing this ground, the nature of the charge, the accused's previous convictions, and any other information advanced by the Crown will be relevant. An extensive, and/or recent, record for offences analogous to that charged might suggest a substantial risk of an established pattern of criminal conduct continuing. However, a risk of further offending cannot be assumed from the mere fact that the accused has a criminal record[14] It is necessary to consider whether any previous convictions are comparable, either in nature or in degree of seriousness, to the charges against the accused. Other considerations relevant to this ground might include an allegation that the accused has threatened to commit further offences. Such an allegation might form part of the charge itself, or might be advanced by the Crown in submissions – for example, if an accused's reply when charged included a threat to harm the complainer.

**4.21** A substantial risk of continued offending might also be established where the charges allege a sustained course of criminal conduct, particularly where the charges are serious. This may arise in domestic abuse cases where particular attention will be paid to previously domestically aggravated offending.

## Substantial risk that accused might interfere with witnesses

**4.22** There may be a risk that the accused, if released, would take action to interfere with witnesses or warn other suspects. The risk must be identifiable and there must be a clear reason to support such a conclusion. That risk may change throughout the life of a case. Again this may be thought to have currency in domestic cases for the reason explained in *Porch* in looking at special conditions -–retraction can take place due to the close intimate and particular relationship between accused and victim/complainer. In some cases the Crown may provide information that the accused has attempted to make contact with witnesses from prison, or that he has threatened to harm a witness. Alternatively, it may be that the charge alleges that the accused has threatened the complainer or another witness. Similarly, an allegation that the accused has approached or contacted a witness in breach of a special condition of bail, or convictions for such conduct, will be relevant when assessing this ground. The court must bear in mind that this risk will often diminish with time.[15] Where the accused has been at liberty for a period of time since the alleged offence and no interference is alleged during that period, the risk of interference pending

14 *Muller v France* (1997) ECHR 11.
15 *Letellier v France* (fn 13 above).

trial may appear less substantial. So the court should have its attention drawn to any periods of time between alleged offending and the case calling; accused might be invited to appear or appear on warrant and the court should factor in any time elapsed in assessing the risk of interference; it must be substantial, noting that, it may be submitted that the risk of interference has increased with the commencement of the criminal proceedings.

### Substantial risk that the accused might (in relation to themself or another person) otherwise obstruct the course of justice

**4.23** This ground may exist where there is reason to conclude that the accused will destroy relevant evidence or warn other suspects if at liberty. Relevant considerations are likely to include the nature of the offence, particularly where the charges allege, for example, an attempt to defeat the ends of justice or to pervert the course of justice. Similarly, the existence of previous convictions for such offences will be relevant. In some cases the Crown may seek to rely on the accused's alleged conduct following detection or arrest. For example it may be alleged that the accused has sought, while in custody, to direct the destruction of evidence. If the accused has previously been on bail and there is no evidence that he or she interfered with the course of justice during that period, this will be a strong factor militating against refusing bail.[16]

### Any other substantial factor which appears to the court to justify keeping the person in custody

**4.24** Bail may be refused in some circumstances if release would provoke public disorder, or place the accused at risk of reprisals, or to ensure that the accused remains at the disposal of the judicial authorities.[17] However, these cases make it clear that on a change of circumstances the question of bail will require to be reconsidered.

## MATERIAL CONSIDERATIONS IN ASSESSING GROUNDS FOR REFUSAL OF BAIL

**4.25** CP(S)A 1995, s 23C(2) states:

> (2) In assessing the grounds specified in subsection (1) above, the court must have regard to all material considerations including

16 *Ringeisen v Austria* 1979–80 EHRR 455, paras 105–106; *IA v France* 1998 ECHR 89, para 109.

17 *Letellier v France* (fn 13 above); *IA v France* (fn 16 above).

(in so far as relevant in the circumstances of the case) the following examples—

(a) the—

(i) nature (including level of seriousness) of the offences before the court;

(ii) probable disposal of the case if the person were convicted of the offences;

(b) whether the person was subject to a bail order when the offences are alleged to have been committed;

(c) whether the offences before the court are alleged to have been committed—

(i) while the person was subject to another court order;

(ii) while the person was on release on licence or parole;

(iii) during a period for which sentence of the person was deferred;

(d) the character and antecedents of the person, in particular

(i) the nature of any previous convictions of the person (including convictions by courts outside Scotland);

(ii) whether the person has previously contravened a bail order or other court order (by committing an offence or otherwise);

(iii) whether the person has previously breached the terms of any release on licence or parole (by committing an offence or otherwise);

(iv) whether the person is serving or recently has served a sentence of imprisonment in connection with a matter referred to in sub-paragraphs (i) to (iii) above;

(e) the associations and community ties of the person.

**4.26** CP(S)A 1995, s 23C(3) states:

'(3) In subsection (1A)(a), "relevant diet" means a diet of the court relating to the offence with which the person is charged—

(a) of which the person has been given due notice, or

(b) at which the person is required by this Act to appear.'

**4.27** The court must have regard to all material considerations. Although they are distinct in CP(S)A 1995, account must be taken of 'all material considerations' when establishing whether one of the 'grounds' exists. The list of examples is non-exhaustive. While the grounds for refusing bail and the material considerations may be closely linked, bail decisions must be based on establishing one or more of the CP(S)A 1995, s 23C(1) grounds, keeping in mind that the material considerations in CP(S)A 1995, s 23C(2) may not, in and of themselves, justify the refusal of bail.

## CP(S)A 1995, s 23C(2)(a)(i): Nature (including level of seriousness) of offence

**4.28** The nature and seriousness of the offence is not of itself a sufficient reason for refusing bail; it is a material but not decisive consideration. In serious cases, the nature and gravity of an offence might support a conclusion that there is a substantial risk that the accused will abscond. Or it might be that the nature of the offence suggests a substantial risk that the accused will commit further offences or interfere with witnesses or abscond[18].

## CP(S)A 1995, s 23C(2)(a)(ii): Probable disposal of the case if the person were convicted of the offence

**4.29** This consideration introduces the proportionality test required by the ECHR. It may be disproportionate to refuse bail in respect of a charge which has no likelihood of resulting in a custodial sentence; the corollary is that the prospect of a substantial custodial sentence may, in some cases, support the conclusion that the accused is likely to abscond. There may be cases in which a custodial sentence is likely on conviction as a result of the accused's record rather than the nature of the offence. It could be argued that a person facing a significant sentence may present with a substantial risk of obstructing the course of justice. that may justify a finding of the ground set out in CP(S) A 1995, s 23C(1)(d) (any other substantial factor).

## CP(S)A 1995, s 23C(2)(b): Whether the accused was on bail at the time of the instant offence

**4.30** In relevant cases, the petition or complaint will usually include a bail aggravation providing the dates of previous bail orders and the courts which granted bail. Existing bail from the High Court may point strongly against a grant of bail. The nature and seriousness of the charge for which the accused is on bail may assist in reaching a decision and if necessary, the Crown should

18 *Monterroso v Secretary of State for the Home Department* 2000 SCCR 974.

be asked to provide information about the matters for which the accused is on bail. This is likely to be a consideration as to whether the ground at CP(S)A 1995, s 23C(1)(b) (substantial risk of further offending) or CP(S)A 1995, s 23C(1)(d) (any other substantial factor) is established. If the accused is on bail for a domestic offence or a domestically aggravated offence, that will be a material factor if further domestic allegations arise.

## CP(S)A 1995, s 23C(2)(c): Whether the offence is alleged have been committed whilst the accused was subject to another order of the court, on licence, parole or deferred sentence

**4.31** This consideration is an update of the so-called Wheatley guidelines,[19] where an accused is in a 'position of trust'. Court orders can now be imposed which put the accused in that position, such as community payback orders (CPO), or drug treatment and testing order (DTTO). This is likely to be a consideration as to whether the ground at CP(S)A 1995, s 23C(1)(b) or (d) is established. This will be particularly so if there is a domestic offence in respect of which the accused is undergoing a domestically related programme requirement of a CPO, or some equivalent.

## CP(S)A 1995, s 23C(2)(d): The character and antecedents of the person

**4.32** This includes a number of more specific considerations as follows:

- the nature of any previous convictions (including convictions from outwith Scotland);
- whether the accused has previously contravened a bail or other court order by committing an offence or otherwise;
- whether the accused has previously breached the terms of any release on licence or parole by committing an offence or otherwise; and
- whether the accused is serving, or has previously served, a sentence of imprisonment in connection with any of the foregoing matters.

**4.33** A history of offending, especially a pattern of similar offending may well establish a ground under CP(S)A 1995, s 23C(1)(b). A history of prison sentences and offending on licence may lend itself to establishing a ground under CP(S)A 1995, s 23C(1)(d). A history of breaching court orders may suggest a likelihood that the accused will not comply with bail conditions. That

19 Set out in *Smith v McCallum* 1982 SCCR 115.

could be said to establish a ground under CP(S)A 1995, s 23C(1)(c). That is more often a consideration in reality for the second part of the test and may not always assist in those terms in assessing if one of the CP(S)A 1995, s 23C grounds exists. It will have to be specifically considered when the court applies its mind to CP(S)A 1995, s 23B(2). Where an accused's record discloses recent convictions for analogous offending, breaching bail, offending against the same victim, breaching a court order such as a disqualification from driving or a community payback order, or interfering with the course of justice, those circumstances may provide material on which to assess all four grounds.

## CP(S)A 1995, s 23C(2)(e): The associations and community ties of a person

**4.34** The absence of community ties in the country may, in some cases, support the conclusion that the accused is likely to abscond. In marginal cases it can be helpful to elicit information about the accused's home circumstances in order to allay, or confirm, any concerns about the likelihood of the accused complying with the conditions of bail. In the wider assessment in the second part of the test, if the accused has a fixed address, family ties and a job or other responsibilities, these can be good indicators that there is less likelihood of them failing to comply with bail conditions. Family ties in domestic abuse cases are often a matter put before the court – contact, childcare commitment or financial dependence, for example. A condition keeping the accused away from the family home may have significant implications for family budgets, for division of childcare or other domestic responsibilities, or contact between parties. These must be balanced against the considerations which favour bail and the imposition of special conditions

## CP(S)A 1995, s 23C(2)(g): Other material considerations

**4.35** As has been said, the list of material considerations provided by CP(S)A 1995, s 23C is non-exhaustive. Other considerations may apply. It was held that the length of time during which a person is likely to remain on remand is a factor in deciding whether to grant bail and one to be given particular weight in light of extended periods of remand during the period of the Coronavirus pandemic.[20] Such considerations might be the health of accused, ongoing treatments, caring responsibilities, parental responsibilities, upcoming examinations, job opportunities

20 *JD v HMA* [2020] HCJAC 15. That case is also a strong authority for the pre-eminent consideration being the risk imposed by the accused.

## PART TWO OF THE TEST

## Public interest and necessity (CP(S)A 1995, s 23B(1A)(b))

**4.36** The public interest test is contained in CP(S)A 1995, s 23B(1A)(b). Once a ground has been established, the court moves on to the second consideration; a good reason for refusing bail can only be established if:

> '(b) having regard to the public interest, and having considered the imposition of bail conditions in accordance with subsection (2), it is necessary to refuse bail—
>
> (i) in the interests of public safety, including the protection of the complainer from a risk of harm, or
>
> (ii) to prevent a significant risk of prejudice to the interests of justice.'

**4.37** This section reflects the policy intention that only those who pose a risk to (i) public safety or (ii) the delivery of justice in a case should be remanded.[21] In considering public safety, CP(S)A 1995, s 23B(8) defines 'complainer' as the person against whom the offence to which the proceedings relate is alleged to have been committed, and the terms 'harm' as physical or psychological harm, and 'psychological harm' as including fear, alarm and distress.

**4.38** In considering prejudice to the interests of justice, CP(S)A 1995, s 23B(9) defines that as:

> '(a) the accused person evading justice as a result of the proceedings being delayed or discontinued, or
>
> (b) the course of justice in the proceedings being impeded or prejudiced as a result of—
>
> (i) the destruction, concealment or withholding of evidence,
>
> (ii) the giving of false or misleading evidence, or
>
> (iii) the quality of evidence, or its sufficiency in law, being diminished.'

## Public safety

**4.39** Where the court is not satisfied that the public interest could be safeguarded by the imposition of conditions, bail may be refused if the court considers it necessary in the interests of public safety (including complainer

21 This might be seen to reflect the decision in *JD v HMA* [2020] HCJAC 15 where the emphasis was very clearly on the risk posed.

safety) – CP(S)A 1995, s 23B(1A)(b) points to 'a risk of harm' to the complainer, compared to 'a significant risk' of prejudice to the interests of justice. In considering public safety, harm is defined as meaning physical or psychological harm. Psychological harm is further defined as including fear, alarm and distress. These are common words which should be given their ordinary meaning. So, public safety may well be compromised by an accused who targets an individual in a domestic relationship. The specific consideration of psychological harm suggests that the court should have regard to similar considerations as in domestic abuse legislation. The policy intention is explicitly to make the safety of complainers a discrete factor in the courts decision-making when assessing public safety to determine the question of bail. It is not however restricted to domestic complainers. It should be borne in mind that the question of special conditions is still a key consideration even if a risk of harm is established by either the record, nature of offence or other information obtained.

## Prejudice of the interests of justice

**4.40** In considering the interests of justice, 'prejudice' means the accused person evading justice as a result of either the proceedings being delayed or discontinued. It also means the course of justice in the proceedings being impeded or prejudiced as a result of the destruction, concealment or withholding of evidence, the giving of false or misleading evidence or the quality or sufficiency of evidence being diminished. The risk must be 'significant', so that some information will be required specific to the accused or to the offence.

## Special conditions – the need to consider if special conditions can safeguard the public interest

**4.41** CP(S)A 1995, s 23B(2) provides that if the court has determined that a CP(S)A 1995, s 23C(1) ground exists, the final step in considering the necessity test (public safety/interests of justice) is to 'consider the extent to which the public interest could, if bail were granted, be safeguarded by the imposition of bail conditions'. Where the court is satisfied that the public interest could be safeguarded through the imposition of conditions, bail may not be refused. CP(S)A 1995, s 24(4) makes mandatory the imposition of the standard conditions above and 'such further conditions as the court … considers necessary to secure (i) that the standard conditions are observed.' In any case where CP(S)A 1995, s 24(2C) applies (allegations of domestic, sexual, stalking offences) and additional conditions are not imposed, the court should state why it considers in the circumstances of the case that such conditions are unnecessary (CP(S)A 1995, s 24(2B)). Special bail conditions may only be imposed where the court considers them necessary to ensure observance of the standard conditions. In all cases it is necessary to ensure that any special condition is precise and readily enforceable. This text focuses on those which might arise in domestic offending; it is important to note that special conditions are not to be used where they could simply be viewed as some kind of punishment or where they are unnecessary to address the question of safeguarding public safety/interests of justice.

**4.42** It is essential that special conditions, such as refraining from contacting a named person or going to a particular address, are explained to the accused from the Bench in plain terms, and for the sheriff to obtain (and note) the accused's undertaking to obey them. This procedure is particularly important in domestic abuse cases. As was recognised in *Porch,* cases of domestic abuse can raise more involved issues in relation to special conditions, a matter recognised by the changes made to the bail provisions.

## Nature of special conditions

**4.43** The imposition of these type of conditions, where the background suggests a pattern of abuse in particular, are intended to ensure a witness's ability to give evidence is not impacted (thus assisting with securing compliance with the standard condition at CP(S)A 1995, s 24(5)(c)). Such additional conditions are also aimed at protecting the complainer from the risk of further abuse (thus assisting with securing compliance with the standard condition at CP(S) A 1995, s 24(5)(b) and (ca)). The imposition of the additional conditions is a matter for the court. Such conditions are commonly requested by the Crown in domestic abuse cases and are often applied by the Court. Such cases can present difficult decisions. It is the practice of the police and the procurator fiscal to obtain and record the complainer's views on the question of bail conditions. If not provided these can be sought from the justice social worker or local court-based third sector agency. The complainer's views are likely to be a relevant (but not a determinative) consideration and, if not volunteered by the Crown, the court may wish to seek them. If enquiries are to be made of the complainer, it is important that that is done by a party who is independent of the accused (for example, the procurator fiscal or a member of an advocacy service) and in a manner which will enable a complainer to speak as freely as possible (ie outwith the presence of the accused or their solicitor). A complainer who is fearful of an accused or who is subject to control or influence is unlikely to be able to so say in the accused's presence: doing so may increase the risk of harm. The complainer should not be made to feel responsible for the outcome of the decision and the consequences for the accused.

# TYPE OF SPECIAL CONDITIONS IMPOSED

## Prohibition of contact with named individual

**4.44** In some cases additional conditions are imposed requiring the accused to refrain from contact with the witness, or to avoid a certain locus.

In some cases these conditions may be an unnecessary precaution, but they are usually accepted, and there is seldom any debate as to the extent to which they are necessary to secure the observation of the standard conditions.[22] Special conditions will ordinarily include a standard request from the crown for conditions not to approach or contact a complainer in domestic abuse or sexual offence cases. It is common to impose a condition that the accused does not approach or contact or communicate with or attempt to approach or contact[23] or communicate with a named person. This is often (but not always) the complainer.[24] The court is often asked to balance the wider public interest with the pleas of a complainer who say that she wishes the accused to be permitted to come home. Consideration of the expressed views of the complainer, their right to family life and the presumption of innocence have to be balanced against the factors identified as arising in domestic abuse cases, such as the psychological effects of sustained domestic abuse and the impact of trauma. Practicalities must be considered; a condition such as, 'not to approach within 50 metres of (a named person)' is not easily enforceable. That standard condition will usually be that an accused must not approach contact or communicate, or attempt to approach contact or communicate with the named person. A condition may be sought to prevent entry to a specific property (a dwelling place, or place of work); care should be taken if an accused is to be prevented from entering a street. The condition should be only such as to assure compliance with the standard conditions; so the length of the street, the fact of it being a main shopping centre, or a transport hub are all considerations.

## Curfew

**4.45** A curfew may assist in avoiding, amongst other things, repeat night-time offending or provide an additional security for public safety. It might be difficult to justify a curfew where there is no course of conduct libelled or where any previous offending was committed during the day. The provision introduced by BRC(S)A 2023, on one view, suggests that a curfew should *always* be considered when otherwise the necessity test has been met. CP(S)A 1995, s 24(2AA)(iii) imposes a duty on the court, when refusing bail, specifically to state:

> 'its reasons for considering under section 23B(1A)(b) and (2) that either it would not be appropriate to impose on the accused bail conditions subject to a requirement to submit to monitoring in accordance with Part 1 of the Management of Offenders (Scotland) Act 2019 (electronic monitoring) or

22 *Porch* (fn 4 above).

23 On indirect contact by an accused with a protected person, by text message, sent to her sister, see *Cottam v McCloy* 2009 GWD 32-534.

24 See, for example, *Ross Pollock-Smith v PF* (Stirling) [2019] HCJAC 67 where the court imposed a condition not to contact the Justice Social worker officer preparing report.

> that doing so would not adequately safeguard the interests of public safety or justice as mentioned in section 23B(1A)(b)(i) or (ii)'.

It should accordingly be considered, although the value of a curfew in the context of domestic offending may be limited, as the protection tends to be required in relation to a named individual.

## The accused's address (domicile of citation)

**4.46** The accused's bail order must specify an address which will be the accused's domicile of citation (as defined in CP(S)A 1995, s 25(3)). The domicile of citation must be within the UK. It should also be the accused's normal place of residence and if the accused ceases to reside there, they must apply to the court within seven days to have their bail address altered.

**4.47** While it is clear that the bail address ought to be the accused's normal place of residence, the court may, on cause shown, direct that a different address be specified as the domicile of citation. This question can arise when the accused is of no fixed abode. The absence of a 'fixed abode' is, of course, a consideration when assessing the grounds for refusal of bail and, in some cases, it will militate against bail. In some courts the social work department's Bail Information Service may provide (or be asked to provide) a report which can be of particular value in assessing whether the accused has a fixed abode. Sometimes, such a report can be obtained (either in writing or orally) before the end of the sitting at which the accused appears and, if the report is positive on the question of accommodation, a custodial remand can be avoided. Some local authority areas have bail hostel accommodation and the Bail Information Service may advise thereon. But the issue of domicile of citation can arise in a domestic context where the crown insist on a condition that the accused leave the matrimonial or family home as a result of the allegations made; the condition may be accepted as a realistic alternative is remand, but there may be limited time/opportunities to identify an alternative address. However, it is submitted that the absence of a fixed address does not, in and of itself, justify the refusal of bail. If bail is otherwise justified, it should not be held up by absence of specific address. In such cases, the court is sometimes asked to specify the accused's solicitor's office as the domicile of citation or a local authority or third sector housing supplier. It is often said that the accused intends, on release, to present themself to the local authority as being homeless. This is argued to be sufficient cause for the court to specify an address which is not the appellant's normal place of residence. It is for the court to decide whether such a departure from the normal rule is justified in the particular circumstances of the case, but if acceding to such a request it is submitted that it is good practice to impose further conditions requiring the accused to report to the local authority within a specified period and, thereafter, to notify the sheriff clerk of their 'normal place of residence', again within a specified period.

## Change to the domicile of citation

**4.48** The Act of Adjournal (Criminal Procedure Rules) 1996, r 4.1 provides a procedure for changing the address in a bail order. It is not a bail review. The application is to be made in writing and the prosecutor is required, in terms of r 4.1(2), to notify the clerk in writing within seven days about whether or not they intend to oppose the application. Sometimes the procurator fiscal does not provide such notification but there is no provision which entitles the court to treat silence as consent to the application. It is suggested that good practice is to have the Sheriff Clerk confirm the Crown's position if necessary. Where the prosecutor does not oppose the application, the court proceeds to dispose of the application and the attendance of the applicant is not necessary (r 4.1(3)). Where the prosecutor notifies the clerk that they intend to oppose the application, a hearing must be fixed (r 4.1(4)).

## Review of bail conditions

**4.49** Both the accused and the prosecutor are entitled to apply to the court for a bail review. The accused may be asking the court to admit them to bail, where bail was previously refused, or to vary the conditions of bail.[25] The prosecutor may be asking the court to remand the accused in custody, where bail was previously granted, or to vary the conditions of bail.[26]

**4.50** A bail review is quite different from a bail application. A bail review can be made at any stage in proceedings, not only when the accused is brought before the court. A bail review can be sought no sooner than five days after the court's original (or first) decision on the accused's bail, and no sooner that 15 days after any subsequent decision on bail.[27]

**4.51** The court can only review its earlier decision where there has been a material change in the accused's circumstances or where there is material information which was not available to the court when it made its original bail decision. In domestic cases, this will often be prompted by a communication sent to the accused's solicitor or to the crown by the complainer or someone representing the complainer, asking for the bail conditions to be relaxed or even for the case to be dropped. The same considerations as narrated in para 4.15 et seq above apply, the complainer's view, while material, is not determinative; the passage of time since the bail order was made can be a factor in demonstrating that there has been no breach, or vouching the negative consequences for the family financially,

25 CP(S)A 1995, s 30.
26 CP(S)A 1995, s 31.
27 CP(S)A 1995, s 30(3).

etc. A review may arise when the accused provides a letter from the partner asking for the bail conditions to be relaxed for childcare, financial support, caring responsibilities ,etc. The decision remains a matter for the court in the exercise of its discretion but both the considerations above and *Porch* will require to be taken into account. The fact that 'there has been a material change in circumstances does not mean the application for review will succeed. It simply means that the court can review the original decision.

**4.52** From a procedural point of view, if there has been an earlier appeal against the sheriff's decision on bail, the correct forum must be used. Where the appeal did not succeed (and the sheriff's original decision was upheld) the sheriff can determine any subsequent application to review the original order. Where an appeal against the sheriff's original decision succeeded, the order admitting the accused to bail, or remanding them in custody, is an order of the Sheriff Appeal Court and cannot, therefore, be reviewed by the sheriff. In that situation any application for review should be made to the Sheriff Appeal Court.[28]

## Bail appeals

**4.53** Bail appeals are governed by CP(S)A 1995, s 32. Appeals may be at the instance of the accused or the Crown. In the case of a Crown appeal, the accused is not released but continues to be detained for a period of up to 72 hours (excluding Sundays and public holidays) from the grant of bail to allow the Crown appeal to be determined. The relevant appeal court can extend this period which failing the accused will be liberated on expiry of the 72-hour period.[29] In petition cases the accused may appeal against the refusal of bail before full committal.[30]

### CONSIDERATION BY THE APPROPRIATE APPEAL COURT

**4.54** Bail appeals are heard in chambers by a single judge of the High Court or the Sheriff Appeal Court. In modern practice, bail appeals have are invariably been held in a closed court room and, since August 2020, bail appeals to the Sheriff Appeal Court have been heard in virtual closed court format, using video-conferencing. Although the accused has a right to be personally present at a Crown bail appeal,[31] in practice this rarely happens. The accused is not

28 *Russell v HMA* [2021] HCJAC 24 (para 30).
29 CP(S)A 1995, s 32(7).
30 CP(S)A 1995, s 32(1) .
31 Act of Adjournal (Criminal Procedure Rules) 1996, r 4.2

entitled to be present at a defence bail appeal.[32] An appellant (or respondent in a Crown appeal), who is legally represented has no right to attend a bail appeal hearing, although the court may, using its powers under CP(S)A 1995, s 32(4) consider that justice requires that the accused be present.[33] The result of the appeal is communicated to the prison or young offenders' institution in which the accused is detained. In the event of a successful appeal by the accused, the bail conditions are served on them there and, if accepted, release follows.

**4.55** The approach to determining bail appeals has generally therefore been treated as one of determining whether the court of first instance has erred in the exercise of its discretion[34] Generally the question for the appeal court will be whether the decision was one which the court of first instance was entitled to reach in the exercise of its discretion, including in the proper consideration of the grounds for refusal of bail specified in CP(S)A 1995, s 23C, the appeal court's powers are not limited to such a review and in light of CP(S)A 1995, s 32(4) the court is given a broad discretion as to how it deals with a bail appeal. The appeal process can allow an appellant to address the public interest and CP(S)A 1995, s 23C grounds in a more focused way or even anew and this is particularly so where more specific information has become available to either party between the time of the bail application and the hearing of the bail appeal.

## ARREST OF OFFENDER FOR BREACH OF BAIL AND POWER OF ORIGINAL COURT

**4.56** The provisions of CP(S)A 1995, s 28 reflect what was a widening out of the previously existing s 28 powers.[35] These provisions ensure that a person can be detained and brought before a court under CP(S)A 1995, s 28 for breaching bail, even although the person has been arrested for a breach of bail under section 27 or was arrested in relation to a separate substantive offence, and it turns out that the circumstances of that offence show that the person was breaching bail[36]. Whenever the police arrest someone in these circumstances they may detain them in custody and make use of the provisions set out in section 28(2)–(6) of the 1995 Act to bring that individual to the court which dealt with the original application for that court to consider recalling or altering the bail order.

32 *DL v HM Advocate* 2007 SCCR 472, also reported as *L v HM Advocate* [2007] HCJ 8, 2008 SCL 25

33 *DL* (fn 32 above).

34 (see, eg *M v HM Advocate*). The decision was characterised as discretionary as long ago as 1878 in *Directors of City of Glasgow Bank* v *HM Advocate* (1878) 6 R (J) 4 at p 8.

35 As revised by the Criminal Justice (Scotland) Act 2016 and the Criminal Proceedings etc (Reform) (Scotland) Act 2007.

36 CP(S)A 1995, s 28 (1)–(1B).

**4.57** The section provides that an accused who is on bail may be arrested without warrant by any constable who has reasonable grounds for suspecting that they have broken, is breaking or is likely to break any condition of the bail. Additionally, a constable may detain a person arrested for any other offence, if they have reasonable grounds for suspecting that they have breached or is likely to breach any bail condition, even if they would otherwise have been obliged to release them.

**4.58** A person so arrested or detained is to be brought wherever practicable to the court to which their original bail application was made, not later than the first day after their arrest, excluding Saturdays, Sundays and court holidays, unless the court is sitting for criminal purposes on such excluded days.[37] If he is in custody only for breach of bail, and a constable is of the opinion that there are no reasonable grounds for suspecting that the person has broken, or is likely to break, a condition of their bail, he must be released from custody immediately.

**4.59** The court to which the original application was made may recall the bail order, release the accused under the original order, or vary the order so that it contains such conditions as the court thinks necessary to ensure compliance with the requirements of CP(S)A 1995, s 24(5)(a) to (d) of the 1995 Act.[38] The court's decision is appealable in the same way as the original order, (although there is no apparent provision for review).[39] Provision is made for accused who have been released on bail in terms of s 65(8C) of CP(S)A 1995.[40]

37 CP(S)A 1995, s 28(2).
38 CP(S)A 1995, s 28(4).
39 CP(S)A 1995, s 28(5) makes provision that the same rights of appeal shall be available as against the original order.
40 CP(S)A 1995, s 28(4A)–(4B) of the Criminal Procedure (Scotland) Act 1995.

# Chapter 5

# Offences

**5.01** This chapter looks at the type of offences most commonly encountered in the context of domestic abuse, both common law and statutory.

**5.02** For years the existing common law with some statutory additions was taken to be sufficient to meet allegations of domestic abuse, where effectively the only difference in the prosecution was that the complainer was the partner or ex-partner of the accused. That was recognised as an inadequate means of dealing with the distinctive issues which arise in domestic offending, so the Scottish government have taken steps to recognise the distinctive nature of offending against a partner or ex-partner. Although many crimes, both statutory and common law, had currency in a domestic context, the nature and scope of domestically related behaviour could not always be fitted easily into the existing criminal law. As will be clear, behaviour which in another context may not meet a criminal threshold, can become criminal in the context of the statutory regime under the Domestic Abuse (Scotland) Act 2018 (DA(S) A 2018) or s 39 of the Criminal Justice and Licensing (Scotland) Act 2010 (CJL(S)A 2010).

**5.03** The first legislative provision specifically recognising the effect of domestic abuse and the need to distinguish it was the Abusive Behaviour and Sexual Harm (Scotland) Act 2016 (ABSH(S)A 2016) which *inter alia* introduced a new statutory aggravation.[1]

**5.04** The 2016 Act was followed by The Domestic Abuse (Scotland) Act 2018 which provided for a specific offence intended to reflect the reality of the experiences of child and adult victims of domestic abuse. The policy memorandum which accompanied the introduction of the bill to the Scottish Parliament explained the purpose of the new offence:

> 'The provisions of this bill will improve how the justice system responds to domestic abuse. The bill will do this by ensuring that the criminal law reflects that domestic abuse can often be a course of conduct which takes place over a sustained period of time. In addition, the course of conduct can consist of psychological and emotional abuse which either cannot be or, at the very least, can be difficult to prosecute under existing laws.'

1 See **Chapter 4** above.

**5.05** The 2018 Act which came into force on 1 April 2019 criminalised psychological domestic abuse, and coercive and controlling behaviour.

## OFFENCES

## ABUSIVE BEHAVIOUR AND SEXUAL HARM (SCOTLAND) ACT 2016

**5.06** As noted by the High Court of Justiciary in *Sutherland (Adam) v HM Advocate Harvie*[2] (a case involving conduct before the coming into force of ABSH(S)A 2016), it is clear that individuals who disclose intimate images on a private basis have little or no control of the image once it has been sent and are vulnerable to considerable embarrassment and upset if that anticipant privacy was not maintained. The terms of ABSH(S)A 2016, s 2 aim to reflect that. The Act provides:

**'2 Disclosing, or threatening to disclose, an intimate photograph or film**

(1) A person ('A') commits an offence if—

(a) A discloses, or threatens to disclose, a photograph or film which shows, or appears to show, another person ('B') in an intimate situation,

(b) by doing so, A intends to cause B fear, alarm or distress or A is reckless as to whether B will be caused fear, alarm or distress, and

(c) the photograph or film has not previously been disclosed to the public at large, or any section of the public, by B or with B's consent.

(2) For the purposes of this section, a photograph or film is disclosed if it, or any data or other thing which is capable of being converted into it, is given, shown or made available to a person other than B.

(3) In proceedings for an offence under subsection (1), A has a defence if any of the following facts is established—

(a) B consented to the photograph or film being disclosed,

(b) A reasonably believed that B consented to the photograph or film being disclosed,

(c) A reasonably believed that disclosure of the photograph or film was necessary for the purposes of the prevention, detection, investigation or prosecution of crime, or

2 [2017] HCJAC 22; 2017 JC 268; 2017 SLT 721; 2017 SCCR 268 at para 26,

(d) A reasonably believed that disclosure of the photograph or film was in the public interest.

(4) For the purposes of subsection (3), consent to the photograph or film being disclosed may be—

(a) consent which is specific to the particular disclosure or (as the case may be) the particular threatened disclosure, or

(b) consent to disclosure generally where that consent covers the particular disclosure or (as the case may be) the particular threatened disclosure.

(5) In proceedings for an offence under subsection (1), A has a defence if the following matter is established—

(a) B was in the intimate situation shown in the photograph or film,

(b) B was not in the intimate situation as a result of a deliberate act of another person to which B did not agree, and

(c) when B was in the intimate situation—

(i) B was in a place to which members of the public had access (whether or not on payment of a fee), and

(ii) members of the public were present.

(6) For the purposes of subsection (3), a fact is established, and for the purposes of subsection (5), the matter is established, if—

(a) sufficient evidence is adduced to raise an issue as to whether that is the case, and

(b) the prosecution does not prove beyond reasonable doubt that it is not the case.

**3 Interpretation of section 2**

(1) For the purposes of section 2, a person is in an 'intimate situation' if—

(a) the person is engaging or participating in, or present during, an act which—

(i) a reasonable person would consider to be a sexual act, and

(ii) is not of a kind ordinarily done in public, or

(b) the person's genitals, buttocks or breasts are exposed or covered only with underwear.

(2) In section 2—

'film' means a moving image in any form, whether or not the image has been altered in any way, that was originally captured by making a recording, on any medium, from which a moving image may be produced, and includes a copy of the image,

'photograph' means a still image in any form, whether or not the image has been altered in any way, that was originally captured by photography, and includes a copy of the image.

**5.07** The provision was considered by the Sheriff appeal Court in *DF v PF Dundee*[3], where the court said:

> '[24] The language of section 2(1)(b) is clear and unambiguous. The mischief which the 2016 Act was designed to address is plain from its terms; it is not restricted to what might commonly be referred to as incidents of 'revenge porn'. As such, there is no need for recourse to parliamentary materials to aid an understanding of legislative intent. Had such recourse been necessary, it would not have supported the appellant's position. We note that an amendment to remove the reference to 'recklessness' was debated and withdrawn during stage 2 of the Bill.
>
> [25] An offence is committed in terms of section 2(1) of the 2016 Act if the individual who has disclosed or threatened to disclose intimate images has acted recklessly, that is, if they failed to give thought to or was indifferent as to the foreseeable effect upon the complainer of such a disclosure. Recklessness is to be inferred or deduced from the conduct of the individual at the time of the circumstances giving rise to the offence.'

## DEFENCE OF CONSENT

**5.08** In considering in terms of ABSH(S)A 2016, s 2(3)(b) whether the complainer consented to a previous disclosure of the photograph or film to the public at large, or a section thereof, consent means free agreement. Whether or not there was free agreement is determined having regard to what the parties did and said to each other. Unlike free agreement insofar as it relates to sexual encounters, where consent must be given at the time,[4] consent to the photograph or film being disclosed may be either consent which is specific to the particular disclosure or threatened disclosure, or consent to disclosure

3 2023 SCCR 118.

4 *GW v HM Advocate* [2019] HCJAC 23 where consent at a time materially remote from the conduct said to be criminal cannot provide a defence in terms of the Sexual Offence (Scotland) Act 2009.

generally, where that consent covers the particular disclosure or threatened disclosure. In considering reasonable belief, simply having an honest belief that the complainer consented to the disclosure or threatened disclosure is not enough. The accused's belief must be held on reasonable grounds.

## ASSAULT

**5.09** An assault is an attack on the person of another with evil intent. An attack is a physical interference with the person of another. The motive for the attack is irrelevant. Evil intent means that the attack has to be intentional, as distinct from being accidental, negligent or reckless. It is not a requirement that the accused intended 'evil consequences' as a result of his acts; ie that that was the motive for his behaviour. There is no need for there to be an intent to injure and to cause bodily harm[5]. The requisite intention is to do the act deliberately. This interpretation might be seen as a departure from the previously understood position that there must be an intention to cause bodily harm, although as the High Court explain, the law was clearly stated by Lord Justice Clerk (Ross) in Lord Advocate's Reference (No 2 of 1992),[6] where he said 'what this means is that assault cannot be committed accidentally or recklessly or negligently'. A deliberate act is enough to constitute assault. Threats or menaces which produce fear or alarm can be assaults if bodily injury is threatened. Spitting on or at someone is an assault.

**5.10** Assaults may be made more serious by any resulting injury allowing the addition of aggravation such as 'to injury', severe injury, permanent disfigurement, permanent impairment, to danger of life. It follows from *Kirkup*[7] that it is not necessary to establish that an accused person intended the particular consequence that arose. All that is required for the aggravation to be established is that it was a consequence of the assault.

**5.11** The aggravation to danger of life need not give rise to injury if the risk existed. So, to push someone out of a window even if no injuries arise could be regarded as an assault to danger of life.

## BREACH OF BAIL

**5.12** This is a common offence in a domestic context where a special bail condition will be imposed (not to contact the complainer or visit an address and there will be an allegation that the accused has breached the terms of the condition. The statutory provision in CP(S)A 1995, so far as relevant, says:

5 *Kirkup v HM Advocate* 2025 HCJAC 9 para [23] following *Dickson v Procurator Fiscal, Kilmarnock* [2023] SAC (Crim) 3.

6 1993 JC 43 (at p 48).

7 2025 HCJAC 9.

**'27 Breach of bail conditions: offences.**

(1) Subject to subsection (7) below, an accused who having been granted bail fails without reasonable excuse—

(a) to appear at the time and place appointed for any diet of which he has been given due notice or at which he is required by this Act to appear; or

(b) to comply with any other condition imposed on bail,

shall, subject to subsection (3) below, be guilty of an offence and liable on conviction to the penalties specified in subsection (2) below.

[…]

(4B) In any proceedings in relation to an offence under subsection (1) above or subsection (7) below, the fact that (as the case may be) an accused—

(a) was on bail;

(b) was subject to any particular condition of bail;

(c) failed to appear at a diet; or

(d) was given due notice of a diet,

shall, unless challenged in the manner described in paragraph (a) or (b) of subsection (4A) be held as admitted.

[…]

(10) A court which finds an accused guilty of an offence under this section may remit the accused for sentence in respect of that offence to any court which is considering the original offence.

(11) In this section "the original offence" means the offence with which the accused was charged when he was granted bail or an offence charged in the same proceedings as that offence.'

## WHAT IS A REASONABLE EXCUSE?

**5.13** The test of reasonable excuse, in the context of CP(S)A 1995, s 27(1)(b) and generally, has not been subjected to much analysis in case law in Scotland but some guidance can be elicited from *R v G*;[8] although an English

8 [2009] UKHL 13 where the court looks at comparators such as possession of an offensive weapon under s 1(1) of the Prevention of Crime Act 1953 and s 47(1) of the Criminal Law (Consolidation) (Scotland) Act 1995, and failure to provide a specimen of blood or urine under s 7(6) of the Road Traffic 1988.

case resulting from a charge under the Terrorism Act 2000, Lord Rodger's opinion reflects Scottish legislation and case law in its analysis of what may constitute a reasonable excuse

**5.14** Lord Rodger said:

> '81 It is comparatively easy to identify examples of excuses which could never be regarded as reasonable. It is similarly easy to give examples of excuses which everyone would regard as reasonable … So the courts have recognised that any decision on whether an accused had a reasonable excuse must depend on the particular circumstances of the case.'

**5.15** Lord Rodger continued:

> '[I]t is impossible to envisage everything that could amount to a reasonable excuse for doing what it prohibits. Ultimately, in this middle range of cases, whether or not an excuse is reasonable has to be determined in the light of the particular facts and circumstances of the individual case. Unless the judge is satisfied that no reasonable jury could regard the defendant's excuse as reasonable, the judge must leave the matter for the jury to decide.'

**5.16** In *Lister v Lees,*[9] the court said (again the context of possession of weapons):

> 'Although "good reason" is a different expression from "reasonable excuse", in our opinion the same approach falls to be adopted when the court is considering whether what has been put forward on behalf of an accused amounts to "good reason". Each case must depend on its own facts and circumstances and, in determining the issue, the court should have regard to the general purpose of the legislation, and where the legislation contains a general prohibition, the court must determine whether the reason advanced appears to constitute a justifiable exception to the general prohibition contained in the legislation.'

**5.17** This was followed in *Frame v Kennedy,*[10] where the court said at para 20:

> 'Obviously, as was said by the Lord Justice Clerk in *Lister v Lees*, every case will turn on its own facts and circumstances, but that in turn must mean that one cannot in advance prescribe the circumstances which will, or will not, amount to a reasonable excuse.'

**5.18** Finally, in *McMillan (David Baillie) v HM Advocate,*[11] the court said:

9 1994 SCCR 513
10 2008 SCCR 382
11 [2010] HCJAC 103

> 'It is recognised that the [Sexual Offences] Act 2003 contains no definition of the words "reasonable excuse". Accordingly one is therefore required to approach the expression by attributing to it its ordinary meaning, having regard to the words used, drawing such assistance as may be available from decisions upon similar language used elsewhere. The word "excuse" does not itself present any difficulty, meaning simply that which is offered as a reason for being excused. However, in the context, the word "reasonable" is of importance. To our mind, the use of that word indicates that Parliament intended that the excuse should possess some objectively recognisable justification.'

**5.19** The accused does not need to prove the existence of a reasonable excuse to any particular standard. It is for the Crown to meet that defence, and to satisfy the court beyond reasonable doubt that it should be rejected.

## CRIMINAL JUSTICE AND LICENSING (SCOTLAND) ACT 2010, S 38

**5.20** **38 Threatening or abusive behaviour**

'(1) A person ("A") commits an offence if—

- (a) A behaves in a threatening or abusive manner,
- (b) the behaviour would be likely to cause a reasonable person to suffer fear or alarm, and
- (c) A intends by the behaviour to cause fear or alarm or is reckless as to whether the behaviour would cause fear or alarm.

(2) It is a defence for a person charged with an offence under subsection (1) to show that the behaviour was, in the particular circumstances, reasonable.

(3) Subsection (1) applies to—

- (a) behaviour of any kind including, in particular, things said or otherwise communicated as well as things done, and
- (b) behaviour consisting of—
  - (i) a single act, or
  - (ii) a course of conduct.'

## Interpretation

**5.21** For the offence to be committed a person must as a matter of fact behave in a threatening or abusive manner, and the behaviour must be likely to cause a reasonable person fear or alarm and it is either intended to cause such fear and alarm or the perpetrator is reckless as to whether that result ensues. Behaviour includes things said, or communicated, as well as things done, and can include a single act or a course of conduct, recognising that the cumulative effect of minor behaviour could breach the threshold. A polite conversational request or compliment or overture will not be construed as threatening merely because it is uninvited or unwelcome[12]. The behaviour does not require to cause a person actual fear or alarm provided the behaviour is such that a reasonable person would be likely to suffer such fear or alarm.

**5.22** In addition, the accused must have the necessary intention to cause such fear or alarm as a result of his behaviour or alternatively, while not intending the result, be reckless as to whether the behaviour in question would have such a result.[13]

## No need for a victim

**5.23** Initially it was understood that there was no requirement for any person to suffer actual fear or alarm; the behaviour had only to be likely to cause such a reaction in a reasonable person;[14] there was a brief period where the test was determined to be that real fear and alarm had been suffered by a real complainer,[15] until the matter was authoritatively determined in *Patterson v Harvie,*[16] where the five-judge bench restored the *Rooney* approach. The Lord Justice General said:

> 'Section 38(1) sets out three clear and concise constituents of the offence. Paragraphs (a) and (b) define the actus reus of the offence. Whether the accused has behaved in a threatening or abusive manner and whether that behaviour would be likely to cause a reasonable person to suffer fear or alarm are straightforward questions of fact. Paragraph (c) sets out the mens rea that is required. It seems to me that the question under paragraph (b) is not whether the complainer suffered actual fear or alarm. If it had been the intention of the Parliament that the complainer must have suffered actual fear or alarm, paragraph (b) could have said exactly that. On the contrary, paragraph (b) sets an objective test. It provides that the requirement of the subsection is made out if the behaviour would be likely to cause a reasonable person to suffer fear or alarm. A reasonable person is someone who is not of abnormal sensitivity. If a reasonable person would have suffered fear or alarm, it follows on the objective test that it is no defence if the behaviour causes no fear or alarm to the individual complainer, who might be, for

12 *Ahmed v HM Advocate* 2020 HCJAC 37; 2021 JC 19; 2020 SCCR 382.
13 *Patterson v Harvie*, 2015 JC 118.
14 *Rooney v Brown* 2013 SCCR 334.
15 *Jolly v HMA*, 2014 JC 1713.
16 2015 JC 118.

example, an intrepid Glasgow police officer. In my view, the essence of the statutory offence is that the accused's conduct is to be judged by an objective test in which the actual effect of the threatening or abusive behaviour on those who experience it is irrelevant. If the requirements of paragraphs (a) and (c) are made out, the crime is complete if the accused's behaviour would be likely to cause fear or alarm to the hypothetical reasonable person.'

**5.24** Accordingly it has been established that there is no requirement for an identified victim for the offence to be committed. There is no need for actual fear or alarm to be caused to any person provided it could be anticipated that a reasonable person would suffer fear or alarm as a result of the behaviour in question.

## Defence

**5.25** Section 38(2) provides a defence that the behaviour was reasonable. The defence of self-defence, arguably available in breach of the peace[17] is not available. In *Urquhart v HMA,*[18] the High Court said the following:

> 'First, it seems to us inevitable that if a person conducts themselves in a manner which accords with the descriptions in parts (i) and (ii) and the reason for him doing so was that he was acting in self-defence in the sense that he genuinely thought he was in danger, he is bound to have intended to cause fear and/or alarm to his assailant. However cogent the case of self-defence might be, it could not, accordingly, prevent part (iii) being established. Secondly, the statutory defence afforded by s 38(2) is plainly wide enough to cover all and anything that an accused person may wish to advance to the effect that he was in fact acting in self-defence. Further, when doing so, it would not be necessary for the accused to meet all the requirements of self-defence that apply when pled as a special defence. The availability of a reasonable alternative means of escape from the danger would not, for instance, deprive him of the defence. There would be no prejudice to the accused in directing him to s 38(2) if he seeks to raise any issue of self-defence. He may in fact be in a better position than if he were constrained by the requirements of the special defence. We are satisfied that the relevant statutory intention clearly was that that is where any such issue should be raised.'

**5.26** The matter was addressed in *Patterson v Harvie*[19] at paragraphs [27]–[28] where the court (in an obiter remark) held that responses elicited by

17 *Derrett v Lockhart* 1991 SCCR 109; the language of the complaint included the words 'struggle and fight with each other' so such a special defence may be restricted to cases where the libel is in similar terms.

18 [2015] HCJAC 101.

19 2015 JC 118.

specific questioning encouraging to articulate feeling and when he was asked several times to clarify was described as presenting 'an irresistible defence to such an unreasonable prosecution.'

## CRIMINAL JUSTICE AND LICENSING (SCOTLAND) ACT 2010, S 39

**5.27** **'39 Offence of stalking**

(1) A person ("A") commits an offence, to be known as the offence of stalking, where A stalks another person ("B").

(2) For the purposes of subsection (1), A stalks B where—

(a) A engages in a course of conduct,

(b) subsection (3) or (4) applies, and

(c) A's course of conduct causes B to suffer fear or alarm.

(3) This subsection applies where A engages in the course of conduct with the intention of causing B to suffer fear or alarm.

(4) This subsection applies where A knows, or ought in all the circumstances to have known, that engaging in the course of conduct would be likely to cause B to suffer fear or alarm.

(5) It is a defence for a person charged with an offence under this section to show that the course of conduct—

(a) was authorised by virtue of any enactment or rule of law,

(b) was engaged in for the purpose of preventing or detecting crime, or

(c) was, in the particular circumstances, reasonable.

(6) In this section— "conduct" means—

(a) following B or any other person,

(b) contacting, or attempting to contact, B or any other person by any means,

(c) publishing any statement or other material—

(i) relating or purporting to relate to B or to any other person,

(ii) purporting to originate from B or from any other person,

(d) monitoring the use by B or by any other person of the internet, email or any other form of electronic communication,

(e) entering any premises,

(f) loitering in any place (whether public or private),

(g) interfering with any property in the possession of B or of any other person,

(h) giving anything to B or to any other person or leaving anything where it may be found by, given to or brought to the attention of B or any other person,

(i) watching or spying on B or any other person,

(j) acting in any other way that a reasonable person would expect would cause B to suffer fear or alarm, and 'course of conduct' involves conduct on at least two occasions.

(8) Subsection (9) applies where, in the trial of a person ("the accused") charged with the offence of stalking, the jury or, in summary proceedings, the court—

(a) is not satisfied that the accused committed the offence, but

(b) is satisfied that the accused committed an offence under section 38(1).

(9) The jury or, as the case may be, the court may acquit the accused of the charge and, instead, find the accused guilty of an offence under section 38(1).'

**5.28** The statutory heading of CJL(S)A 2010, s 39 describes it as stalking; it effectively means harassing or persecuting with unwanted attention. An accused person stalks another if they engage in a course of conduct, as a result of which the subject of the stalking suffers fear or alarm. And to be convicted of this offence, an accused must either have intended that the other person would suffer fear or alarm as a result of the course of conduct carried out by the accused or alternatively have known (or ought in all the circumstances to have known) that engaging in that course of conduct would be likely to cause the other person to suffer fear or alarm. The offence is only committed where the accused's behaviour in fact causes the person subject to the behaviour to suffer fear or alarm (in contrast with the approach to CJL(S)A 2010, s 38 in *Paterson v Harvie*[20] above and DA(S)A 2018) The court is considering what has been proved to have been said or done and then considering what can be inferred or deduced from these proven facts. The test is objective. In the light of all the circumstances should the accused have known that the other person was likely to suffer fear or alarm as a result of their behaviour?[21]

20 2015 JC 118; 2014 SLT 857; 2014 SCL 606; 2014 SCCR 521.

21 *Miller v HM Advocate* 2022 JC 33.

**5.29** A course of conduct means conduct on at least two occasions. There is an overlap with the evidential approach to be taken in relation to s 1 of DA(S) A 2018. The offence of stalking occurs when the accused person engages in a course of relevant conduct within the meaning of CJL(S)A 2010, s 39(6).

**5.30** The conduct in question does not need of itself to be criminal, if viewed in isolation– so for example turning up at the complainer's home, providing unwanted gifts, trying to communicate with a complainer at their workplace, and ignoring requests to desist can constitute the conduct required. The section provides that *any* conduct can be caught by the section if it can be expected to cause the other person to suffer fear or alarm. But it has been held that proffering apologies to an estranged wife, or to make enquiries about her whereabouts are not per se conduct engaging the act unless the person was made aware of the contact and was in fact frightened or alarmed and the accused had the necessary intention or knowledge as to the effect. The court should distinguish between lawful conduct (an apology for example) and the criminal conduct charged.[22] In relation to this category of behaviour, reference to a 'reasonable person' simply means the ordinary man or woman in the street.

## Defence

**5.31** CJL(S)A 2010, s 39 provides that it is a defence for a person charged with the offence of stalking to show that the course of conduct was authorised by virtue of any enactment or rule of law, was engaged in for the purpose of preventing or detecting crime, or was, in the particular circumstances, reasonable. The first two are self-explanatory. In relation to whether the course of conduct was reasonable in the particular circumstances, factors to be considered will be the nature of the conduct concerned, including its frequency, the effect of the conduct on the complainer, the circumstances in which the conduct arose, and any explanation given by the accused for the conduct.

## Alternative

**5.32** If the court is not satisfied that the Crown have proved the charge of stalking against the accused, then the judge or jury, as the case may be, is required to consider whether it is satisfied that the accused behaved in a threatening and abusive manner in terms of CJL(S)A 2010, s 38.[23] CJL(S) A 2010, s 38 is an alternative verdict which may be brought in when a person is charged with the offence of stalking.

22 *Miller* (fn 21 above) para [58].
23 See **5.20**, above.

## COMMUNICATIONS ACT 2003, S 127

**5.33** **'127 Improper use of public electronic communications network**

(1) A person is guilty of an offence if he–

(a) sends by means of a public electronic communications network a message or other matter that is grossly offensive or of an indecent, obscene or menacing character; or

(b) causes any such message or matter to be so sent.

(2) A person is guilty of an offence if, for the purpose of causing annoyance, inconvenience or needless anxiety to another, he–

(a) sends by means of a public electronic communications network, a message that he knows to be false,

(b) causes such a message to be sent; or

(c) persistently makes use of a public electronic communications network.

[…]

(4) Subsections (1) and (2) do not apply to anything done in the course of providing a programme service (within the meaning of the Broadcasting Act 1990 (c. 42)).'

**5.34** A message or material includes written messages, such as letters or emails, as well as images such as pictures or photographs. It also includes the spoken word such as things said during a call or recorded, for example, in a voicemail. A 'public electronic communications network' means an electronic communications network provided wholly or mainly for the purpose of making electronic communications services available to members of the public. Therefore, things said over the phone, or things communicated by text message, on social media, or by email are communicated by a public electronic communications network

## Components of the offence

**5.35** In *DPP v Collins* (at para 8),[24] the House of Lords held that it was plain from s 127(1)(a) of the Communications Act 2003 that the actus reus of the offence was the sending of a message of the proscribed character by the defined means. The offence was complete when the message was sent. Therefore, it made no difference that the message was never received. The

24 [2006] 1WLR 2223.

offence did not depend on whether a message was received by a person who for any reason was deeply offended, or by a person who was not.

**5.36** The court continued in relation to offensiveness at para 9:

> 'The parties agreed with the rulings of the Divisional Court that it is for the justices to determine as a question of fact whether a message is grossly offensive, that in making this determination the justices must apply the standards of an open and just multiracial society, and that the words must be judged taking account of their context and all relevant circumstances. I would agree also. Usages and sensitivities may change over time. Language otherwise insulting may be used in an unpejorative, even affectionate, way, or may be adopted as a badge of honour ('Old Contemptibles'). There can be no yardstick of gross offensiveness otherwise than by the application of reasonably enlightened, but not perfectionist, contemporary standards to the particular message sent in its particular context. The test is whether a message is couched in terms liable to cause gross offence to those to whom it relates.'

**5.37** So it was for the court, applying the standards of an open and just multiracial society and taking account of the context and all relevant circumstances, to determine as a question of fact whether a message was grossly offensive; and it was necessary to show that the defendant intended his words to be grossly offensive to those to whom the message related, or that he was aware that they might be taken to be so.

## The position in Scotland

**5.38** The provision was looked at by the Sheriff Appeal Court in *Brown v PF Ayr*.[25] The accused had sent two messages to a former partner which were alleged to be grossly offensive The accused made a submission of no case to answer arguing that the messages were not threatening or menacing. In allowing the appeal and adopting the approach taken in *Collins*, the court said that the messages required to be considered objectively in the context in which they are sent. Conviction of this offence did not depend upon the message being received or the recipient's reaction or state of mind following receipt of the message. The reaction of the recipient or complainer was not the determining factor. For the purpose of criminal liability the court should not only have regard to that background but must undertake an objective assessment of the words deployed. Giving the opinion of the court Sheriff Principal Stephen said.

25 2016 SCCR 564.

> 'That analysis should allow the court to recognise whether the boundary has been crossed between words which may be unwelcome, intemperate or even upsetting and words which are menacing and threatening.'

**5.39** That provision was further considered by the Sheriff Appeal Court in *Sutinyte v P F Glasgow,*[26] where the accused sent messages to an elected representative. The sheriff considered that although not characterised by the recipient as grossly abusive, they could, objectively, be seen as such. The accused was convicted and appealed; the sheriff appeal court upheld the conviction. Giving the opinion of the court, Sheriff Principal Murray said at para [9]:

> 'On objective assessment, the messages included language which was intrinsically offensive, which conveyed personal insult, and which wished physical harm to the recipient, who was acting as a public servant. We agree that, in context, the messages went beyond merely offensive, and were grossly offensive. To quote Lord Bingham the appellant "used language which is beyond the pale of what is tolerable in our society"'.

**5.40** Sheriff Principal Murray's reference to 'objective assessment' reflects the approach (if not in identical language) in Collins where Lord Bingham said that 'the respondent's messages were grossly offensive and would be found by a reasonable person to be so.' [27] It is accordingly a question of fact whether a message is grossly offensive. In making that determination, it is the standards of an open and just multiracial society that must be applied. The words should be judged taking account of their context and all relevant circumstances. The test is whether a message is couched in terms liable to cause gross offence to those to whom it relates.

## DOMESTIC ABUSE (SCOTLAND) ACT 2018

### Background

**5.41** The existing criminal law was seen as inadequate, failing as it did to recognise the sustained nature of the behaviour, and the difficulty of prosecuting where no physical violence or threats arose. The advantage of the ability to prosecute a course of conduct was to show context and provide for the fact that psychological abuse can more easily be identified in an ongoing course of behaviour. The number of prosecutions under the Act has increased as the Act

26 2022 SCCR 22; 2022 SLT (Sh Ct) 127.
27 Collins at para [13].

beds in.[28] The impact that it has had on victims or survivors will require further time to properly evaluate.[29]

**5.42** The primary policy objective of DA(S)A 2018, s 1 was to ensure that the criminal law reflected the view that domestic abuse can be a course of conduct which takes place over a sustained period of time, and the course of conduct can consist of both physical violence and threats, and psychological and emotional abuse.[30] The offence was defined as a course of conduct so as to reflect how victims actually experienced domestic abuse. The desire of the Scottish Government was to create a general offence to cover the wide range of conduct that can constitute a pattern of abusive behaviour within a relationship.

**5.43** The wrong identified as coercive control may well have been the original focus of the legislation, but it was not the limit. Behaviour that falls short of, or differs from, coercive control can still give rise to a conviction. So coercive control is not a *sine qua non* of a conviction under the terms of the Act; what is required is a course of abusive behaviour which is likely to cause physical or psychological harm, and that it is intentional or the perpetrator is reckless about the harmful effect.

## The 2018 Act

**5.44** The Domestic Abuse (Scotland) Act 2018 is in the following terms, so far as relevant to this chapter:

**'1 Abusive behaviour towards partner or ex-partner**

(1) A person commits an offence if—

(a) the person ('A') engages in a course of behaviour which is abusive of A's partner or ex-partner ('B'), and

(b) both of the further conditions are met.

28 Domestic Abuse (Scotland) Act 2018: interim reporting requirement January 2023. Criminal proceedings data indicated an increase in the number of people convicted of the new offence (from 212 in 2019/20 to 383 in 2020/21). Similarly, the figures showed an increase in the use of the new statutory sentencing aggravation intended to reflect the harm caused to children by domestic abuse since the Act came into force, from 39 in 2019/20 to 90 in 2020/21 (around a quarter of all convictions for the offence). The impact of the pandemic made it difficult for the report to draw firm conclusions about the criminal justice statistics presented in the report.

29 Domestic Abuse (Scotland) Act 2018 and the Criminal Justice System Women's experiences two years in; the emerging findings (January 2022), collated and written by Dr Nancy Lombard, Dr Katy Proctor, and Dr Nel Whiting, Glasgow Caledonian University. The research concluded that it was too early to evaluate the effectiveness of the legislation, especially as its inception happened shortly before the COVID 19 pandemic. However, to date, the authors concluded that the findings from this small sample of victims/survivors did not show any substantive evidence of DA(S)A 2018 having had a positive impact on practice and women's experiences of the criminal justice system.

30 Scottish Government Policy Memorandum on the Domestic Abuse (Scotland) Bill.

(2) The further conditions are—

(a) that a reasonable person would consider the course of behaviour to be likely to cause B to suffer physical or psychological harm,

(b) that either—

(i) A intends by the course of behaviour to cause B to suffer physical or psychological harm, or

(ii) A is reckless as to whether the course of behaviour causes B to suffer physical or psychological harm.

(3) In the further conditions, the references to psychological harm include fear, alarm and distress.

**2 What constitutes abusive behaviour**

(1) Subsections (2) to (4) elaborate on section 1(1) as to A's behaviour.

(2) Behaviour which is abusive of B includes (in particular) —

(a) behaviour directed at B that is violent, threatening or intimidating,

(b) behaviour directed at B, at a child of B or at another person that either—

(i) has as its purpose (or among its purposes) one or more of the relevant effects set out in subsection (3), or

(ii) would be considered by a reasonable person to be likely to have one or more of the relevant effects set out in subsection (3).

(3) The relevant effects are of—

(a) making B dependent on, or subordinate to, A,

(b) isolating B from friends, relatives or other sources of support,

(c) controlling, regulating or monitoring B's day-to-day activities,

(d) depriving B of, or restricting B's, freedom of action,

(e) frightening, humiliating, degrading or punishing B.

(4) In subsection (2) —

(a) in paragraph (a), the reference to violent behaviour includes sexual violence as well as physical violence,

(b) in paragraph (b), the reference to a child is to a person who is under 18 years of age.

[...]

**4 Evidence of impact on victim**

(1) The commission of an offence under section 1(1) does not depend on the course of behaviour actually causing B to suffer harm of the sort mentioned in section 1(2).

(2) The operation of section 2(2) (b) does not depend on behaviour directed at someone actually having on B any of the relevant effects set out in section 2(3).

(3) Nothing done by or mentioned in subsection (1) or (2) prevents evidence from being led in proceedings for an offence under section 1(1) about (as the case may be) —

(a) harm actually suffered by B as a result of the course of behaviour, or

(b) effects actually had on B of behaviour directed at someone.

**5 Aggravation in relation to a child**

(1) This subsection applies where it is, in proceedings for an offence under section 1(1) —

(a) specified in the complaint or libelled in the indictment that the offence is aggravated by reason of involving a child, and

(b) proved that the offence is so aggravated

(2) The offence is so aggravated if, at any time in the commission of the offence—

(a) A directs behaviour at a child, or

(b) A makes use of a child in directing behaviour at B.

(3) The offence is so aggravated if a child sees or hears, or is present during, an incident of behaviour that A directs at B as part of the course of behaviour.

(4) The offence is so aggravated if a reasonable person would consider the course of behaviour, or an incident of A's behaviour that forms part of the course of behaviour, to be likely to adversely affect a child usually residing with A or B (or both).

(5) For it to be proved that the offence is so aggravated, there does not need to be evidence that a child—

(a) has ever had any—

(i) awareness of A's behaviour, or

(ii) understanding of the nature of A's behaviour, or

(b) has ever been adversely affected by A's behaviour.

(6) Evidence from a single source is sufficient to prove that the offence is so aggravated.

(7) Where subsection (1) applies, the court must—

(a) state on conviction that the offence is so aggravated,

(b) record the conviction in a way that shows that the offence is so aggravated,

(c) take the aggravation into account in determining the appropriate sentence, and

(d) state—

(i) where the sentence imposed in respect of the offence is different from that which the court would have imposed if the offence were not so aggravated, the extent of and the reasons for that difference, or

(ii) otherwise, the reasons for there being no such difference.

(8) Each of subsections (2) to (4) operates separately along with subsection (5), but subsections (2) to (4) may be used in combination along with subsection (5).

(9) Nothing in subsections (2) to (5) prevents evidence from being led about—

(a) a child's observations of, or feelings as to, A's behaviour, or

(b) a child's situation so far as arising because of A's behaviour.

(10) In subsections (4) and (5), the references to adversely affecting a child include causing the child to suffer fear, alarm or distress.

(11) In this section, the references to a child are to a person who—

(a) is not A or B, and

(b) is under 18 years of age.

**6 Defence on grounds of reasonableness**

(1) In proceedings for an offence under section 1(1), it is a defence for A to show that the course of behaviour was reasonable in the particular circumstances.

(2) That is to be regarded as shown if—

(a) evidence adduced is enough to raise an issue as to whether the course of behaviour is as described in subsection (1), and

(b) the prosecution does not prove beyond reasonable doubt that the course of behaviour is not as described in subsection (1).

**7 Presumption as to the relationship**

(1) In proceedings for an offence under section 1(1), the matter of B being A's partner or ex-partner is to be taken as established—

(a) according to the stating of the matter in the charge of the offence in the complaint or indictment, and

(b) unless the matter is challenged as provided for in subsection (2).

(2) The matter is challenged—

(a) in summary proceedings, by—

(i) preliminary objection before the plea is recorded, or

(ii) later objection as the court allows in special circumstances,

(b) in proceedings on indictment, by giving notice of a preliminary objection in accordance with section 71(2) or 72(6) (b) (i) of the Criminal Procedure (Scotland) Act 1995.

[…]

**10 Meaning of references to behaviour**

(1) Subsections (2) to (4) explain what is meant by the references to behaviour in this Part.

(2) Behaviour is behaviour of any kind, including (for example) —

(a) saying or otherwise communicating something as well as doing something,

(b) intentionally failing—

(i) to do something,

(ii) to say or otherwise communicate something.

(3) Behaviour directed at a person is such behaviour however carried out, including (in particular) —

(a) by way of conduct towards property,

(b) through making use of a third party,

as well as behaviour in a personal or direct manner.

(4) A course of behaviour involves behaviour on at least two occasions.

**11 Meaning of partner and ex-partner**

(1) Subsections (2) and (3) describe who is a person's partner or ex-partner as referred to in this Part.

(2) Someone is a person's partner if they are—

(a) spouses or civil partners of each other,

(b) living together as if spouses of each other, or

(c) in an intimate personal relationship with each other.

(3) Whether someone is a person's ex-partner is to be determined accordingly.'

## TWO PRELIMINARY POINTS

### Subjective element

**5.45** It is not a requirement of the offence for actual physical or psychological harm to be caused. But the wording of the statute imposes a subjective element to the crime; the question is whether a reasonable person would determine that the actual victim (the 'person B' in the language of the statute) would suffer.[31] Therefore, the court is entitled to take account of any particular vulnerability of the complainer in considering whether the accused's behaviour would be likely to cause them to suffer physical or psychological harm.

**5.46** Notwithstanding the subjective element, an accused cannot submit that by showing or purporting to show that the complainer is in some way used to, or hardened to, or immune to abuse, or capable him- or herself of being abusive, the protection afforded by the act is not thereby neutralised. The complainer's behaviour does not and cannot inform the question of whether the complainer was him- or herself subjected to abuse in terms of the act.

**5.47** In *CH v HM Advocate*,[32] albeit in the context of an application under CP(S)A 1995, s 275, the High Court considered that matter. The accused

31 DA(S)A 2018, s 1(2)(a).
32 [2025] HCJAC 29.

sought to elicit evidence that the complainer had abused the appellant and that the allegations he faced were an extension of the abuse. The High Court in holding that the evidence was inadmissible said

> '[28] The evidence sought to be elicited is plainly irrelevant and collateral to the true issues in the case, which are simply whether the Crown can prove the charges on the indictment. The proposed evidence does not bear directly on a fact in issue or make a fact in issue more or less probable (*CJM v HM Advocate* 2013 SCCR 215). There is no legitimate link between the matters in the application and the charges. It is conceivable that evidence concerning the complainer's conduct towards the appellant might be admissible in his defence if such conduct took place in the course of the particular events libelled on the indictment.
>
> [29] The application appears to have been drafted on the misconceived basis that the implication of the Crown's having libelled a course of abusive conduct against the appellant is that this somehow opens the door to his being entitled to lead such evidence as he chooses to lead concerning the behaviour of the complainer towards him during the period of the libel regardless of whether there is any temporal or other link with the allegations featuring in the charges. Such an approach would potentially allow a person facing a charge under section 1 of the 2018 Act to blacken the character of the complainer by dredging up instances of allegedly inappropriate behaviour on her part from the past history of the relationship. This would serve only to undermine the clear policy and purpose of the 2018 Act.'

## The place of sexual offending within DA(S)A 2018

**5.48** The course of abusive behaviour towards a partner or ex-partner which DA(S)A 2018, s 1 criminalises can include anything that amounts to sexual violence, or any sexual offending which would amount to abusive behaviour;[33] accordingly sexual offences can be included in a single omnibus or cumulative charge under s 1 if they form part of a single alleged course of conduct by an accused towards his or her partner or ex-partner. Although entirely consistent with the terms of the Act, that consequence was not necessarily foreseen and was subject to challenge initially on the basis that the sheriff court was not competent to hear an allegation of conduct which amounted to rape within the context of an allegation under s 1. In *Mackenzie v HM Advocate,*[34] the High Court made it clear that there was nothing incompetent in libelling what could also be charged as rape within a charge under DA(S)A 2018, s 1 of the Act, and there was no requirement that such a case be tried in the High Court.

33 DA(S)A 2018, s 3(4)(a) provides that reference to violent behaviour includes sexual violence as well as physical violence.

34 2024 JC 121.

**5.49** Accordingly sexual offences, (including rape) which would otherwise have required separate charges (and indeed the need for separate and stand-alone corroboration), can be included in DA(S)A 2018, s 1 charges, where the requirement is instead for corroboration of the course of abusive behaviour (see **Chapter 7** below).

## OVERVIEW

**5.50** These are three key elements of the offence. DA(S)A 2018 provides that a person commits an offence if that person:

(1) engages in a course of behaviour which is abusive of their partner or ex-partner; and

(2) that a reasonable person would consider that the course of behaviour would be likely to cause the complainer to suffer physical or psychological harm; and

(3) that the accused either intended that their course of behaviour caused the complainer to suffer physical or psychological harm, or else was reckless as to whether their course of behaviour would cause such physical or psychological harm.

## THE COMPONENTS OF THE OFFENCE

### A course of behaviour

**5.51** A 'course of behaviour' involves behaviour on at least two occasions (DA(S)A 2018, s 10(4)). A single incident of abuse, however serious, cannot constitute an offence under DA(S)A 2018, s 1; such behaviour may be prosecuted on its own, and may attract an aggravation under s 1 of the Abusive Behaviour and Sexual Harm (Scotland) Act 2016. It will be for the court to determine in the particular circumstances of a case whether two incidents occurring far apart in time, with no evidence that they formed part of any wider pattern of behaviour, truly amounted to a course of behaviour.

**5.52** Behaviour which would not necessarily be criminal in another context can constitute criminal behaviour in the context of domestic abuse.[35] The conduct or behaviour need not be thematically the same to form a course of conduct; not all discrete incidents when viewed cumulatively can form a course of behaviour, but separate types of behaviour can form part of a course of conduct.

35 *Walker v Procurator Fiscal, Dunoon* 2022 SAC (Crim) 9: 'Mere presence at a locus may be covered by this definition.'

**5.53** Attending at a workplace, locking a person in the family home, and then perpetrating an assault could form a course of conduct. A perpetrator who makes threats directly through text, social media or phone, and through a third party, could not argue that because the means or medium of communication was different, there was no course of conduct. Each case must be looked at on its own facts and circumstances.[36]

**5.54** Some guidance may be gained from the approach taken by the High Court in relation to other areas, although care should be taken to avoid reading across too much. In *Donegan v HM Advocate,*[37] looking at the Moorov doctrine, Lady Dorrian said:

> 'However, where there are both similarities and dissimilarities in the relevant incidents, the applicability of the doctrine should be left to the jury unless it can be said that on no possible view could there be a connection between the charges'.

**5.55** This was adopted and reframed in *GS v HM Advocate*[38] where the court said:

> '[23] It is only where it is impossible to say on the evidence that the individual incidents were component parts of a single course of conduct persistently pursued that there will be an insufficiency of evidence as a matter of law …The test of impossibility is obviously a high one. If that test is not capable of being met, the issue becomes one of the weight to be given to the evidence. In our system, questions of weight are for the jury, not the judge.'

**5.56** Similarly with special defences, the court in *Carr v HM Advocate,*[39] which although relating to self-defence has been interpreted as applying more widely, said at para 13;

> '…[withdrawal of a special defence is] always a strong step and it is only appropriate to do so if there is no evidence from which it can possibly be inferred that the accused was acting in self-defence at the relevant time. To put it another way, so long as there is any possibility of the jury being satisfied that an accused acted in self-defence, or in the light of evidence given in support of the plea of self-defence, entertaining a reasonable doubt as to his guilt, the issue must be left for them to determine.'

**5.57** Accordingly, it is suggested that unless on no possible view could the separate episodes of behaviour amount to a course of behaviour, the statutory test is met.

36 *Walker*, para 13.
37 2019 JC 81, para 42.
38 2024 JC 35.
39 2013 SCCR 471.

## Partner or ex-partner

**5.58** The definition of partner or ex-partner will rarely be an issue in offences charged as domestic abuse because of the need for a course of behaviour, but someone is a person's partner if they are: (a) spouses or civil partners of each other; (b) living together as if spouses of each other; or (c) in an intimate personal relationship with each other.[40] Ex-partner is to be determined accordingly.[41] In terms of DA(S)A 2018, s 7, the matter of B being A's partner or ex-partner is taken to be established unless the matter is challenged by preliminary objection. So if a challenge is to be taken, representatives of the alleged perpetrator must be alert to the need to challenge timeously.

# WHAT IS 'BEHAVIOUR' AND WHEN IS IT 'ABUSIVE'?

## Behaviour

**5.59** In terms of DA(S)A 2018, behaviour is behaviour of any kind[42] including, but not restricted to, the examples given in DA(S)A 2018, s 10(2): (i) saying or otherwise communicating something as well as doing something; and (ii) intentionally failing to do something, saying or otherwise communicating something. Behaviour can include things said, or done or things not said (giving the 'silent treatment') or not done, all and any of which, depending on the circumstances, can cause psychological harm and can thereby be abusive; it also provides that behaviour directed at a person includes behaviour carried out with or through a third party, striking at, for example, arranging for another person to follow or monitor the complainer.

**5.60** For behaviour to be abusive, DA(S)A 2018, s 2(2) of the Act provides that abusive behaviour will include (but is not restricted to):

(a) behaviour directed at B that is violent, threatening or intimidating;

(b) behaviour directed at B, at a child of B or at another person that either:

  (i) has as its purpose (or among its purposes) one or more of the relevant effects set out in subsection (3): or

  (ii) would be considered by a reasonable person to be likely to have one or more of the relevant effects set out in subsection (3).'

**5.61** The section thereby identifies two alternative approaches to what constitutes abusive behaviour.

40 DA(S)A 2018, s 11(2).
41 DA(S)A 2018, s 11(3).
42 *Walker v PF Dunoon* (fn 36 above).

## The first approach

**5.62** The behaviour identified in DA(S)A 2018, s 2(2)(a) is self-evidently abusive. This will generally be of the kind that could be prosecuted under existing laws. The reference to violent behaviour includes sexual violence as well as physical violence.[43] But such behaviour may form a component or episode in relation to a pattern or course of abuse, being behaviour on one of the two or more occasions required by the Act.

## The second approach

**5.63** This covers behaviour which is regarded as abusive because of the effect which it has on the person subjected to the behaviour. That captures the kind of behaviour which is abusive because it is coercive, or controlling, or manipulative or otherwise constitutes psychological or emotional abuse. There is no necessity that the behaviour has as its effect some degree of coercive control; the effect of the provision is that, even absent evidence of some isolation or dependence or control, the offence can be committed. The intention of DA(S)A 2018 was to provide that conduct of a kind which would not normally allow prosecution under the existing criminal law was included within the definition of abusive behaviour. Some abusive behaviour may of course have several of the listed effects on the victim or may be capable of prosecution under existing offences.

**5.64** There is a subjective element to the crime, and the court is entitled to take account of any particular vulnerability of the complainer in considering whether the accused's behaviour would be likely to cause them to suffer physical or psychological harm. It is not a requirement of the offence for actual physical or psychological harm to be caused.[44] To be abusive in the context of DA(S)A 2018, the behaviour has to have as its purpose or among its purposes one of more of the relevant effects set out in DA(S)A 2018, s 2(3).

## RELEVANT EFFECTS

**5.65** Examples of the relevant effects include: behaviour frightening, humiliating, degrading or punishing the victim; and violent behaviour including sexual violence as well as other physical violence. It is enough that the behaviour has one or more of these effects as its purpose, or among its purposes, or that it would be considered by a reasonable person likely to have one or more of these effects. Behaviour making the victim dependent or subordinate to the perpetrator; isolating the victim from friends and family; controlling, regulating

43 DA(S)A 2018, s 3(4)(a).
44 DA(S)A 2018, s 4.

or monitoring the victim's day-to-day activities; depriving the victim of, or restricting the victim's freedom of action; frightening, humiliating, degrading or punishing the victim; violent behaviour include sexual violence as well as other physical violence.[45]

**5.66** It is enough that the behaviour has one or more of these effects as its purpose, or among its purposes, or that it would be considered by a reasonable person likely to have one or more of these effects. It is not necessary that the perpetrator is aware of the effect of the behaviour; reckless behaviour giving rise to a relevant offence is capable of supporting a conviction.[46]

## DIRECTED AT THE OTHER PARTY

**5.67** The behaviour, in order to give rise to the offence under DA(S)A 2018, s 1 must be 'directed at B'[47] (if it is violent, threatening, or intimidating) or 'directed at B, at a child of B or at another person' (if it has as its purpose, or would be considered by a reasonable person likely to have, one or more of the 'relevant effects'). 'Behaviour directed at a person' is behaviour, however carried out; it includes conduct towards property and conduct through making use of a third party, as well as behaviour in a personal or direct manner.[48]) The reference to 'conduct towards property' is designed to include matters including vandalism of personal property. The definition is deliberately wide but the behaviour must still be 'directed' at a person. So behaviour that might cause the complainer to be humiliated but is not *directed at* the complainer is not caught.[49]

## A REASONABLE PERSON WOULD CONSIDER THE COURSE OF BEHAVIOUR TO BE LIKELY TO CAUSE THE VICTIM TO SUFFER PHYSICAL OR PSYCHOLOGICAL HARM

**5.68** This has two purposes;

(1) to ensure that routine decisions or innocent behaviour which might have one of the relevant effects (financial dependence by one party on the other

45 Unusually, the explanatory notes to the Act give examples of the effects.

46 In *Walker v PF, Dunoon* the SAC were critical of the absence of a finding in fact that the accused was aware of the effect on the complainer (para 13). That is not a necessary component of the offence.

47 *Walker v PF Dunoon,* para15.

48 DA(S)A 2018, s 10(3).

49 The Policy Memorandum provides as an example: if a person has an affair, then that might cause his or her partner to be humiliated, but it is not, without more, *directed at* the partner.

due to choices about work/caring commitments) are not inadvertently brought within the offence; and

(2) it provides that a course of behaviour that is plainly intended to cause the other person to suffer physical or psychological harm is still caught by the legislation even if the other person does not in fact suffer any harm.

As has been said, in respect of behaviour directed at the other person, or their child or 'another person', there is no requirement to show that the behaviour actually had any of the relevant effects in DA(S)A 2018, s 2(3).[50]

**5.69** It was considered that requiring proof of harm would require the victim to give evidence of that harm, and risk re-traumatisation, so it was appropriate to allow the court to take into account any particular vulnerability of the victim, without the need for evidence from the complainer. It is suggested that in practical terms any such offence is unlikely to be established without the evidence of the victim in some form. However, DA(S)A 2018 itself does not preclude the Crown from leading evidence of the harm[51]

## THE ACCUSED INTENDED BY THE COURSE OF ABUSIVE BEHAVIOUR TO CAUSE B TO SUFFER PHYSICAL OR PSYCHOLOGICAL HARM, OR WAS RECKLESS AS TO THE CAUSING OF SUCH HARM

**5.70** This is the mens rea of the offence.

**5.71** The accused must either intend that their course of behaviour causes the complainer to suffer physical or psychological harm, or else be reckless as to whether their course of behaviour would cause such physical or psychological harm (DA(S)A 2018, s 1(2)(b)). So a person who is persistently verbally abusive and demeaning towards their partner may claim that they did not intend that their behaviour to cause psychological harm to their partner. If the court is satisfied that their behaviour was such that the accused person was, at the very least, reckless as to whether their behaviour would cause such harm, then this condition would be met. The need for a course of behaviour deals with the need for such conduct to be persistent.

**5.72** The intention of the provision is said to be to maintain the focus of the Act on the offender's behaviour, so that a prosecution for behaviour which otherwise arises under the Act it is not dependent upon the victim's reaction to the behaviour.[52]

50 DA(S)A 2018, s 4(2).
51 DA(S)A 2018, s 4(3).
52 See the Policy Memorandum.

## DEFENCE: THE REASONABLENESS DEFENCE

**5.73** The Act provides a defence if the course of behaviour was reasonable in the particular circumstances.[53] DA(S)A 2018, s 6(2) places an evidential burden on the defence to adduce sufficient evidence to put the defence in issue and a legal burden on the prosecution to negative the defence.

**5.74** That is to be regarded as shown if:

(a) there is evidence adduced which is enough to raise an issue as to whether the course of behaviour is reasonable, and;

(b) the prosecution does not prove beyond reasonable doubt that the course of behaviour is not reasonable.

**5.75** This can give rise to complexities in relation to special defences; if it is contended for example that a sexual offence forms a component of the behaviour, the provisions of DA(S)A 2018, s 6 do not allow for consent as a discrete defence; it has been established that consent cannot be a defence to a physical assault, or to the infliction of pain.[54]

**5.76** DA(S)A 2018, s 1 charges often contain within them allegations of assault, threatening or abusive behaviour. There is not yet an appeal court decision addressing the appropriateness or otherwise of these special defences in a DA(S)A 2018, s 1 charge. There is authority that a special defence of self-defence has no relevance to a charge under s 38(1) of the Criminal Justice and Licensing (Scotland) Act 2010[55] in which the court reasoned that the statutory defence of reasonableness is broader than self-defence. Someone acting in self-defence is likely to intend to cause fear or alarm, a component part of the statutory offence, so that it cannot be an answer to it. Self-defence may remain relevant to any alternative verdict of common law assault whether under s 38 or s 39 of the Criminal Justice and Licensing (Scotland) Act 2010 or DA(S)A 2018, s 1. It is suggested that no notice of special defence need be lodged in order to argue under the reasonableness defence, that the actions taken were reasonable because of the complainer's consent or the reasonable belief in consent or that the accused acted in self defence – the practical difficulties relating ot special defences arising from the inclusion of sexual offences in the component of DA(S)A 2018 charges have not been addressed in terms by any decision of the High Court of Justiciary.

53 DA(S)A 2018, s 6(1).

54 *Kirkup v HM Advocate* 2025 SLT 234.

55 *Urquhart v H M Advocate* 2016 JC 93 at para 15, (approved in *Thomson v H M Advocate* 2021 JC 109 at para 24).

## DEFENCE IN RAPE OR OTHER SEXUAL ASSAULTS

**5.77** There is likewise no appeal court decision on the appropriateness of a special defence of consent to rape or sexual assault included within a DA(S)A 2018, s 1 charge. Under s 78 and s 288C(4) of the Criminal Procedure (Scotland) Act 1995, where the court is satisfied there appears to be a substantial sexual element to the commission of the offence, and an accused intends to rely on a defence of consent, notice of consent will be required. In such circumstances directions on consent and any reasonable belief in consent that arises would it is submitted be appropriate. Until there is a definitive decision from the High Court, the matter remains uncertain. There seems therefore, no harm in addressing the issue with the court at an intermediate diet, first diet or preliminary hearing, as the case may be.

## ALTERNATIVE VERDICTS

**5.78** If the facts proved are not sufficient for a conviction under DA(S) A 2018, then the accused may, if there is sufficient evidence, be convicted of either;

(a) an offence under s 38(1) of the Criminal Justice and Licensing (Scotland) Act 2010, (threatening or abusive behaviour); or

(b) an offence under s 39 (offence of stalking) of that Act.

## EXTRA-TERRITORIAL JURISDICTION

**5.79** The terms of DA(S)A 2018, s 3 provide that an offence under DA(S) A 2018, s 1 can be constituted by a course of behaviour engaged in by the perpetrator even if the course of behaviour occurs wholly or partly outside the UK; the terms of DA(S)A 2018, s 3 apply only if the alleged perpetrator is habitually resident in Scotland or is a UK national. The offence can be prosecuted in the sheriff court district where the accused is apprehended or in custody, or in a sheriff court district determined by the Lord Advocate, 'as if the offence has been committed entirely in that district.' Once the sheriff court district has been determined, the offence is then deemed to have been committed in the relevant district.

## SEXUAL OFFENCES

**5.80** Sexual offences will appear within a DA(S)A 2018, s 1 libel.[56] Behaviour which is abusive includes behaviour directed at the complainer that

56 The Explanatory Notes to DA(S)A 2018 make this clear at para 23.

is violent, threatening or intimidating.[57] Such behaviour, if non-violent, may also be abusive because it may have a 'relevant effect,' such as frightening, humiliating, degrading, or punishing the complainer. And such behaviour may also be considered to have the relevant effect of threatening or intimidating the complainer. Although attempts were made to challenge the prosecution of rape as a component of DA(S)A 2018, s 1 offending, the matter was determined in *McKenzie v HM Advocate*.[58] The argument was that DA(S)A 2018 had not anticipated that rape (normally the exclusive preserve of the High Court) could be prosecuted in the sheriff court as part of a DA(S)A 2018, s 1 offence; the court said

> '[8] In *DF v HM Advocate*, unreported, 10 August 2021, Lord Matthews explained (at para [28]) that section 1 of the Domestic Abuse (Scotland) Act 2018 extended to sexual behaviour. There was nothing incompetent in libelling what could also be charged as rape within a charge under that section. There was nothing incompetent in an indictment with such a libel. That being so, there is no requirement that the case be tried in the High Court. Section 3(6) of the Criminal Procedure (Scotland) Act 1995 does not exclude the jurisdiction of the sheriff court in a case such as the present.
>
> [9] There is no breach of Article 6 of the European Convention in terms of fair notice. The libel is entirely clear. The Crown set out a number of incidents involving what is said to be abusive behaviour, including sexual violence. Fair notice is given in terms of the indictment itself, together with the lists of witnesses and productions and no doubt supplemented by the disclosure regime.'

## THE SEXUAL OFFENCES (SCOTLAND) ACT 2009

**5.81** This section looks briefly at the Sexual Offences (Scotland) Act 2009 (SO(S)A 2009). The nature and extent of sexual offences in Scotland is beyond the scope of this book.[59]

**5.82** The Sexual Offences (Scotland) Act 2009 made fundamental changes to the framework of sexual offences in Scotland, promulgated because the

57 DA(S)A 2018, s 2(4) expressly provides that this reference to violent behaviour includes sexual violence as well as physical violence.

58 [2024] HCJAC 6; 2024 JC 121.

59 For more detailed analysis of the law see the recent and comprehensive book Turnbull and Harvie, *The Law of Sexual offences in Scotland* (Bloomsbury Professional, 2025).

existing law was perceived as out of date and derived from a time when sexual attitudes were very different from those of contemporary society.[60]

**5.83** Part One of SO(S)A 2009 defines the offences of rape, sexual assault by penetration, sexual assault, sexual coercion, coercing a person to be present during sexual activity, coercing a person to look at an image of sexual activity, communicating indecently, sexual exposure, voyeurism, and administering a substance for sexual purpose. The principal offences are defined as follows.

## Rape

**5.84** Rape is defined[61] as penetration by the penis of the vagina, anus or mouth, without consent and without reasonable belief of consent. Accordingly, rape is extended from the common law offence which was restricted to vaginal intercourse. The offence is gender neutral in respect of both the perpetrator and the victim. 'Penetration', 'penis' and 'vagina' are all defined.

## Sexual assault by penetration

**5.85** Sexual assault by penetration[62] occurs if a person penetrates sexually (using part of their body or anything else) the vagina or anus of the victim without consent and without reasonable belief of consent. There must be either an intention to do so, or a recklessness about whether there is penetration.

## Sexual assault

**5.86** Sexual assault[63] covers a variety of conduct deemed to constitute assault, including penetration, reckless or intentional touching, sexual activity which involves physical contact, and the intentional or reckless emission of some bodily fluids. Again the offence is only committed if there is no consent and no reasonable belief of consent.

## Sexual coercion

**5.87** The offence of sexual coercion[64] applies where a person causes another person, without that person's consent, to participate in sexual activity.

60 See for example comments in *Webster v Dominick* 2005 1JC 65 at para [58]: 'Whether a particular act is indecent will depend on the circumstances of the case judged by social standards that will change from age to age … These will be the standards that would be applied by the average citizen in contemporary society.'

61 SO(S)A 2009, s 1.

62 SO(S)A 2009, s 2.

63 SO(S)A 2009, s 3.

64 SO(S)A 2009, s 4.

Whereas the offences relating to rape and sexual assault all require some degree of physical contact between the perpetrator and victim, the offence of sexual coercion does not. An obvious example would be where the perpetrator forces the victim, under threat of violence, to undertake a solo sexual act.

## Non-physical sexual offending

**5.88** While the offences of rape, sexual assault (whether by penetration or otherwise) and sexual coercion all require some form of physical violation of the victim, there are many sexual offences which do not. While such conduct may not involve the victim in a physical act, they violate the victim's sexual autonomy – so sending an unsolicited and sexually explicit image, performing a sexual act in front of an unsuspecting passer-by, or watching an unknowing person undress are all acts by which the perpetrator places the victim in a sexual situation to which they did not consent. The Act makes provision for five types of conduct which fall into this category: coercing a person to be present while another engages in a sexual act;[65] coercing a person to look at a sexual image;[66] communicating indecently;[67] sexual exposure;[68] and voyeurism.[69]

**5.89** For these 'non-physical' act offences, it must be proved that the perpetrator's purpose was either to obtain sexual gratification, or to humiliate, distress or alarm the victim. That requirement is absent from the 'physical act' offences of rape, sexual assault and sexual coercion, on the basis that one or other of these purposes is implicit in the nature of such conduct.

**5.90** All of the offences in Part 1 of SO(S)A 2009 require the absence of the victim's consent and the absence of a reasonably held belief that the victim was consenting. Consent is defined as 'free agreement'.[70] Mere compliance or acquiescence, or even saying 'yes', may not always amount to consent. Evidence from the complainer that she had agreed to sexual intercourse in order to defuse a situation in which she had been assaulted and abducted does not amount to evidence of consent in any real sense[71]. The Court in *HM Advocate v SM* considered that the definition of consent as 'free agreement' in the 2009 Act, did not mark a departure from what was understood to be meant by consent under the pre-existing common law.

65 SO(S)A 2009, s 5.
66 SO(S)A 2009, s 6.
67 SO(S)A 2009, s 7.
68 SO(S)A 2009, s 8.
69 SO(S)A 2009, s 9 as interpreted by s 10.
70 SO(S)A 2009, s 12.
71 *HM Advocate v SM* 2019 SCCR 255 which, although involving conduct prior to SO(S)A 2009 coming force, considered the implications of the Act.

**5.91** SO(S)A 2009, s 13 sets out certain factual situations in which the law deems there to be no consent at all. These are not evidential presumptions. The section prescribes certain factual situations which, if proved, legally exclude the possibility of valid consent or 'free agreement' existing between the parties, including: where the conduct occurs at a time when the complainer is incapable of consenting because of the effect of alcohol or any other substance; or where the complainer agrees or submits to the conduct because of violence, threats of violence, unlawful detention, or deception; or where the consent is expressed only by someone other than the victim. In addition, SO(S)A 2009, s 14 provides that 'a person is incapable, while asleep or unconscious, of consenting to any conduct.' On the basis that consent requires to be continuing, consent expressed by the person in advance of falling asleep or becoming unconscious cannot provide a defence: see *GW v HM Advocate*.[72]

**5.92** SO(S)A 2009 also provides guidance as to particular issues concerning consent or the lack thereof. Consent to conduct does not, of itself, imply consent to any other conduct and consent to conduct may be withdrawn at any time before, or in the case of continuing conduct, during, the conduct. If the conduct takes place, or continues to take place, after consent has been withdrawn, it takes place, or continues to take place, without consent.[73]

**5.93** For each of the SO(S)A 2009', Part 1 offences, it must also be proved that the accused had no reasonable belief that the complainer was consenting. That means that it must be shown that the accused either knew that the complainer was not consenting or, at least, that if the accused believed the complainer to be consenting, that belief was not a reasonable one to hold. An honest belief that the complainer was consenting is no longer a defence where that belief was unreasonable. Furthermore, a person is expected to take responsibility for establishing whether another person consents to sexual activity. SO(S)A 2009 provides that when a determination is being made, by the court or jury, as to whether an accused's belief in a complainer's consent or knowledge was reasonable, 'regard is to be had as to whether the person took any steps to ascertain whether there was consent or, as the case may be, knowledge, and if so, what those steps were'.[74]

## Threats

**5.94** The making of threats to another, oral or written, can constitute a criminal offence. It is the effect on the other person that matters, not how the threat was made. The threat may be to do violence to the recipient, to destroy

72 2019 SCCR 175; that is also authority for the proposition that if the victim is asleep there can be no reasonable belief – see para 27.

73 SO(S)A 2009, s 15.

74 SO(S)A 2009, s 16.

their property, or to menace or intimidate them. It is not criminal to threaten to do something which one is entitled to do – so to threaten to raise proceedings for residence or contact for example, would not be criminal unless such a threat is made in an improper context (such as threatening such proceedings as an inducement to drop criminal proceedings).

**5.95** This categorisation arises from *James Miller*[75] where the Lord Justice Clerk explained (pp 244–246) that there were two classes of threats: first, those which involved 'grievous bodily harm, or to do any serious injury to his property …', and secondly, those in a 'much larger class' which contemplated lesser or vaguer harms. Only the former were criminal per se, while the latter might acquire criminal status if they were used for an unlawful purpose, (such as extortion or robbery or as part of behaviour caught by s 1 of DA(S)A 2018).

**5.96** The common law of threats had receded in its use in court but, prompted by the decision in *Harris v HM Advocate,*[76] regained some attention. In *Harris* the accused had been charged with a breach of the peace. The High Court held that the charge was irrelevant because the threats (made to a police officer) were not capable of breaching the public peace. What was necessary for the offence to be committed was a need that the 'offending conduct should, in some sense at least, cause or threaten disturbance to the public peace.' There had to be a public-facing element of the offence for it to constitute a breach of the peace. The court did however conclude that, given the conduct, the common law of threats might have been invoked.

**5.97** The law of threats was then considered in *H M Advocate v Baillie,*[77] where the High Court said:

> 'For the crime to be completed, it is not enough that the threat simply be spoken or written. It must be communicated to a third party' (Macdonald (above) p 128). However, it is not a requirement that the threat be conveyed directly to the party threatened. Communication to a third party will suffice (John Jaffray)'.[78].

**5.98** The court went on:

> 'As with almost all common law crimes, the act must be done deliberately. The accused must have intended to do the act. Threatening a person is no doubt, in the ordinary case, motivated by a desire to cause that person, or a third party to whom the threat is communicated, fear and alarm and/or to do something which he would not otherwise have done. However, it is

75 (1862) 4 Irv 238.
76 [2009] HCJAC 80, 2009 SLT 1078, 2010 SCL 56.
77 2013 SCCR 285, 2013 SCL 550
78 (1815) Hume i, 441,

not necessary, for a libel to meet the test of relevancy, that it specify either motive or result. Unlike breach of the peace, where the acts may not be unlawful when looked at in isolation, the communication of a threat of serious harm to the potential object of the harm or to a third party, is itself unlawful. The necessary criminal intent is inferred from the carrying out of the act itself (Elizabeth Edmiston (1866) 5 Irv 219, LJC (Inglis) at 223). It is no defence that, for example, the act was intended to amuse in a situation where, objectively, it was likely to cause fear and alarm.'

**5.99** As is clear, the crime is committed as soon as the words are spoken, the message sent, or the letter posted. Why the threat was made, and the accused's purpose in making it is irrelevant. It does not matter that the accused never intended to carry it out. It is no defence that it was meant to be a joke.

*Chapter 6*

# Statutory Aggravations to Charges in the Context of Domestic Offending

**6.01** In practice when dealing with prosecutions involving domestic abuse, the charge libelled will contain one or more statutory aggravations which might have a significant bearing on the charge itself and will almost certainly be of significance in relation to the question of sentence. In considering the question of aggravations in a domestic context, these fall within two categories:

(1) specific statutory aggravations applicable to domestic abuse; and

(2) general statutory aggravations applicable to any category of offence.

**6.02** It is entirely possible that domestic offending might include both of the foregoing categories; so, for example, an offence aggravated by virtue of the Abusive Behaviour and Sexual Harm (Scotland) Act 2016, may also be aggravated by the offender being on bail, or aggravated in terms of the Hate Crime and Public Order (Scotland) Act 2021. All of these factors may require to be taken into consideration by the sentencing court.

**6.03** In recognition of the corrosive effect that domestically aggravated offences have on society, there has been considerable legislative activity in recent years, resulting in a number of statutory interventions designed specifically to address this particular area of offending. In this regard the most commonly encountered statutory aggravations will relate to offences aggravated either by virtue of the Abusive Behaviour and Sexual Harm (Scotland) Act 2016, or the Domestic Abuse (Scotland) Act 2018.

**6.04** In relation to general statutory aggravations, perhaps the most common form of aggravation encountered in practice in a domestic context are offences which are aggravated by virtue of the fact that at the time of the commission of the offence the accused was subject to conditions of bail. These conditions can be court imposed or imposed as part of police investigative or undertaking bail (see **Chapters 3 and 4**). Perhaps less commonly encountered in the domestic context are offences aggravated by prejudice, namely by race, religious prejudice, disability, sexual orientation or transgender identity.

## SPECIFIC STATUTORY AGGRAVATIONS APPLICABLE TO DOMESTIC ABUSE

**6.05** In general terms, it is now a common element of such charges that the offence libelled have involved the abuse of a partner or ex-partner of the accused. This factor is an aggravation of the charge. The principal source of statutory domestic abuse aggravations derive from the terms of the Abusive Behaviour and Sexual Harm (Scotland) Act 2016.

## BACKGROUND TO THE ABUSIVE BEHAVIOUR AND SEXUAL HARM (SCOTLAND) ACT 2016

**6.06** The background and purpose of the Abusive Behaviour and Sexual Harm (Scotland) Act 2016 (ABSH(S)A 2016) was to support the aims of the Scottish Government's Equally Safe strategy introduced in June 2014 to protect, largely, women and children from a wide range of abusive behaviour, both psychological and physical. The Scottish Government consulted widely on this subject and the 2016 Act came into force on 3 July 2017. The Act's overarching objective was to improve how the justice system responds to abusive behaviour, including domestic abuse and sexual harm and to improve public safety by ensuring that perpetrators are appropriately held to account for their conduct.[1]

**6.07** ABSH(S)A 2016 introduced a new aggravation, to be applied to existing offences where the offence relates to the abuse of a partner or ex-partner and is in the following terms:

> **'1 Aggravation of offence where abuse of partner or ex-partner**
>
> (1) This subsection applies where it is—
>
> (a) libelled in an indictment or specified in a complaint that an offence is aggravated by involving abuse of the partner or ex-partner of the person committing it, and
>
> (b) proved that the offence is so aggravated.
>
> (2) An offence is aggravated as described in subsection (1)(a) if in committing the offence—
>
> (a) the person intends to cause the partner or ex-partner to suffer physical or psychological harm, or
>
> (b) in the case only of an offence committed against the partner or ex-partner, the person is reckless as to causing the partner or ex-partner to suffer physical or psychological harm.

1 2016 Act Explanatory Notes.

(3) It is immaterial for the purposes of subsection (2) that the offence does not in fact cause the partner or ex-partner physical or psychological harm.

(4) Evidence from a single source is sufficient to prove that an offence is aggravated as described in subsection (1)(a).

(5) Where subsection (1) applies, the court must—

(a) state on conviction that the offence is aggravated as described in subsection (1)(a),

(b) record the conviction in a way that shows that the offence is so aggravated,

(c) take the aggravation into account in determining the appropriate sentence, and

(d) state—

(i) where the sentence imposed in respect of the offence is different from that which the court would have imposed if the offence were not so aggravated, the extent of and the reasons for that difference, or

(ii) otherwise, the reasons for there being no such difference.

(6) For the purposes of this section, a person is a partner of another person if they are—

(a) spouses or civil partners of each other,

(b) living together as if spouses of each other, or

(c) in an intimate personal relationship with each other,

and the references to a person's ex-partner are to be construed accordingly.

(7) In this section—

- "cause" includes contribute to causing (and "causing" is to be construed accordingly),
- "psychological harm" includes fear, alarm or distress.'

**6.08** The terms of ABSH(S)A 2016, s 1 make clear therefore that where it is libelled in a charge that the offence has been aggravated by involving abuse of the partner or ex-partner of the accused and that it has been so proved,[2] on

2 ABSH(S)A 2016, s 1.

conviction the court must state that the offence has been so aggravated.[3] This fact must be recorded.[4]

**6.09** The court must also take this aggravation into account when sentencing the offender.[5] As part of this process the court must state what difference this aggravation has made to the sentence were it not for the aggravation,[6] or, where there is no difference in the sentence which has been imposed, the court must state the reason for there being no difference.[7]

**6.10** The offence is aggravated for the purposes of ABSH(S)A 2016, s 1 where the offender in committing that offence has either intended to cause their partner or ex-partner to suffer physical or psychological harm,[8] or has been reckless as to whether they have caused their partner or ex-partner to suffer physical or psychological harm. [9] In the context of this section the reference to 'causing' includes contributing to causing and the reference to 'psychological harm' includes causing fear, alarm, or distress. [10]

**6.11** Further, it is immaterial for the purposes of ABSH(S)A 2016, s 1(2) that the offence did not in fact cause the partner or ex-partner harm.[11]

**6.12** It is also important to note that the aggravation libelled does not in itself require corroboration, and that whilst the offence itself must be corroborated, evidence from a single source is sufficient to prove that an offence is aggravated as described in ABSH(S)A 2016, s 1(1)(a).[12]

## APPLICATION OF THE ABUSIVE BEHAVIOUR AND SEXUAL HARM (SCOTLAND) ACT 2016

**6.13** In the case of *McGowan (Christopher) v HM Advocate,*[13] a punishment, part of 23 years in respect of a life sentence, was imposed on an accused convicted of murdering his partner, with a domestic abuse aggravation. The court specifically stated in this case that whilst the Abusive Behaviour and Sexual Harm (Scotland) Act 2016 did not stipulate any fixed percentage or other level of additional penalty in respect of an abuse of partner aggravation,

3 ABSH(S)A 2016, s 1(5)(a).
4 ABSH(S)A 2016, s 1(5)(b).
5 ABSH(S)A 2016, s 1(5)(c).
6 ABSH(S)A 2016, s 1(5)(d)(i).
7 ABSH(S)A 2016, s 1(5)(d)(ii).
8 ABSH(S)A 2016, s 1(2)(a).
9 ABSH(S)A 2016, s 1(2)2(b).
10 ABSH(S)A 2016, s 1(7).
11 ABSH(S)A 2016, s 1(3).
12 ABSH(S)A 2016, s 1(1)(4).
13 2024 JC 359.

that it had to be assumed that although Parliament was content to leave the overall sentence to the judge's discretion, it was intended that a significant penalty should normally be added to that which would have attended a similar crime not aggravated by partner abuse.

**6.14** This case might however be contrasted with the approach of the sentencing judge in the earlier case of *Rizzo (Keith) v HM Advocate,*[14] where it was stated that the sentence was not enhanced to reflect the aggravation in terms of ABSH(S)A 2016, s 1(1), given that it was stated that regard had been had to the domestic relationship in selecting the punishment part.

**6.15** This decision might perhaps now be seen as out of step with the correct approach to be adopted in selecting sentences, particularly having regard to the later case of *McGowan,*[15]

**6.16** See also the case of *HM Advocate v CM,*[16] which involved serious charges of rape, and which contained aggravations in terms of ABSH(S) A 2016, s 1. In that case reference was made to the fact that although the sentencing judge had stated that he had had regard to the 2016 Act when fixing the sentence, he had failed to comply with the statutory direction contained in ABSH(S)A 2016, s 1(5)(d). Specifically, he did not state why the sentence imposed in respect of the offence was different from that which would have been imposed were the offence not so aggravated, nor did he state the extent of and the reasons for that difference.[17] In this case, the Appeal Court specifically stated that in relation to the sentence of nine years' imprisonment which was imposed, seven months was attributable to the aggravation in terms of ABSH(S)A 2016, s 1(1) of the 2016 Act.

**6.17** In the case of *HM Advocate v AP,*[18] the sentencing judge was said to have failed to comply with the terms of ABSH(S)A 2016, s 1(5)(d). The sentence was quashed and an alternative sentence was imposed.

**6.18** It should be noted that where a plea of guilty has been tendered by an accused to an offence with an aggravation in terms of the ABSH(S)A 2016, it means that it has been accepted by the accused that they intended to cause their partner or ex-partner to suffer physical or psychological harm, or had at least been reckless as to causing physical or psychological harm. If found guilty of an offence so aggravated, there should be a finding to that effect.

14 2020 SCCR 397.
15 Fn 13 above.
16 2025 JC 39.
17 *Ibid*, para 17.
18 2024 JC 398.

**6.19** The current prevailing approach therefore in dealing with such matters appears to be to stress that the terms of ABSH(S)A 2016, s 1(5) must be complied with, and that not only should there be an element of the sentence imposed attributable to the aggravation, but also that this element is properly recorded.

## DEFINITION OF PARTNER OR EX-PARTNER

**6.20** In terms of ABSH(S)A 2016, s 1(6), the question of whether a person is a partner or ex-partner of another person is a matter of fact, but it will be held to apply if the parties are spouses or civil partners of each other,[19] living together as if spouses of each other,[20] or in an intimate personal relationship with each other.[21]

## PRESUMPTION AS TO THE RELATIONSHIP

**6.21** It is also worth noting that the definition of the term 'partner or ex-partner' in terms of ABSH(S)A 2016 is to be regarded as a special capacity in that where the capacity of being a partner or ex-partner is libelled in the charge, in the complaint or indictment then that status is to be taken as established, unless the matter has been challenged.[22]

**6.22** In summary proceedings, the challenge must be made by way of a preliminary objection before the plea is recorded,[23] or at such later stage as the court allows in special circumstances,[24] or in proceedings on indictment, by way of notice of a preliminary objection in accordance with ss 71(2) or 76(6)(b)(i) of the Criminal Procedure (Scotland) Act 1995.[25]

## THE DOMESTIC ABUSE (SCOTLAND) ACT 2018

**6.23** The Domestic Abuse (Scotland) Act 2018 (DA(S)A 2018) introduced a further aggravation of relevance in relation to cases involving domestic abuse, namely those offences which are aggravated by reason of involving a child.

**6.24** DA(S)A 2018, s 1 specifies that a person commits an offence if they engage in a course of behaviour that is abusive of their partner or ex-partner,[26]

19 ABSH(S)A 2016, s 1(6)(a).
20 ABSH(S)A 2016, s 1(6)(b).
21 ABSH(S)A 2016, s 1(6)(c).
22 ABSH(S)A 2016, s 1A(1)(a).
23 ABSH(S)A 2016, s 1A(2)(a)(i).
24 ABSH(S)A 2016, s 1A(2)(a)(ii).
25 ABSH(S)A 2016, s 1A(2)(b).
26 DA(S)A 2018, s 1(1).

The conditions set out in DA(S)A 2018, s 1(2) must be met, namely that a reasonable person would consider that the course of behaviour would be likely to cause their partner or ex-partner to suffer physical or psychological harm,[27] and that they either intended by the course of that behaviour to cause them to suffer physical or psychological harm,[28] or were reckless as to whether that course of behaviour caused them to suffer physical or psychological harm.[29] DA(S)A 2018, s 1 also specifies that any reference to psychological harm includes fear, alarm or distress.[30]

**6.25** Given the impact that domestic abuse often has on children, and in recognition of the fact that children are often effectively 'weaponised' by perpetrators of domestic abuse, DA(S)A 2018 specifically introduced a statutory aggravation whereby an offence in terms of DA(S)A 2018, s 1(1) is aggravated if it involves a child. The terms of DA(S)A 2018, s 5(1) specifically provides:

> **'5 Aggravation in relation to a child**
>
> (1) This subsection applies where it is, in proceedings for an offence under section 1(1)—
>
> (a) specified in the complaint or libelled in the indictment that the offence is aggravated by reason of involving a child, and
>
> (b) proved that the offence is so aggravated.'

**6.26** DA(S)A 2018 goes on to specify that the offence in terms of DA(S) A 2018, s 1(1) is aggravated in terms of this section if the offender directs behaviour at a child,[31] or makes use of a child in directing behaviour at the partner or ex-partner. [32]

**6.27** An offence is also to be regarded as so aggravated if a child sees or hears or is present during an incident that the offender directs at the partner or ex-partner.[33] The offence is also to be regarded as aggravated if a reasonable person would consider that the course of behaviour or an instance of that behaviour is likely to adversely affect a child usually residing with either party or both.[34]

27 DA(S)A 2018, s 1(2)(a).
28 DA(S)A 2018, s 1(2)(b)(i).
29 DA(S)A 2018, s 1(2)(b)(ii).
30 DA(S)A 2018, s 1(3).
31 DA(S)A 2018, s 5(2)(a).
32 DA(S)A 2018, s 5(2) (b).
33 DA(S)A 2018, s 5(3).
34 DA(S)A 2018, s 5(4).

**6.28** For it to be proved that the offence is so aggravated, there does not need to be evidence that a child—

(a) has ever had any:

  (i) awareness of A's behaviour; or

  (ii) understanding of the nature of A's behaviour; or

(b) has ever been adversely affected by A's behaviour.[35]

**6.29** Further, evidence from a single source is sufficient to prove that the offence is so aggravated.[36]

**6.30** In terms of conviction, the fact that the offence was so aggravated must be recorded and the effect on any sentence must be recorded. Specifically, DA(S)A 2018, s 5(7) states that the court must:

(a) state on conviction that the offence is so aggravated;[37]

(b) record the conviction in a way that shows that the offence is so aggravated;[38]

(c) take the aggravation into account in determining the appropriate sentence;[39] and

(d) state:

  (i) where the sentence imposed in respect of the sentence is different from that which the court would have imposed if the offence were not so aggravated, the extent of and the reasons for that difference;[40] or

  (ii) otherwise, the reasons for there being no such difference.[41]

**6.31** The terms of DA(S)A 2018, s 5(7) can be seen to mirror the terms of s 1(5) of the Abusive Behaviour and Sexual Harm (Scotland) Act 2016 in relation to the recording of the domestic abuse aggravations and the effect (or lack of effect) that this will have on sentencing.

35 DA(S)A 2018, s 5(5).
36 DA(S)A 2018, s 5(6).
37 DA(S)A 2018, s 5(7)(a).
38 DA(S)A 2018, s 5(7)(b).
39 DA(S)A 2018, s 5(7)(c).
40 DA(S)A 2018, s 5(7)(d)(i).
41 DA(S)A 2018, s 5(7)(d)(ii).

## STATISTICS: STATUTORY DOMESTIC ABUSE AGGRAVATIONS IN SCOTLAND

**6.32** Both offences involving the statutory aggravation of domestic abuse, in terms of the Abusive Behaviour and Sexual Harm (Scotland) Act 2016 and aggravations of domestic abuse in relation to a child in terms of the Domestic Abuse (Scotland) Act 2018 are recorded by Police Scotland and COPFS and give some indication of the incidence and application of these aggravations.

**6.33** The new statutory domestic abuse aggravation, introduced in ABSH(S)A 2016, was used for the first time in 2017/18, and applied to 30,100 charges with a domestic abuse identifier in 2023/24. In the same period there were 4,859 convictions with a domestic identifier in the period April 2024 to December 2024. During that time the vast majority of people convicted of an offence with a domestic abuse statutory aggravation were male (86%), and the most common crime types with a domestic abuse statutory aggravation were:

- **offences involving threatening and abusive behaviour**, which made up 37 per cent of domestic abuse convictions (2,410 convictions) – of these breach of the peace type convictions, the vast majority of convictions were for offences of 'threatening or abusive behaviour' (2,242), with the others for stalking (146) and breach of the peace (22);
- **crimes against public justice which includes breach of bail charges** (31% or 1,996 convictions); and
- **common assault** (22% or 1,450 convictions).

**6.34** In relation to the domestic abuse aggravation involving a child, there were 90 convictions with a statutory aggravation for domestic abuse in relation to a child in 2020/21.[42]

## GENERAL STATUTORY AGGRAVATIONS

**6.35** In relation to general statutory aggravations which apply to all offences, perhaps the most common aggravation encountered in practice is that the offence was committed whilst the accused was subject to conditions of bail.

**6.36** The question of bail is dealt with elsewhere (see **Chapter 4**), but in the context of domestic offences, a perpetrator, being subject to bail at the time of the commission of the offence is a significant aggravator. That is because the perpetrator was in a position of trust, having been released by the courts, (or in specific circumstances as set out in **Chapter 3**), by the police, and inter alia subject to the condition that they must not commit any offences whilst on bail.

42 See COPFS statistics available on https://www.copfs.gov.uk.

**6.37** Questions of bail are governed by Part III of the Criminal Procedure (Scotland) Act 1995, as amended by the Bail and Release from Custody (Scotland) Act 2023. Section 24 of the Criminal Procedure (Scotland) Act 1995 confirms that all crimes and offences are bailable,[43] and also sets out the standard conditions of bail which apply in every case, specifically that the accused:[44]

> '(a) appears at the appointed time at every diet relating to the offence with which he is charged of which he is given due notice or at which he is required by this Act to appear;
>
> (b) does not commit an offence while on bail;
>
> (c) does not interfere with witnesses or otherwise obstruct the course of justice whether in relation to himself or any other person;
>
> (ca) does not behave in a manner which causes, or is likely to cause, alarm or distress to witnesses;
>
> (d) makes himself available for the purpose of enabling enquiries or a report to be made to assist the court in dealing with him for the offence with which he is charged
>
> (e) where the (or an) offence in respect of which he is admitted to bail is one listed in subsection (7A)(b), does not seek to obtain, otherwise than by way of a solicitor, any precognition of or statement by the complainer in relation to the subject matter of the offence.'

## SPECIAL CAPACITY

**6.38** The status of being on bail is a special capacity and if this capacity is libelled then unless timeously challenged it will be held as admitted.[45] In summary proceedings timeous challenge is by a preliminary objection prior to the tendering of a plea, or in solemn proceedings by the giving of a preliminary objection in terms of ss 71(2) or 72(6)(b)(i) of the Criminal Procedure (Scotland) Act 1995 (CP(S)A 1995).[46]

**6.39** If the fact that the accused was subject to bail is challenged, then it will be for the Crown to prove that the accused was subject to bail at the relevant time. This is usually done by producing a certified copy bail order and minutes of court proceedings to establish that the accused was released on

43 Criminal Procedure (Scotland) Act 1995, s 24(1).
44 Criminal Procedure (Scotland) Act 1995, s 24(5).
45 CP(S)A 1995, s 255.
46 CP(S)A 1995, s 27 (4A).

bail on the date libelled and that the bail order had not fallen at the time of the commission of the new offence.

**6.40** In terms of CP(S)A 1995, s 27(3), where it is alleged in an indictment or complaint that an offence contained within that indictment or complaint was committed while the offender was subject to bail conditions, then that is not a separate offence,[47] However, the sentencing court must have regard to the fact that the offence was committed while on bail as well as the number of bail orders to which the person was subject when the offence was committed,[48]

**6.41** The court must also take account of any previous convictions of the accused for offences under CP(S)A 1995, s 27(1)(b) above (in relation to breaches of special conditions of bail),[49] and the extent to which the sentence or disposal in respect of any previous conviction(s) of the accused differed, by virtue of this subsection, from that which the court would have imposed but for this subsection.[50]

**6.42** The CP(S)A 1995 provides therefore that where an accused person is subject to bail when committing a further offence, this should be reflected in an increased sentence for the offence subsequently committed.

**6.43** The terms of CP(S)A 1995, s 27(5) provide that where there is a maximum penalty provided by statute, then it may be increased by an amount equivalent to level 3 on the standard scale in the event of a fine being imposed, and by 60 days in the JP Court or by six months in the High Court or Sheriff Court in the event of a custodial sentence being imposed,[51] notwithstanding that this enhanced penalty might otherwise exceed the ordinary statutory maximum of the court. Despite the wording of the legislation it appears that the enhanced penalty can also be applied to common law offences.[52]

**6.44** In respect of specific breaches of bail conditions in terms of CP(S) A 1995, s 27(1)(b), an offender will be liable to a fine not exceeding level 3 on the standard scale if a financial penalty is to be imposed, and 60 days if the conviction is in the JP Court and 12 months in any other case. [53]

**6.45** Given that many bail orders imposed in relation to cases involving domestic abuse include special conditions of bail, the terms of this section are of particular relevance. It is extremely common for accused persons in

47 CP(S)A 1995, s 27 (3).
48 CP(S)A 1995, s 27 (3)(a).
49 CP(S)A 1995, s 27 (3) (b).
50 CP(S)A 1995, s 27 (3) (c).
51 CP(S)A 1995, s 27 (5).
52 *Kyle v HM Advocate*, 2010 SCCR 458.
53 CP(S)A 1995, s 27 (2).

domestic abuse cases to be subject to additional conditions to the effect that they do not approach, contact or communicate with the complainer (or attempt to do so), or prohibiting entering a particular address. Accordingly, where further offending takes place, this will mean that the offender will be liable to be sentenced in relation to that offence, aggravated by the fact that the offender was on bail at the relevant time, but they will often also face a separate charge alleging breach of a special condition in terms of CP(S)A 1995, s 27(1)(b) (see **5.12** above). That matter will fall to be sentenced separately from the substantive offending itself.

## OTHER STATUTORY AGGRAVATIONS

**6.46** In relation to domestic offending, other statutory aggravations encountered in practice are aggravations relating to various types of prejudice. The Hate Crime and Public Order (Scotland) Act 2021 (HCPO(S)A 2021) was passed by the Scottish Parliament on 11 March 2021 and received Royal Assent on 23 April 2021. The Act came into effect on 1 April 2024 and applies to offences committed from that date onwards. Any offences committed before that date will continue to be reported and prosecuted under relevant existing legislation.

**6.47** Section 1(1) of HCPO(S)A 2021 specifically provides that an offence will be aggravated by prejudice, if, at the time of committing the offence, or immediately before or after doing so, the offender demonstrates malice and ill-will towards the victim, and that malice and ill-will is based on the victim's membership or presumed membership of a group defined by reference to a characteristic mentioned in HCPO(S)A 2021, s 1(2). This aggravation applies whether or not there is a specific victim of the offence.[54]

**6.48** At the present time the protected characteristics as set out in HCPO(S) A 2021, s 1(2) are:

(a) age;

(b) disability;

(c) race, colour, nationality (including citizenship), or ethnic or national origins;

(d) religion or, in the case of a social or cultural group, perceived religious affiliation;

(e) sexual orientation;

(f) transgender identity; or

(g) variations in sex characteristics.

54 HCPO(S)A 2021, s 1(1).

**6.49** Further detail about the meaning of the specific characteristics is provided in HCPO(S)A 2021, s 11.

**6.50** Accordingly, in practice, an offence committed by an offender in a domestic context may contain an aggravation that the offender demonstrated ill-will and malice towards the victim based on their membership or presumed membership of one of the protected groups (or perceived affiliation in the case of a social or cultural group).

**6.51** The terms of HCPO(S)A 2021 specifically provide that it is immaterial whether or not the offender's ill will and malice is also based, to any extent, on any other factor,[55] specifically allowing for the situation that an offence already aggravated by the terms of another Act such as ABSH(S)A 2016, can also be aggravated where the offender also evinces ill- will and malice on the basis of the victim's possession of one of the protected characteristics.

**6.52** It is also the case that the proof of an aggravation does not require to be corroborated and evidence from a single source is sufficient to establish this.[56]

**6.53** HCPO(S)A 2021 makes specific provision for the treatment of offences said to have been aggravated by prejudice.[57]

**6.54** Accordingly, where it is libelled and has been proved in an indictment, or complaint, that an offence has been aggravated by prejudice,[58] the court must state on conviction that the offence has been aggravated by prejudice,[59] and the relevant form of prejudice having regard to one or more of the characteristics mentioned in HCPO(S)A 2021, s 1(2).[60] There is a duty on the court to record the conviction in a way that demonstrates that that the offence is aggravated by prejudice,[61] and to record the type of prejudice by which the offence is aggravated by reference to one or more of the characteristics mentioned in HCPO(S)A 2021, s 1(2).[62] Thereafter, the court is obliged to take the aggravation into account in determining the appropriate sentence,[63] and to state, where the sentence in respect of the offence is different from that which the court would have imposed, if the offence were not so aggravated, the extent

55 HCPO(S)A 2021, s 1(3).
56 HCPO(S)A 2021, s 1(4)
57 HCPO(S)A 2021, s 2
58 HCPO(S)A 2021, s 2(1)
59 HCPO(S)A 2021, s 2(2)(a)(i)
60 HCPO(S)A 2021, s 2(2)(a)(ii)
61 HCPO(S)A 2021, s 2(2)(b)(i)
62 HCPO(S)A 2021, s 2(2)(b)(ii)
63 HCPO(S)A 2021, s 2(2)(c)

of and the reasons for that difference,[64] or otherwise, the reasons for there being no such difference.[65]

**6.55** These provisions very closely echo the provisions of the 2016 Act, and demonstrate that the court may have a number of factors to consider in terms of aggravations in the sentencing process.

## AGGRAVATIONS APPLICABLE TO OFFENCES BEFORE 1 APRIL 2024

**6.56** For offences committed prior to the commencement of the Hate Crime and Public Order (Scotland) Act 2021, see the following statutes:

- race – Crime and Disorder Act 1998, s 96:
- religion – Criminal Justice (Scotland) Act 2003, s 74:
- disability – Offences (Aggravation by Prejudice) (Scotland) Act 2009, s 1; and
- sexual orientation or transgender identity – (Aggravation by Prejudice) (Scotland) Act 2009, s 2.

64 HCPO(S)A 2021, s 2(2)(d)(i)
65 HCPO(S)A 2021, s 2(2)(d)(ii)

# Chapter 7

# Evidence

## GENERAL

**7.01** The onus of proof is on the crown; the crown has to establish that crime has been committed beyond reasonable doubt, and it must do so on the basis of corroborated evidence. The crown is not required to prove every detail of a charge or every word by corroborated evidence; it has to establish that a crime was committed and that it was committed by the person accused of being the perpetrator. Where there is a single episode of continuous criminal activity, it is not necessary for each of the elements of the libel to be corroborated. So in an assault where a number of blows are inflicted, it is not necessary for each of the blows to be corroborated.[1]

## CORROBORATION

**7.02** The law of evidence is well served by material dealing with proof, so a brief analysis only of the requirements of the law is given. In general corroboration is required to prove what may properly be regarded as separate crimes, including different episodes of assault, even where these have been libelled as part of one composite charge. This does not apply where the components are correctly to be regarded as simply component parts of a single offence of assault, where they are 'all of a piece'.[2]

**7.03** In *Wilson v HM Advocate,*[3] a case involving an omnibus charge of assault, including several incidents occurring over a period of a month, the court concluded that these had to be viewed as separate crimes, requiring corroboration, rather than as elements of the one assault. The court recognised that a different approach required to be taken towards s 1 of the Domestic Abuse (Scotland) Act 2018 (DA(S)A 2018). At para 37, the court stated:

1 *Campbell v Vannet* 1998 SCCR 207 approved in *CA v HM Advocate* 2023 JC 8 para [9] and see In *Yates v HM Advocate* 1977 SLT (Notes) 42, a case in which the complainer gave evidence that she was compelled by threats with a knife to go to a secluded place where the appellant had raped her; the court concluded on appeal that distress was capable of corroborating her account and it was not necessary for there to be distinct corroboration for the use of the knife. Although there was no corroboration from any source that a knife was used, the jury was entitled to convict of rape leaving the reference to the knife in the libel.

2 *Campbell* (fn 1 above).

3 2019 SCCR 273.

> 'Separate episodes of assault do not constitute a separate crime known as a course of conduct in which only one incident requires to be corroborated as if it were an element in a single episode of assault as in *Campbell v Vannet* (cf. lewd and libidinous practices: *Stephen v HM Advocate* and now the Domestic Abuse (Scotland) Act 2018 s.1(1) ).'

**7.04** The basic rule of corroboration was re-stated in *Lord Advocate's Reference No 1 of 2023*.[4] No-one can be convicted on the testimony of one witness alone; corroboration (that is, evidence from another source) is required. The crown is required to prove, by evidence from two sources, that the crime libelled was committed and that it was the accused who committed it. The evidence against the accused can come from any of the following: the eyewitness testimony of two or more witnesses or from one eyewitness and circumstantial evidence; or from two or more sources of circumstantial evidence. But there must be two sources of evidence.[5]

## Nature of corroborating evidence

**7.05** The corroborating evidence does not need to be incriminating in itself and does not even need to be more consistent with the direct evidence than with the accused's account: evidence can corroborate a principal source of evidence if it confirms or supports or fits with that evidence that direct evidence. The need for two sources of evidence does not mean two eyewitnesses. Corroboration can be supplied by another witness also giving direct evidence, or by a witness giving evidence of facts and circumstances which are capable of supporting the direct evidence. Corroboration may also be found in an agreed fact in a joint minute; the conclusive proof of a fact in a joint minute may itself constitute full legal proof of an essential fact or facts, for example if it is set out in a joint minute that the accused penetrated the complainer's vagina with his penis, then there is no further evidence required for identification. Corroboration of a complainer's account may be found in a statement made by an accused person, whether orally or by way of electronic message or social media posting, or from evidence from CCTV footage and from the res gestae. Also corroboration of a complainer's evidence can be based on circumstantial evidence and the emotional disturbance or distress observed by another witness. The court determined in *Lords Advocate's Reference no 1 of 2023* that where a witness hears the complainer's account de recenti (that is, within a short period of time of the incident concerned), and sees and speaks to emotional disturbance, then both the distress and the complainer's reported account are viewed as real evidence, independent from the complainer, and thus corroborative of her account that she was raped or

4 2023 HCJAC 40; 2024 JC 140; 2023 SLT 1115; 2023 SCCR 340.

5 *Lord Advocate's Reference No 1 of 2023*, paras [1] and [235].

assaulted as the case may be[6]. And even absent distress, the court determined that a witness reporting a complainer's statement, if made res gestae or de recenti, is of itself apt to corroborate her evidence of the commission of the crime. In the Lord Advocate's References Nos 2 and 3 of 2023[7] the majority of the court, eight judges, also determined that a complainer's statement *res gestae* or *de recen*ti, spoken to by another witness, is a separate source and capable of corroborating the complainer's evidence identifying the accused as perpetrator. But such evidence would still require evidence from the complainer, or from another source. A *de recenti* statement spoken to by a witness can only provide one source of evidence

## The extent of the corroborative evidence

**7.06** Corroboration concerns the quantity and not the quality of testimony. The modern authority is *Fox v HM Advocate,*[8] where a full bench held that it was sufficient that there was independent evidence that confirmed or supported the direct evidence. To be corroborative, the evidence did not need to be incriminating in itself. The full bench in *Lord Advocate's Reference No 1 of 2023* referred to *Fox* approvingly (see paras 193 and 220), and LJG Carloway had explained in *Garland v HM Advocate,*[9] at para 21:

> '... where the question is whether proof of certain facts and circumstances affords sufficient corroboration of direct testimony, it is not necessary for those facts and circumstances to be more consistent with the direct evidence than an explanation or account given by an accused. It is sufficient that they are capable of confirming or supporting the complainer's testimony. It is a matter for the jury to determine whether to accept the facts and circumstances as corroborative or to interpret their meaning in a different manner.'

**7.07** So the corroborative evidence requires only to be consistent with or give support to or fit in with the principal evidence.

## Additional forms of evidence relevant to domestic abuse cases

### *Admissions*

**7.08** Anything said by an accused person is evidence against him or her; it is an exception to the general rule against hearsay. An accused's admissions

6 [2023] HCJAC 40.
7 [2024] HCJAC 43.
8 1998 JC 94.
9 2020 HCJAC 46.

whether express or implied, or open to more than one interpretation, can be corroborative of the account of the complainer or other evidence:

> 'Whether, and to what extent, a comment or reply made by an accused person may properly be regarded as an admission is a fact specific question, the answer to which depends on the nature and content of the comment and the circumstances in which it is made. The contextual situation is important.'[10]

**7.09** In relation to admissions, it has been established that it is not just clear and unequivocal admissions which have evidential value. In *Greenshields v HM Advocate,*[11] a reply (to a caution and charge for murder) of 'You don't think I did it myself do you; but I'm telling you nothing about it until I see my lawyer', was considered to be capable of constituting an implied admission to murder. It remains a matter for the court what is to be made of any purported admission It was sufficient if the admission was capable of providing support for, or confirmation of, or fitted with, the principal source of evidence. The matter was addressed in *CR v HM Advocate*[12] as follows:

> 'It has often been said that if there is a clear and unequivocal admission of guilt, then very little evidence in corroboration of such an admission is required … [I]t is not appropriate that this approach to what is required to corroborate a clear and unequivocal confession should be described as a rule … there is a risk that, by describing the requirement in minimal terms by using the words such as "very little" and then elevating it into a rule, there will be a weakening of the principle that there must be a sufficient independent check of the confession to corroborate it.'

**7.10** The court continued at para 15:

> 'Whether and to what extent a comment or reply made by an accused person may properly be regarded as an admission is a fact specific question the answer to which depends on the nature and context of the comment and the circumstances in which it is made. The contextual situation is important.'

**7.11** But in relation to whether support is provided by the admission, note should be taken of *M (W) v HM Advocate,*[13] where the court stressed that it was important to distinguish, on the one hand, a case where an admission is relied upon as the primary evidence in a circumstantial case, and on the other where it is relied upon as corroboration of other evidence which constitutes the primary

10 *CR v HM Advocate* 2022 SCCR 227; and see also *Kelly v HM Advocate* 2024 JC 354

11 1989 SCCR 637

12 [2022] HCJAC 25

13 2022 JC 248 [para 12] See also *PF Livingston v H(J)* 2021 SLT (Sh Ct) 415 where the accused admitted he had struck the complainer, saying he meant it as a joke; that could corroborate the complainer's account of being assaulted

evidence. In the former, the nature of the surrounding circumstances may be such that only a clear and unequivocal admission, made in the context of a specific allegation, or lack of reaction to a clear allegation, may be sufficient for the purpose. Everything depends on the context.

### *Admissions to police during questioning*

**7.12** Similarly, an admission, if made to police, can be used, but it must be borne in mind that in any case where the admissibility of answers by a suspect to police questioning becomes an issue, it will be necessary to consider the whole relevant circumstances in order to discover whether or not there has been unfairness on the part of the police; unfairness may take many forms, but:

> '[I]f answers are to be excluded they must be seen to have been extracted by unfair means which place cross examination, pressure and deception in close company' ...[W]here in the opinions [in] the decided cases the word "interrogation" or the expression "cross examination" are used in discussing unfair tactics on the part of the police they are to be understood to refer only to improper forms of questioning tainted with an element of bullying or pressure designed to break the will of the suspect or to force from him a confession against his will.'
>
> *Lord Advocate's Reference (No 1 of 1983)*[14]

**7.13** The judge will exclude evidence of a statement if it was taken in circumstances which render it inadmissible under any rule laid down by the law. In other cases the judge will admit the statement if the Crown satisfy the judge that it would be fair to do so, by proving that the statement was made freely and voluntarily and was not extracted by unfair or improper means.[15]

## Corroboration from an implied admission or failure to respond

**7.14** In *M (W) v HM Advocate,*[16] there were admissions in general terms to assaulting children and a failure (in the same conversation) to respond to the statement 'Well, stop hitting them'. The Appeal Court found that the same principles on admissions apply where the significance of the evidence is that an accused has failed to respond to, or react to an allegation in circumstances where that failure could be regarded as criminative. In M (W)'s case, the failure to respond to the statement also had to be read in the context of the general admissions made.

14 1984 JC 52, 1984 SCCR 62.
15 *Thompson v Crowe* 1999 SCCR 693.
16 2022 JC 248.

**7.15** An accused's reaction in the absence of any express words can also be corroborative. In *Adamson v HM Advocate*[17], where the fact that the accused, upon being told that an allegation of rape was not to be reported to the police, sat down and began crying, could be corroborative. It was for the jury or fact finder to choose whether the reaction was relief that a well-founded accusation of rape was not to be investigated by the authorities, or relief that an ill-founded, malicious accusation of that kind was not to be taken further. The fact finder could find that it was consistent with or fitted with the complainer's account[18]. In *McGill v HM Advocate*,[19] the court determined that the accused's reaction (to the finding of drugs) could point to the 'substantial possibility' of the accused knowing of the drugs, so reactions could be taken onto account.

**7.16** In *CR v HM Advocate*,[20] where the appellant was charged with specific crimes of lewd, indecent and libidinous practices against two complainers, the court agreed with the trial judge that it was open to the jury to find corroboration from implied admissions made in response to a non-specific allegation of sexual abuse. Similarly it was open to the jury to find corroboration when a non-specific allegation by one of the complainers was met with the appellant replying: 'I couldn't help myself but I'm not like those people you hear about on the radio, on the news.' The court rejected the suggestion that the detail of the conduct in question had to be put to the appellant (to which his answers were a response) before the answers could be regarded as an admission. The court distinguished *Gracie v HM Advocate*[21] and *G v HM Advocate*,[22] before explaining:

> '[19] If the impression has been gained from *Gracie* and *G* that only unequivocal admissions in the clearest terms may provide corroboration of a crime, that is not consistent with long established authority. In the first place, such an approach would not be consistent with the law on corroboration. In order to be corroborative, evidence does not require to be more consistent with guilt than with innocence. It is sufficient if it is capable of providing support for or confirmation of, or fits with, the principal source of evidence on an essential fact (*Fox v HMA*). The trial judge properly directed the jury that where there is a primary source such as an eye witness,
>
> > "all that is required for corroboration is evidence that provides support for or confirmation of, or fits with the main source of evidence about an essential fact".'

17 2012 JC 27.
18 As in *Fox v HM Advocate* 1998 JC 94.
19 2000 SCCR 25.
20 2022 SCCR 227.
21 2003 SCCR 105.
22 2012 SLT 999.

**7.17** So an admission, even an equivocal admission, can provide corroboration of an essential fact, as long as it might be reasonably inferred from what was said and its context that it was indeed an admission which confirmed or supported or fitted with the principal evidence relating to the fact. But the question of whether it was reasonably capable of bearing the inference is a question of law for the judge. This was discussed in *LC v HM Advocate,*[23] a case of rape constituted by penetration continuing after the withdrawal of consent. The appeal court decided that the jury could not reasonably infer that the appellant's answers at police interview was an admission capable of corroborating the complainer's evidence. The first answer was 'I went in too hard'. The second, in response to being asked whether the complainer sustained any injuries, was 'she said that she was very sore and obviously it was … I guess it's my fault cause I'd gone in sort of thing' (para 20). The court held that in context the responses were not capable of being regarded as admissions that he persisted with consent after consent was withdrawn. The court held that the only reasonable inference was that he accepted responsibility for the complainer feeling sore. The trial judge's direction to the jury that it could constitute corroboration was found to be a material misdirection. So context is all for statements said to be admissions, however the statements are made

## MUTUAL CORROBORATION – THE *MOOROV* DOCTRINE

**7.18** The doctrine of mutual corroboration has been associated with the decision in *Moorov v HM Advocate*[24], although *Moorov* was part of the evolution of the doctrine rather than the genesis; the decision effectively is a baseline for developments since then, stating as it did the limitations and boundaries of the law of mutual corroboration.

**7.19** The testimony of one witness about one crime may be corroborated by a second witness's testimony about another crime where there are similarities in time, place and circumstances in the crimes 'such as demonstrate that the individual incidents are component parts of one course of conduct persistently pursued by the accused' (*MR v HM Advocate*[25]).

**7.20** In *KH v HM Advocate,*[26] the court said at para [24]:

> 'Mutual corroboration is not about whether the evidence of a witness should be accepted (although it may assist in that exercise), it assumes that the evidence is accepted. It is about the existence of a sufficiency in terms of the requirement for corroboration.'

23 [2022] HCJAC 47

24 1930 JC 68

25 2013 JC 212, LJC (Carloway), delivering the opinion of the Full Bench, at para [20] and citing *Ogg v HM Advocate* 1938 JC 152, LJC (Aitchison) at 157 describing the ratio of Moorov

26 2015 SCCR 242

**7.21** The Moorov doctrine allows mutual corroboration of evidence in cases where an accused is charged with more than one crime, if those crimes are sufficiently connected in time, character, and circumstance to be considered part of a single course of criminal conduct. The evidence of one witness to one crime can corroborate the evidence of another witness to a different, but related, crime. The evidence of multiple witnesses, each speaking to a different incident, can mutually support each other, even without independent corroboration for each incident. Before the doctrine can apply, the alleged crimes must be part of a course of conduct persistently or systematically pursued, so the separate crimes must not be isolated incidents but rather component parts or episodes of a more extensive course of conduct persistently pursued by the accused. Whether those similarities exist will be a question of fact and degree.[27] It is only where 'on no possible view' could it be said that the individual incidents were component parts of the one course of conduct persistently pursued by the accused that a no case to answer submission should be upheld [28]

**7.22** For much of its history, the development of this doctrine involved analysis of similarities and differences between the charges (both in the types of charges libelled, and the specific conduct alleged) as well as looking at any time gaps between the various episodes to determine whether the doctrine can apply. So, if the differences between the charges outweighed the similarities, or the time gaps were regarded as too long between the charges, the matter was brought to an end by the upholding of a submission of no case to answer, or quashed convictions. But there has been an increasing shift towards leaving the decision as to whether the doctrine can apply to the jury or fact finder, culminating in the full bench in *Duthie v HM Advocate*[29] making it clear that a submission of no case to answer should only be sustained when, 'on no possible view', could it be said that the individual incidents were component parts of a course of conduct persistently pursued by the accused. Before looking for proof of a course of conduct, there first had to be a search for similarities in the time, character and circumstances. When analysing the similarities in circumstances, the mutually corroborative testimony did not have to relate to incidents which carried the same *nomen criminis*.[30]

**7.23** The court continued in *Duthie* at para [21]:

27 *HM Advocate v SM (No 2)* 2019 SCCR 262, LJG Carloway at para [6].

28 *HM Advocate v SM (No 2)* 2019 SCCR 262; *Donegan v HM Advocate* 2019 SCCR 106, LJC (Lady Dorrian) at para [39].

29 2021 JC 207; interestingly a full bench was convened in recognition of the Appeal Court's concern that there may have been a continuing tension between some of the appellate decisions of the High Court in these areas over the previous decade.

30 *R v HM Advocate* [2013] HCJAC 8, 2013 JC 212, [2013] 1 WLUK 197, applied. Therefore, a sexual offence of a relatively minor type might corroborate more serious sexual conduct: *Watson (Graham) v HM Advocate* [2019] HCJAC 51, 2019 JC 187, [2019] 7 WLUK 218, applied.

'Although the Domestic Abuse (Scotland) Act 2018 reflected important advances in society's understanding of the nature and effects of sexual abuse, it did not alter the position that rape was different from a physical assault, given the need for penetration. The Crown's central contention that testimony about physical assaults could afford corroboration of rapes was rejected.

[22]. Although a person, who is of a controlling disposition, may perpetrate a number of different types of crime against his partners, perhaps including not only physical or sexual assaults but also theft, malicious mischief and contraventions of the Communications Act 2003, that does not make these offences 'similar' for the purposes of mutual corroboration. Dishonest persons may have a propensity to commit a variety of lucrative crimes, from theft to drug dealing and from extortion to embezzlement; that does not make them similar crimes for those purposes. It is not sufficient that the incidents relied upon demonstrate a propensity to commit the crimes of the nature libelled; the test of similarity must first be met. That test is a necessary precursor to the search to see if the inference of a course of conduct persistently pursued is met. The Crown's central contention that testimony about physical assaults can afford corroboration of rapes is rejected.'

**7.24** So from that can be taken that the doctrine of mutual corroboration still requires offending to be similar; that does not of course mean that the different components of the course of behaviour under s 1 of DA(S) A 2018 must be similar; the restriction applies to how such matters are corroborated.

## Single complainer *Moorov*

**7.25** The case of *HM Advocate v Ricky Taylor*[31] was another significant case in the development of the doctrine; like *Moorov* itself, the decision did not innovate in the law but simply clarified the extent of the law. The normal rule is that each incident in a single, composite charge required corroboration, where the incidents were a course of conduct systematically pursued, the corroboration could be by mutual corroboration. Such mutual corroboration did not depend on whether the separate incidents were charged in separate charges or a single, composite charge. The court also held that mutual corroboration did not require multiple complainers and it could equally apply to a course of conduct against a single complainer. So a succession of criminal acts against a single complainer was as redolent (perhaps more so) of a single

31 2019 JC 71; although the case arose from a decision in a summary complaint, it is reported as if a solemn case.

course of conduct persistently pursued as a succession of acts against different individuals.

**7.26** The accused in *Taylor* was charged (in one charge) with intentionally engaging in a sexual activity in the presence of the same complainer on four separate occasions within one month in that he repeatedly exposed his penis at windows of his home and masturbated. The court held that the evidence of the complainer's husband in respect of the last incident of four could corroborate the evidence of the complainer in the first three incidents. It was evidence from a separate source which enabled all four incidents to be corroborated.

**7.27** The principle derived from *Moorov* remains the same; if such incidents share the conventional similarities in time, place and character of commission such that they can properly be said to form part of a single course of criminal conduct persisted in by the accused, evidence given in relation to one such incident can be used to corroborate evidence given in relation to others; that is so regardless of whether the incidents are charged in one charge or in several. The point is that evidence concerning one incident may corroborate evidence concerning another incident, even against the same complainer, provided that there is relevant evidence from more than one source. It cannot matter whether the corroborating evidence is given by another complainer or by some other individual who observed and is able to speak to the relevant events.[32]

## Omnibus charges or composite charges

**7.28** It is competent to libel in one 'composite' charge a number of instances of criminal behaviour; that has always been the case, particularly where a course of conduct is alleged. This is frequently done in practice in connection with charges under DA(S)A 2018. Where, albeit within a single composite charge, the incidents of criminal behaviour are separate and distinct, possibly separated by substantial periods of time between them, each such incident requires to be proved by corroborated evidence.[33]

**7.29** However, even in such a case, if the separate incidents of criminal behaviour libelled in the composite charge show similarities in time, place and character of commission such that they can properly be said to form part of a single course of criminal conduct persisted in by the accused, corroboration may be provided by the principle of mutual corroboration. The requirement for corroboration will depend on whether the charge libelled is a charge libelling a number of separate events, (each of which constitutes a separate crime) or a charge libelling a single event involving different elements, occurring at or

32 *Taylor*, para [16].
33 *Dalton v HM Advocate* 2015 SCCR 125; *Spinks v Harrower* 2018 JC 177.

about the same time or as part of an uninterrupted continuum[34] or a statutory charge constituted by a 'course of conduct', comprising elements that constitute separate crimes and elements that might not otherwise be criminal but become so because they are part of that course of conduct, most relevantly for this text such as a contravention of DA(S)A 2018, s 1, or s 39 of the Criminal Justice and Licensing (Scotland) Act 2010).

**7.30** In *RM v HM Advocate*[35] the Appeal Court determined that there was no requirement to break down a composite charge into its different elements to be addressed separately by the jury in delivering their verdict.

**7.31** A number of cases have discussed the importance of being clear in this context about the difference between a charge libelling a number of separate events, each of which constitutes a separate crime, and a charge libelling a single event 'involving different elements, occurring at or about the same time or as part of an uninterrupted continuum'.[36] In the case of the latter, it is not necessary that each element is corroborated, provided there is corroboration of the essential elements of the crime.

**7.32** Where what is libelled in a charge comprises a series of separate crimes over a period of time, to convict of any of the separate elements there has to be corroborated evidence in relation to each separate element. The court will still deliver one verdict upon the charge, notwithstanding it contains elements constituting separate crimes.[37] For example, in a case involving a number of allegations of rape over significant passages of time[38] or a case alleging eight allegations of assault over four years[39] each incident of criminal behaviour required to be proved by corroborated evidence.

## Single continuing crime or series of crimes

**7.33** Whether what is charged is a single continuing crime or series of separate crimes may itself in certain cases be a matter for the jury to determine[40] This may particularly be the case in charges libelling statutory offences that are constituted by a 'course of conduct' or 'course of behaviour' involving a number of incidents, some of which on their own might not amount to criminal conduct.[41]

34 *Ryasamaowski v HM Advocate* 2020 JC 84.
35 2012 SCCR 611.
36 *Rysamanowski v HM Advocate* 2020 JC 84 per LJG Carloway at para [17].
37 A jury should be made aware that they can delete an element from the libel if they are not satisfied that that element has been proved: *Afzal v HM Advocate* 2013 SCCR 703.
38 *Dalton v HM Advocate* 2015 SCCR 125.
39 *Spinks v Harrower* 2018 SCCR 179.
40 *Wilson v HM Advocate* 2019 SCCR 273.
41 *Finlay v HM Advocate* 2020 SCCR 317.

## How is the question of sufficiency of evidence addressed in this context of a composite of omnibus change?

**7.34** The requisite corroboration may, depending on the evidence, be afforded by any of the usual mechanisms, *Moorov* can apply even where each incident in an omnibus/composite charge has the same complainer, provided that there are two sources of evidence to prove crucial facts. In *Rysamanowski v HM Advocate*,[42] the court said:

> 'The principle can apply to the evidence of a single complainer who speaks to separate offences, which are all committed against her, where there is a separate witness who speaks to one or more of these offences and the whole series constitutes the requisite course of conduct'.[43]

**7.35** In instances where the charge consists of a number of allegations occurring over a short period of time with similarities in the character of commission, provided there are two sources of evidence to prove the crucial facts, the complainer in the allegations does not require to be different.[44] The fact that the separate episodes of criminal behaviour are libelled as one single charge is of no consequence. What is required in such circumstances is that there is evidence from one source relating to each separate charge or each separate aspect of a single charge.[45]

**7.36** The Appeal Court addressed the matter specifically in *Rysamanowski*[46] in the following terms:

> '[17]. It is apparent that this area of the law is continuing to cause difficulties in practice. It need not do so. First, although the Crown may be allowed considerable latitude when framing a criminal charge involving young children (Allison, Practice 256; Hume, Crimes ii, 222–223) that has no bearing on the need to corroborate each separate criminal act, whether these form part of a course of conduct or not and whether the crimes are sexual in nature or not. Secondly, the need for corroboration may be satisfied as a result of the application of mutual corroboration. In this case, the events libelled, which occurred on separate days over a period of time during which the complainer was otherwise living normally with her family, were separate criminal acts (*Spinks v Harrower*, LJG (Carloway), delivering the opinion of the court, at para.13; cf, *Stirling v McFadyen*). Corroboration could not be supplied in the same manner as in

42 2020 JC 84.
43 per Lord Carloway, at para [21], referring to *HM Advocate v Taylor* 2019 JC 71.
44 *Wilson v HM Advocate* 2017 JC 64.
45 *Taylor* paras 18_20.
46 2020 JC 84.

> a single assault, involving different elements, occurring at or about the same time or as part of an uninterrupted continuum. However, thirdly, applying mutual corroboration, the mother's evidence about the final episode could corroborate the earlier episodes spoken to by the complainer, and vice versa. For a conviction of the whole charge, the jury would have to hold that each episode was a component part in a single course of conduct persistently pursued by the appellant. That in turn requires the jury to examine the similarities and dissimilarities in time, place and circumstances. It is important to recognise in all of this that the phrase "course of conduct" has no significance in relation to sufficiency of evidence other than in the context of mutual corroboration.'

**7.37** The court went on to say:

> '[21]. The principle of mutual corroboration is well understood. Corroboration of separate offences can, in defined circumstances, be provided by different complainers. The principle can apply to the evidence of a single complainer who speaks to separate offences, which are all committed against her, where there is a separate witness who speaks to one or more of these offences and the whole series constitutes the requisite course of conduct (*HM Advocate v Taylor*). In these circumstances, the route to verdict must include the conventional directions in a mutual corroboration case. There is no other route involving corroboration of a course of conduct.'

## COURSE OF CONDUCT

**7.38** Where the charge is of a statutory crime involving a 'course of conduct' or 'course of behaviour', which is defined as conduct or behaviour on at least two occasions, (some elements of which may constitute individual crimes and others which may not in themselves be criminal but have become so, because they are part of that course of conduct or behaviour), there must be corroboration of the course of conduct or behaviour. This applies even though the phrase 'course of conduct' or 'course of behaviour' is not used in the charge as libelled, if the existence of such a course of conduct or behaviour is clearly implicit in how the libel is framed. What is required is corroboration of at least two elements of the behaviour libelled and a connection between all of the various elements, such that they demonstrate a 'continuity of purpose'.

**7.39** In *Finlay v HM Advocate,*[47] the court held that:

47 2020 SCCR 317, at [14].

> 'Where the alleged commission of the crime is by a course of conduct, there would require to be corroborating evidence of that course of conduct, ie evidence relating to two or more of the incidents referred to in the libel from which the jury could conclude that these were not isolated acts but truly part of a course of conduct. Corroboration of one incident alone might be sufficient for corroboration of the crime restricted to that one incident or a single act...but not for a course of conduct'.

## Corroboration and the Domestic Abuse (Scotland) Act 2018

**7.40** DA(S)A 2018, s 1 and the question of corroboration was examined in detail by the Appeal Court in *CA v HM Advocate.*[48] The court provides a succinct synopsis of the offence at paras 2–4.as follows:

> '[2]. Section 1 of the Domestic Abuse (Scotland) Act 2018 makes it an offence to engage in a course of behaviour which is abusive of a partner or ex-partner, in circumstances where a reasonable person would consider that course of behaviour to be likely to cause physical or psychological harm, and where the offender either intended the behaviour to cause such harm or was reckless as to whether it did so. References to psychological harm include fear, alarm and distress.
>
> [3]. Guidance as to what constitutes abusive behaviour for the purpose of the Act is given in section 2, which provides that abusive behaviour includes (in particular) behaviour which is violent, threatening or intimidating; has as a purpose, or would be considered by a reasonable person to be likely to have, certain effects on a complainer, namely: making them dependent on, or subordinate to, the accused; isolating them from friends, relatives or other sources of support; controlling, regulating or monitoring their day-to-day activities; depriving them of, or restricting their, freedom of action; and frightening, humiliating, degrading or punishing them. References to violent behaviour include sexual violence. The instances of behaviour alleged in the charge were all capable of coming within the ambit of this guidance.
>
> [4]. Section 10 provides that behaviour means 'behaviour of any kind', and includes doing, saying or otherwise communicating something as well as intentionally failing to do, say or otherwise communicate something. It includes behaviour carried out directly, but also through a third party or by conduct towards property. Section 10(4) provides: "A course of behaviour involves behaviour on at least two occasions".'

48 [2022] HCJAC 33.

**7.41** The sheriff at first instance had directed that it was the course of behaviour which required to be proved on corroborated evidence; the appellant argued that each of distinct averments of abusive conduct libelled in a single charge required corroboration.[49] The court endorsed the approach taken by Lord Matthews (in an unreported DF case), stating:

> '[10] …The [2018] Act specifically creates a new offence which, in the words of the Lord Justice General, constitutes "a separate crime known as a course of conduct". It is the course of behaviour which is the core of the offence, and it is thus the course of behaviour – in other words proof of behaviour "on at least" two occasions – which must be established by corroborated evidence. Once there is corroborative evidence of this kind it is open to the jury to determine that other incidents equally form part of the course of conduct, even though spoken to by only one witness. Where the commission of a course of conduct is the core element of an offence, it is the proof of a course of conduct which constitutes the relevant essential element of the offence.
>
> [11] In these circumstances the "course of behaviour" may be equiparated with the evidential position which applies in relation to a single charge of assault: in the case of a single episode of assault, there is no need for every element of the libel to be corroborated. In the same way that one must look for corroboration of a single charge of assault, without demanding corroboration of every individual element thereof, in a case such as this it is the course of behaviour which must be established, without any requirement for corroboration of every single element of that course of behaviour. There is one single offence which lies in a course of conduct.'

**7.42** The approach to corroboration set out in *CA* was endorsed in *McKenzie v HM Advocate*;[50] the Court reiterated that the offence was committed by engaging in a course of behaviour, that it would be sufficient to prove two incidents of the course of behaviour and that this would entitle the jury to convict of the remaining, (otherwise uncorroborated), aspects if these incidents were part of the same course of conduct saying at para [9]:

> 'The nature of the evidence required to prove the charge has been set out in *CA v HM Advocate*, 2023 J.C. 8, in which it was explained, adopting the language of *DF v HM Advocate*, that the offence under section 1 was committed by engaging in a course of behaviour. It would be sufficient to

49 The appellant founded on decisions in *Dalton v HM Advocate* 2015 SCCR 125, *Spinks v Harrower* 2018 JC 177, *Wilson v HM Advocate* [2019] HCJAC 36 and *Rysmanowski v HM Advocate* 2020 JC 84.

50 2024 JC 121.

prove two incidents of the course of behaviour. That would entitle the jury to convict of the remainder, albeit uncorroborated, aspects, if they were part of the same course of conduct (*CA v HM Advocate*, LJC (Dorrian) at para [13], adopting *DF v HM Advocate*[51] at para [31] and citing *Finlay v HM Advocate*, 2020 S.C.C.R. 317 at para [14]).'

**7.43** Two of the incidents or episodes in the libel must, therefore, be proven by corroborated evidence. Thereafter, the court can find the remainder of the incidents proven on the evidence of one witness, if those incidents are part of the same course of abusive behaviour as the two corroborated incidents. Corroboration of the minimum two incidents can be provided in the conventional sense, or by way of mutual corroboration, whether by *Moorov* or *Taylor*.

**7.44** That approach was similarly adopted in *Bain v HM Advocate,*[52] where the Appeal Court said at para 8:

> 'The nature of the evidence required to prove the charge has been set out in *CA v HM Advocate*, 2023 J.C. 8, in which it was explained, adopting the language of *DF v HM Advocate*, that the offence under section 1 was committed by engaging in a course of behaviour. It would be sufficient to prove two incidents of the course of behaviour. That would entitle the jury to convict of the remainder, albeit uncorroborated, aspects, if they were part of the same course of conduct. (*CA v HM Advocate,* LJC (Dorrian) at para [13], adopting *DF v HM Advocate* at para [31] and citing *Finlay v HM Advocate*, 2020 S.C.C.R. 317 at para [14]).'

**7.45** The court endorsed the trial judge's direction to the jury that they could only return a verdict of guilt on an element which was only spoken to by one witness (ie the complainer) if it was 'part of the same course of abusive behaviour'. The court observed that the jury must have believed the complainer in relation to the sexual element under consideration and must have accepted that the sexual element formed part of the course of conduct (para 9).

**7.46** The issue of whether there is a course of abusive behaviour (including whether any averments of sexual misconduct form part of that course of behaviour) may now be seen as a jury question so that a DA(S)A 2018 course of abusive behaviour now falls to be considered in the same way as any other course of conduct: it will only be when on no possible view could it be said that the individual incidents were component parts of a course of conduct that submission of no case to answer (either on the libel or an averment in it) should be upheld and the matter withdrawn from the jury.

51 Unreported 10 August 2021.
52 2024 JC 326.

# Chapter 8

# Witnesses

## VULNERABLE AND CHILD WITNESS LEGISLATION – ITS DEVELOPMENT

**8.01** Over the last 20 years there has been increasing recognition of the need to better accommodate the needs of vulnerable witnesses and complainers in the criminal justice system. Legislative reforms allow such witnesses to give their evidence at trial using 'special measures' or, in the case of taking evidence by commissioner, to have their evidence captured at an earlier stage and introduced at trial in a recording.

**8.02** The Vulnerable Witnesses (Scotland) Act 2004 (VW(S)A 2004) formalised and extended measures founded in common law to help child and adult vulnerable witnesses give the best evidence possible. The 2004 Act defined 'vulnerable witnesses' as those with a mental disorder and anyone for whom there is a significant risk that the quality of their evidence will be diminished through fear or distress. It introduced an assumption that all children under the age of 18 years are vulnerable and are automatically entitled to special arrangements in court unless a judge considers such arrangements unnecessary. Further special provision is made for child witnesses under the age of 12.

**8.03** The Victims and Witnesses (Scotland) Act 2014 (VW(S)A 2014) was subsequently enacted to ensure that Scotland complies with Directive 2012/29/EU of the European Parliament and of the Council of 25 October 2012, establishing minimum standards on the rights, support and protection of victims of crime. The aim of the 2014 Act is to improve the support available for victims and witnesses. The Act amends the Criminal Procedure (Scotland) Act 1995, the Vulnerable Witnesses (Scotland) Act 2004, the Criminal Justice (Scotland) Act 2003 and the Sexual Offences Act 2003.

**8.04** Section 11 of VW(S)A 2014 inserted two new categories of vulnerable witness:

(1) the 'deemed vulnerable' witness: this category includes victims of alleged sexual offences, human trafficking, and victims of an offence the commission of which involves domestic abuse or stalking who are giving evidence in proceedings which relate to that particular offence; and

(2) witnesses who are considered to be at significant risk of harm by reason only of them giving evidence.

**8.05** The Vulnerable Witnesses (Criminal Evidence) (Scotland) Act 2019 (VW(CE)(S)A 2019) gave legislative effect to the recommendations of the Evidence and Procedure Review[1] aimed at improving the means by which vulnerable witnesses can be supported in the criminal justice system. The provisions are intended to increase the use of pre-recorded evidence captured in advance of trial and create a regime around 'taking evidence by commissioner', meaning a witness does not have to give evidence at court in the course of a trial. Rather, questioning of the witness by both prosecution and defence is video recorded and that recording played at trial, to comprise the witness' evidence. Practice Note No 1 of 2024[2] replaced Practice Note No 1 of 2017 and sets out guidance for practitioners in assessing whether a commission is required, as well as necessary steps in preparation for seeking a commission, and the conduct of the hearing. The benefits of a commission include early capture of evidence, reducing the effect of the passage of time on a witness' recollection, and removing the uncertainty and delay that can be encountered in the scheduling and commencement of a trial.

**8.06** As at the time of writing (September 2025), the provisions have been commenced in respect of child witnesses in serious cases. VW(CE)(S)A 2019 has provisions to extend to 'deemed vulnerable' adult witnesses, with an implementation plan[3] for the next stages of commencement updated in April 2024. As currently advised, by April 2026 the provision should extend to child witnesses in certain sheriff and jury cases, including domestic abuse.

## DEFINITION OF 'VULNERABLE WITNESS'

**8.07** The relevant provisions are to be found at s 271 of the Criminal Procedure (Scotland) Act 1995 (CP(S)A 1995), as amended, which sets out the definition of 'vulnerable witness':

> '1. For the purposes of this Act, a person who is giving or is to give evidence at, or for the purposes of, a hearing in relevant criminal proceedings is a vulnerable witness if —
>
> (a) the person is under the age of 18 on the date of commencement of the proceedings in which the hearing is being or is to be held,
>
> (b) there is a significant risk that the quality of the evidence to be given by the person will be diminished by reason of —

1 www.scotcourts.gov.uk/media/qftkkfek/evidence-and-procedure-review.pdf [accessed 21 August 2025].

2 www.scotcourts.gov.uk/media/tlqhmogc/practice-note-2024-taking-of-evidence-of-a-vulnerable-witness.pdf [accessed 21 August 2025].

3 www.gov.scot/publications/vulnerable-witnesses-criminal-evidence-scotland-act-2019-implementation-plan/ [accessed 21 August 2025].

(i) mental disorder (within the meaning of section 328 of the Mental Health (Care and Treatment) (Scotland) Act 2003), or

(ii) fear or distress in connection with giving evidence at the hearing,

(c) the offence is alleged to have been committed against the person in proceedings for —

(i) an offence listed in any of paragraphs 36 to 59ZL of Schedule 3 to the Sexual Offences Act 2003,

(ii) an offence under section 22 of the Criminal Justice (Scotland) Act 2003 (traffic in prostitution etc.)

(iii) an offence under section 4 of the Asylum and Immigration (Treatment of Claimants, etc.) Act 2004 (trafficking people for exploitation),

(iiia) an offence of human trafficking (see section 1 of the Human Trafficking and Exploitation (Scotland) Act 2015), or

(iv) an offence the commission of which involves domestic abuse, or

(v) an offence of stalking, or

(d) there is considered to be a significant risk of harm to the person by reason only of the fact that the person is giving or is to give evidence in the proceedings.'

**8.08** The definition includes 'persons under 18 at the 'commencement of proceedings' which is defined in CP(S)A 1995, s 271(3):

'(3) For the purposes of subsection (1)(a), section 271B(1)(b) and sections 271BZA to 271BZC, proceedings shall be taken to have commenced —

(a) where it is relevant to a court's consideration of whether to authorise the use of the special measure of taking evidence by commissioner (on its own or in combination with any other special measure) and the accused has appeared on petition, on the date when the accused appeared on petition, or

(b) in any other case, on the date when the indictment or, as the case may be, complaint is served on the accused.'

**8.09** Thus, for cases reported to the Procurator Fiscal on or after 1 September 2015, child witnesses (aged under 18 at the commencement of proceedings) and adult witnesses who are deemed to be vulnerable are entitled to one or more *standard* special measures. The standard special measures are use of a screen, a supporter, or use of live TV link from the court building or a remote site.

**8.10** The *non-standard* special measures are: evidence in chief in the form of a recorded prior statement; evidence taken by a commissioner (this is now a standard special measure for a child under the age of 18 in all High Court cases – see VW(CE)(S)A 2019); and excluding the public from the court while the witness gives evidence (closed court). There is no automatic entitlement to these but they can be applied for if criteria are met.

**8.11** In summary cases, commencement of proceedings is the date of service of the complaint. In solemn cases this refers to the date of service of the indictment. If cases are deserted and subsequently re-raised it is the date of service of the new complaint or indictment that applies.

**8.12** Other than those adult witnesses who are deemed to be vulnerable in terms of CP(S)A 1995, s 271(1)(c), there is no *automatic* entitlement for other adult witnesses to give their evidence with the assistance of a special measure. It is for the party calling the witness to consider if the witness is vulnerable in terms of s 271(1)(b) of CP(S)A 1995 in that there is a significant risk that the quality of their evidence will be diminished by reason of mental disorder, or fear and distress in connection with giving evidence at trial; or where there is considered to be a significant risk of harm to the person by reason only of the fact that the person is giving or is to give evidence in the proceedings.

**8.13** In determining whether a person is vulnerable, the court has to take into account various factors mentioned in s 271(2) of CP(S)A 1995. The degree of vulnerability may relate to a variety of factors including personal characteristics, personal circumstances, and the nature of the dispute or offence.

**8.14** Section 10(e) of VW(S)A 2014 inserts subsection (4A) into CP(S)A 1995, s 271 which requires the court to consider the best interests of the witness and views of the witness in deciding whether they are vulnerable, either because the quality of their evidence is likely to be diminished (CP(S)A 1995, s 271(1)(b)), or they are likely to be at significant risk from harm in giving their evidence (CP(S)A 1995, s 271(1)(d)).

**8.15** Accordingly, for the interests of this chapter, a witness to an offence, the commission of which involves domestic abuse, will be deemed vulnerable, and the legislation operates on an assumption of the use of special measure/s at court by such a witness. The Crown will likely make an automatic or default application for use of special measures of screens and/or supporter in these cases at summary level. In solemn cases, a different combination of special measures may be in contemplation.

**8.16** The Advocate's Gateway provides useful guidance[4] on identifying vulnerability in witnesses and on the questioning of witnesses with different types of vulnerability.

## THE VULNERABLE ACCUSED

**8.17** Notably, vulnerable witnesses can include an accused person. An application can be made for an accused to have available the use of special measures. The statutory scheme for special measures for an accused is different from that for witnesses and is limited to the accused giving evidence. Some statutory provisions explicitly exclude the accused (for example CP(S)A 1995, s 271BZA regarding commissions). Section 271F of CP(S)A 1995 sets out modifications to the provisions for vulnerable witnesses insofar as they apply to the accused giving evidence. Judges may be invited by the accused's representative to consider what other measures may be required, including breaks and the involvement of advocacy workers. Such measures may allow an accused to participate in a trial.

## SEEKING SPECIAL MEASURES

**8.18** A vulnerable witness notice must be lodged with the court in relation to any child or deemed vulnerable witness for the use of standard special measures, of non-standard special measures, a combination of standard and non-standard special measures, or for the giving of evidence without special measures.

**8.19** In summary cases, the vulnerable witness notice will be lodged at least one week prior to the Intermediate diet where possible. Vulnerable witness notices and applications must be lodged no later than 14 days before the trial diet in summary cases. In solemn cases, vulnerable witness notices should be lodged:

- 14 clear days before the preliminary hearing in high court cases; and
- 7 clear days before the first diet in sheriff and jury cases.

4 www.theadvocatesgateway.org/ [accessed 20 August 2025].

**8.20** The grant of special measures can, of course, be reviewed and amended up until and even during a trial, until a witness completes their evidence. On the day, a witness may decline the use of special measures already granted; or a witness who has had no application made for use of special measures may have the situation reviewed by the court. Necessarily, there may be practical difficulties in the last minute availability of non-standard special measures.

**8.21** In preparing a vulnerable witness notice or application, practitioners must have regard to the statutory tests and have regard to the best interests of the witness/accused.

**8.22** Objections cannot be lodged in relation to notices which contain a request for standard special measures alone (CP(S)A 1995, s 271A(4A)(a)). With an application for non-standard special measures the sheriff clerk will hold the application for seven days to allow for objections to be lodged. If no objections are lodged after the expiry of the seven days, the clerk will send to the sheriff/judge for consideration. If objections are lodged, the clerk will assign a hearing and intimate the date to parties. Depending on the available time, the objection hearing may be assigned for the same date as the intermediate diet hearing or first diet in the sheriff court or preliminary hearing in the High Court. There may be occasions where a notice includes both standard and non-standard special measures. When this occurs, the notice must be held for seven days to allow for any objections to be lodged. Objections may also be lodged in relation to vulnerable witness applications lodged on behalf of witnesses who are not deemed vulnerable under the Act. In practice, objections are rare, the principle of support for vulnerable witnesses being well-established.

## SIMPLIFIED NOTIFICATION PROCEDURE FOR STANDARD SPECIAL MEASURES FOR VULNERABLE WITNESSES

**8.23** A new, simplified procedure for notifying courts of the intention to use standard special measures when certain vulnerable witnesses are giving evidence came into force on 27 June 2025 through commencement of s 6 of the Vulnerable Witnesses (Criminal Evidence) (Scotland) Act 2019 which adds a new provision—s 271AA—to CP(S)A 1995. It is intended to reduce the demands on both the parties and the courts which are associated with notifying the use of standard special measures.

**8.24** Where an indictment or complaint is served on or after 27 June 2025, parties proposing to cite a vulnerable witness are not required to lodge a vulnerable witness notice under CP(S)A 1995, s 271A where they intend to use *only* standard special measures. Instead, there is a simplified notification procedure which removes the requirement for notices to use standard special measures to be reviewed by a judge and limits the amount of information which needs to be provided to the court.[5]

**8.25** This new procedure applies only to witnesses deemed to be vulnerable and child witnesses. If the party lodges a notice with the clerk of court by the required time, the witness is entitled to the benefit of the standard special measure or measures specified in the notice as if the use of that measure or measures were authorised by an order made by the court under CP(S)A 1995, s 271A(5)(a)[6].

**8.26** There are certain exceptions in the legislation in relation to the use of the new procedure for children. The new procedure cannot be used for children covered by the presumption in favour of pre-recorded evidence as set out at CP(S)A 1995, s 271BZA, nor for children under the age of 12 who are giving evidence in cases that involve serious sexual and violent offences as set out at CP(S)A 1995, s 271B.

**8.27** Where standard special measures are sought for taking the evidence of other groups of vulnerable witnesses, parties must submit a vulnerable witness application in accordance with CP(S)A 1995, s 271A as described above.

**8.28** To qualify for the new procedure, the notice must be submitted to the courts within a certain timeframe.[7] The required time is:

- any time before a date has been fixed for a preliminary hearing in the High Court, the first diet in the sheriff court or a hearing at which evidence is to be given or,
- if the date has been fixed, no later than 14 days before the preliminary hearing in the high court, or no later than seven clear days before the first diet in sheriff court indictment proceedings, or in a case in which the proceedings are not to take place in the High Court or on indictment in the sheriff court, for a hearing at which the evidence is to be given, no later than 14 clear days before that hearing.

**8.29** Where these timescales are not met, the vulnerable witness notice procedure in terms of s 271A will continue to apply, although the court must be satisfied on cause shown.[8]

## COMMON LAW POSITION

**8.30** At common law there is no definition of 'vulnerable witness'. The court has a common law power to protect any vulnerable witness who would

5 CP(S)A 1995, s 271AA (2).
6 CP(S)A 1995, s 271AA (4).
7 CP(S)A 1995, s 271AA (6).
8 CP(S)A 1995, s 271AA (5).

be placed at a disadvantage by having to give evidence in the normal way. Accordingly, these common law powers may apply to any 'persons who are vulnerable to attack, or fear of attack, or intimidation arising out of their giving evidence' (see *Hampson v HM Advocate*[9]).

**8.31** In *Hampson*, the Appeal Court held that the judge had the power to allow the rape complainer to give evidence from behind a screen. The Lord Justice General (Cullen) said: '[I]t is well recognised that there are witnesses who would be placed at an unfair disadvantage by the normal procedure, and on that account are regarded as vulnerable and in need of special measures to protect them. Such witnesses may normally be found within one or more of the following groups of person

(1) children;

(2) persons whose ability to hear, see or communicate is impaired, or who have a problem with their health, whether physical or mental; and

(3) persons who are vulnerable to attack, or fear of attack, or intimidation arising out of their giving evidence.

We have said 'within' such a group or groups, since whether an individual witness should be given such protection depends on, inter alia, the degree of his or her vulnerability.'

## THE SPECIAL MEASURES – AN OVERVIEW

**8.32** It is helpful to understand the operation of each of the special measures in considering the making of an application or service of a notice to meet a child or vulnerable witness' needs.

**8.33** The special measures provided for in the legislation are:

- the taking of evidence by a commissioner in accordance with CP(S) A 1995, s 271I;
- use of a live television link in accordance with CP(S)A 1995, s 271J;
- use of a screen in accordance with CP(S)A 1995, s 271K;
- use of a supporter in accordance with CP(S)A 1995, s 271L;

9 2003 SCCR 13, at para [7]; the Appeal Court makes it clear that common law powers subsist following the coming into force of vulnerable witness legislation, at paras 13 and 14.

- the giving of evidence in chief by prior statement in accordance with CP(S)A 1995, s 271M; and
- the exclusion of the public while taking evidence per CP(S)A 1995, s 271HB (amended by VW(S)A 2014, s 20).

**8.34** Section 19 of VW(S)A 2014 amends CP(S)A 1995 to include temporary additional special measures within CP(S)A 1995, s 271HA. This allows for the expansion by Scottish Ministers of the categories currently listed in CP(S)A 1995, s 271H.

**8.35** As noted above, deemed vulnerable witnesses will be automatically entitled to the use of certain special measures known as *standard* special measures (previously only child witnesses had this routine entitlement). These standard special measures are the use of a live television link, a screen (to avoid the witness seeing the accused), and a supporter. In addition, the procedures for child witnesses are expanded to encompass deemed vulnerable witnesses.

## Use of screens

**8.36** Section 271K of CP(S)A 1995 permits positioning a physical screen in court in order that the accused is concealed from the sight of the witness. A pause in proceedings may be required for the screen to be put in place for a vulnerable witness in the course of a trial. In order to secure the accused's Convention rights to view their accuser, arrangements must be in place to ensure the accused can see and hear the witness give their evidence. In practise, a camera positioned to view the witness relays the live feed to a monitor viewed by the accused. The screen does not interfere with the view of either the witness or the accused by the judge or, in solemn proceedings, the jury. It is important that the witness understand that they will be seen by the accused; it is their view of the accused which is screened.

## Use of a supporter

**8.37** A supporter may accompany a witness to court and sit close to the witness as they give evidence. They must not prompt or otherwise influence the witness or interfere in the proceedings. The Witness Service is a voluntary service run by Victim Support Scotland. Trained volunteers are available to provide practical and emotional support in connection with giving evidence. They may accompany the witness in the courtroom, as they give their evidence. If a witness is giving evidence by live television link, a Witness Service volunteer may be present in the room in which the witness is located. The Witness Service may also assist with pre-trial court familiarisation visits and practical arrangements in attending and waiting at court.

## Via live TV link

**8.38** Different courts will operate different facilities and practitioners should familiarise themselves with local arrangements.

**8.39** Where a live television link is to be used in proceedings in a sheriff court, but that court lacks accommodation or equipment necessary for the purpose of receiving such a link, the sheriff may order the transfer of the proceedings to any other sheriff court in the same sheriffdom which has such accommodation or equipment available.

**8.40** Section 12 of VW(S)A 2014 amends CP(S)A 1995, s 271A to expand the meaning of a standard special measure so that, to qualify as a standard special measure, a live television link no longer has to be in another room within the court, and the use of a supporter no longer has to be only in conjunction with either a live television link or a screen (under CP(S)A 1995, s 271A(14)).

**8.41** Remote sites are few but provision is being expanded. More generally, a witness will be placed in a room within the court building with a camera linked to screens within the courtroom, on which they will be viewed by those present in the courtroom. The presiding judge will have a view of the witness and the surrounding room, in order to be satisfied that no one is interfering with the witness as they give evidence. The judge will switch between cameras positioned to allow the witness a view of the practitioner asking questions at any point in time. The judge thereby controls the witness's view of individual personnel within the courtroom.

**8.42** On a practical level, it will be easier in the sheriff court for practitioners to remain seated when questioning a witness via CCTV as the cameras are positioned at seated level. In contrast, in the High Court the camera points to the lectern, so that counsel or solicitors advocate remain standing when questioning the witness giving evidence via TV link.

## Use of prior statement

**8.43** Section 271M of CP(S)A 1995 applies where the special measure to be used in respect of a vulnerable witness is giving evidence in chief in the form of a prior statement. Prior statements can be used as the witness's evidence in chief in whole or part. Section 271M provides that a statement by a vulnerable witness lodged in evidence is admissible as, or as part of, the witness's evidence in chief, without the witness being requested to adopt or otherwise speak to it.

**8.44** In terms of CP(S)A 1995, s 271M(5), 'statement' has the meaning given in CP(S)A 1995, s 262(1), namely:

> 'a "statement" includes—
>
> (a) any representation, however made or expressed, of fact or opinion; and
>
> (b) any part of a statement,
>
> but does not include a statement in a precognition other than a precognition on oath'.

A statement is:

> 'contained in a document where the person who makes it
>
> (a) makes a statement personally;
>
> (b) makes a statement which is, with or without his knowledge, embodied in a document by whatever means or by any person who has direct knowledge of the making of the statement; or
>
> (c) approves a document as embodying the statement'.[10]

**8.45** This measure envisages the witness's evidence in chief being comprised of a statement given at an earlier stage to an investigating authority, most likely the police. The statement may be in written or verbal form. In the case of a child witness it may be a video recording of a joint investigative interview conducted by police and social work.

**8.46** Prohibited evidence cannot be admitted. In serious cases, proceeding at solemn level, the court is likely to expect that a transcript of the interview be provided. The court will wish to ensure inadmissible material is not included, unless there is a good reason advanced by parties as to why such evidence might be permitted, eg where the defence is content to bring out that the accused was in custody for some evidential reason. The question of editing of the recording and/or the transcript may arise and that will be for the party seeking to introduce the interview to undertake.

**8.47** It is common for an application or notice to seek that the special measures of use of a prior statement and taking evidence by commissioner are combined – see below. Even before the commencement of VW(CE)(S) A 2019, it had become common to encounter vulnerable witness applications

10 CP(S)A 1995, s 262(2).

under CP(S)A 1995, s 271I to take evidence by commissioner, in combination with CP(S)A 1995, s 271M, whereby evidence in chief is in the form of a prior statement.

**8.48** Practice Notes No 1 of 2019[11] and No 1 of 2024[12] govern how such applications under CP(S)A 1995, ss 271I and M are to be approached. VW(CE)(S)A 2019 introduced ground rules hearings to be held before evidence is taken by a commissioner, to ensure preparedness. The provision also allows pre-recording of evidence before indictment if appropriate.

## Taking of evidence by a commissioner

**8.49** Section 271I of CP(S)A 1995 provides that an application may be made to the High Court of Justiciary or the sheriff court, respective to the forum of criminal proceedings, to have a vulnerable witness's evidence taken by commissioner, rather than at trial. The commissioner must be a high court judge in high court proceedings or a sheriff in any other proceedings. The prerequisites and considerations for evidence to be taken on commission are the same as for a CCTV link or screens application. Proceedings before a commissioner appointed shall, if the court so directed when authorising such proceedings, take place by means of a live television link, the link to take place between where the commissioner is sitting and the place from which the witness is giving their evidence. Proceedings before a commissioner must be video recorded.

**8.50** An accused must not, except by leave of the court on special cause shown, be present in the room where such proceedings are taking place; or if such proceedings are taking place by means of a live television link, the accused cannot be in the same room as the witness. The accused is however entitled by such means as seem suitable to the court, to watch and hear the proceedings. The commission may be held at the witness's home or some other suitable venue. The witness is sworn, examined, cross-examined, and re-examined, as necessary. The recording of the commission proceedings is received in evidence without being sworn to by witnesses.

**8.51** This measure is frequently deployed in combination with use of a prior statement (see above). Practise Note No 1 of 2019 provides a great deal of detail about evidence on commission and the necessary arrangements to support its use. This merits further explanation and detail is provided below, in paras **8.59** et seq.

11 www.scotcourts.gov.uk/media/plnf2tpp/criminal-courts-practice-note-number-1-of-2019-vulnerable-and-child-witnesses-written-questions.pdf [accessed 21 August 2025].

12 www.scotcourts.gov.uk/media/tlqhmogc/practice-note-2024-taking-of-evidence-of-a-vulnerable-witness.pdf [accessed 21 August 2025].

**8.52** Parties are encouraged – both Crown and defence – to address their minds at a suitably early stage to the question of whether a commission is necessary for a witness to give their best evidence. Early conduct of a commission has benefits not only in the earlier capture of the evidence but also in giving more time for addressing issues around admissibility and any necessary editing of the commission recording.

### Closed court: CP(S)A 1995, ss 271(1) and 271HB

**8.53** Section 20 of VW(S)A 2014 amended the list of special measures in CP(S)A 1995, s 271H(1) to add an additional special measure of having a closed court (ie excluding the public during the taking of evidence from the vulnerable witness). Section 20 also inserted a new s 271HB into CP(S) A 1995, detailing how this special measure is to operate. This section provides that members or officers of the court, parties to the court, counsel or solicitors or other persons otherwise directly concerned in the case, bona fide representatives of news gathering or reporting organisations present or such other persons as the court may specially authorise to be present, should not be excluded from the court.

**8.54** This special measure does not apply where the vulnerable witness is the accused (CP(S)A 1995, s 271F(8)). Section 92(3) of the 1995 Act states:

> 'From the commencement of the leading of evidence in a trial for rape or the like the judge may, if he thinks fit, cause all persons other than the accused and counsel and solicitors to be removed from the courtroom.'

It will be noted that this section excludes a greater class of persons than those mentioned in CP(S)A 1995, s 271HB.

## IDENTIFICATION EVIDENCE AND INTERPLAY WITH SPECIAL MEASURES

**8.55** Use of certain special measures will preclude a witness being able to identify an accused person in court. Other means will require to be deployed by the Crown to achieve the necessary evidence of identification. In practice, the defence are invited regularly to state at an early stage – usually a hearing on bail or petition committal – whether the evidence of identification of a witness, who can be expected to be vulnerable in terms of the legislation, can be agreed. Agreement will be noted in the court minutes.

**8.56** Alternatively, the Crown may make an application in terms of CP(S) A 1995, s 267B for the accused to attend an identification parade. Section 281A(1) of CP(S)A 1995 provides:

'(1) Where in a trial the prosecutor lodges as a production a report naming—

(a) a person identified in an identification parade or other identification procedure by a witness, and

(b) that witness,

it shall be presumed, subject to subsection (2) below, that the person named in the report as having been identified by the witness is the person of the same name who appears in answer to the indictment or complaint.

(2) That presumption shall not apply—

(a) unless the prosecutor has, by the required time, served on the accused a copy of the report and a notice that he intends to rely on the presumption, or

(b if the accused—

(i) not more than 7 days after the date of service of the copy of the report, or

(ii) by such later time as the court may in special circumstances allow, has served notice on the prosecutor that he intends to challenge the facts stated in the report.

(3) In subsection (2)(a) above, 'the required time' means—

(a) in the case of proceedings in the High Court—

(i) not less than 14 clear days before the preliminary hearing; or

(ii) such later time, being not less than 14 clear days before the trial, as the court may, in special circumstances, allow;

(b) in any other case, not less than 14 days before the trial.'

**8.57** Other methods of identification are also available. Such evidence could be the subject of agreement in a joint minute. Where an offence is alleged to have been committed in any special capacity, such as by the husband of a complainer, if she refers in her evidence to her husband another witness may give evidence as to the fact the accused is the husband of the complainer. That witness can provide court identification of that fact.[13]

13 CP(S)A 1995, s 255, and *P v Williams*, 2005 SLT 508. *Muldoon v Herron*, 1970 JC 30.

**8.58** If the prosecutor has failed to serve the necessary notice in terms of CP(S)A 1995, s 281A, it is possible to lead the evidence of police officers who witnessed the complainer identify the accused as the perpetrator at an identification parade.

## TAKING EVIDENCE BY COMMISSIONER – WHEN AND HOW?

**8.59** SCTS has invested in a number of sites where specialist commission suites are available to conduct the growing number of commission hearings granted. Noting the current schedule to roll out the extended provisions, use of this special measure currently focuses on cases proceeding at High Court level, with some cases identified at sheriff and jury level.

**8.60** The Practice Note gives guidance as to:

(a) when practitioners should consider whether a commission is required;

(b) what practitioners must do in preparation for seeking authorisation to take the evidence of a vulnerable witness by a commissioner;

(c) what issues the court will expect practitioners to address in an application in relation to taking of evidence by a commissioner.

**8.61** Parties need to consider proactively at an early stage whether any witness is, or may be, a vulnerable witness. In High Court proceedings, if the Crown intends to seek the special measure of a commission that must be intimated to the defence at the earliest opportunity so that appropriate legal aid cover can be arranged without delay. Similarly, the defence must intimate any such intention to seek a commission as soon as possible.

**8.62** In cases where it is intended to rely on a prior statement as evidence in chief, it is particularly important that the commission should proceed at as early a stage as possible, having regard to the observations of the court in the case of *MacLennan v HM Advocate*[14] at paras 21 and 28.

**8.63** As the numbers of commissions have increased, problems, particularly relating to the quality and audibility of commission recordings, have become more common. Cases have reached trial before it is discovered that a recording is inaudible.

14 2016 JC 117.

**8.54** In order to ensure that problems are identified early, Practice Note No 1 of 2024 at para 13 requires confirmation by parties to the court within 14 days of the recording being made available for borrowing that they have listened to and viewed the recording and it is of sufficient quality for trial purposes. This allows any problems to be addressed, preserving the trial diet. Section 75A procedure is to be used to convene a preliminary hearing in the event that the intervention of the court is required.

**8.65** Witnesses report a benefit from meeting both the prosecutor and defence representative before the commission itself ,and it is presumed this will be accommodated by practitioners in the absence of any reason advanced to the court seeking excusal.

## VIEWING THE COMMISSION BY ACCUSED

**8.66** Whilst accused persons are entitled to view a commission hearing they do not have to do so. Section 271I(3)(b) of CP(S)A 1995 creates an entitlement and not an obligation. The commission hearing is not part of the trial in terms of CP(S)A 1995, s 92 and so does not have to take place in the presence of the accused.

**8.67** If an accused person wishes to view the commission hearing, then arrangements are in place for those in custody to do so.

**8.68** For accused persons on bail who wish to view the commission hearing, arrangements are in place for them to attend at court premises and practitioners should familiarise themselves with local arrangements. Practical considerations for planning the commission hearing must include ensuring a means for the accused to communicate with their legal representative in the course of the hearing. There are standard protocols that communication can take place by telephone or text between a legal representative located remotely with the accused, and the legal representative in the commission room, conducting the hearing (with legal aid supporting this arrangement). This allows any issue from the accused's perspective to be raised with the commission judge.

**8.69** Unless, exceptionally, the court has ordered otherwise, an accused person must not attend at the actual Commission Centre. Defence representatives must ensure their clients understand these arrangements.

**8.70** A memorandum from the Lord Justice General (January 2020) explains what might be done where an accused who is on bail fails to attend a commission hearing. In short, the accused does not have to attend and it is competent, and may well be appropriate, to proceed with the commission in the absence of the accused.

## WITNESSES' RIGHTS

### Recovery of personal information – right to be heard

**8.71** *WF v Scottish Ministers*[15] was a petition for judicial review arising from sheriff and jury proceedings involving domestic abuse. The petitioner, a complainer in the criminal proceedings, applied for legal aid so as to enable her to be represented at a hearing before the sheriff of the accused's petition for recovery of her medical records. She argued that recovery of such documents would infringe her Convention rights to private and family life. The Scottish Ministers refused to make legal aid available for this purpose, arguing inter alia that she had no right to be heard or represented in front of the sheriff on the application.

**8.72** The petitioner sought reduction of that decision. She also sought declarator that the failure of the Scottish Ministers to promulgate such legislation as may be required to enable her to be represented before the sheriff in opposition to the application for recovery of her medical records was incompatible with, and a breach of, her Convention rights under Article 8 and/or Articles 6 and 14.

**8.73** In his Opinion, Lord Glennie addressed the issue of the petitioner's right to be heard and concluded as follows:

> 'I conclude, therefore, that a haver and any person whose Article 8 rights may be infringed by an order for recovery of medical records and other sensitive documents must have the application for recovery intimated to them and must be given the opportunity to be heard in opposition to the application before an order is made or, at least, before the documents are handed over to the party seeking them. I put it in this way because there may be many stages at which that person may be heard. It may be that they should be heard on every application. It may be that they should only be heard if, having had the application intimated on them and been given the opportunity of objecting, they indicate that they wish to be heard. Or it may be that they should only be heard once the court has determined that the documents pass the test of relevancy and should be recovered subject to any objection on Article 8 grounds. In this connection it may be possible to devise rules applying to applications in the criminal process a procedure similar to that which exists in civil proceedings. That is a matter for the framers of any new rules to determine. In the meantime it will be a matter for a sheriff hearing the application to determine how best to ensure that a party seeking to vindicate his or her Convention rights is heard before medical and other sensitive records are allowed to be released.'

15 [2016] CSOH 27.

**8.74** If medical records (or other sensitive personal data) are sought by petition, the petition must be intimated to the complainer or the subject of the records/data. The court will likely first consider the question of relevancy of the material sought to the proceedings. If a complainer has indicated an objection to production of the records on Article 8 grounds, the complainer will be given an opportunity to argue in opposition to the petition.

**8.75** As a result of this case, COPFS revised its policy on the recovery of sensitive personal records of rape complainers for use as evidence. Before the Crown attempts to recover sensitive personal information, such as medical records, the consent of the witness in question should be obtained. If consent is not forthcoming, the Crown may take further action, after careful consideration of the full facts and circumstances and any reasons for refusal offered by the witness.

**8.76** If the witness is uncontactable or consistently fails to engage despite repeated efforts, consideration may be given to seeking the authority of the court to seize the records. COPFS should intimate the application and date of the hearing to the witness by recorded delivery or by personal service.

**8.77** Where the need to recover the records has been explained to the witness but the witness has refused to provide consent, the prosecution may consider seeking a court order to recover the records without the witness' consent, or consider whether the prosecution or the affected charge/s be discontinued. In some exceptional cases, service of the public interest may require recovery of the records without the witness' consent, eg if discontinuation is the outcome of not recovering the records and the accused is believed to pose a significant risk to the complainer or the public. In those circumstances the witness will be advised:

- that COPFS intends to apply for a court order to recover the records;
- they will have the right to tell the court that they object to recovery of their records;
- the witness has a right to legal aid to pay for legal advice and representation in order to tell the court that they object;
- the court will decide whether or not to grant authority to recover the records; and
- if the Court refuses authority to recover the records, then all or part of the prosecution may have to be discontinued.

**8.78** COPFS policy is:

- In solemn proceedings, where the accused has appeared on petition but the indictment has not yet been served, to apply to the Sheriff for a common law warrant to seize the records.

- In solemn proceedings where the indictment has been served, or in summary proceedings where the accused has answered the complaint, COPFS should apply to the Court in terms of CP(S)A 1995, s 301A(3)(b) for an order for the production of the records.
- request in the crave that the Court fix a hearing on the matter (to allow the witness to make representations to the court); and
- intimate the application and date of the hearing to the witness by recorded delivery or by personal service so that the witness can instruct a solicitor to attend on their behalf.

**8.79** A parallel can be seen in *PF Falkirk v BM*,[16] where an accused sought to recover the complainer's telephone records. The Sheriff Appeal Court held that the application engaged the complainer's Article 8 rights and should have been intimated to her. She should also have been informed of her right to be heard and the possibility of obtaining legal aid and an execution of service should have been lodged with the court. Various observations about the necessary specification in such an application and other procedures to be followed are also discussed in the judgment.

## WITNESS DIGNITY AND PRIVACY – CONDUCT OF CROSS-EXAMINATION

**8.80** A number of appeal cases address the cross-examination of vulnerable witnesses, particularly in cases of sexual allegations. It is clear that rules articulated by the Appeal Court about the content and conduct of cross-examination apply equally to all witnesses and, in criminal matters, to the accused, when giving evidence. These considerations will be particularly relevant in respect of questioning of vulnerable complainers in domestic abuse cases.

- Cross-examination should test a witness's evidence, but should be 'properly directed and focused' (*Begg v HMA*,[17] at para 39).
- Irrelevant questions should be stopped (*MacDonald v HMA*,[18] at para 47).
- The tone of questioning can be an issue. Whilst difficult questions may need to be asked of witnesses, questioning should not be in a tone that suggests incredulity at a witness' answer, or in a belligerent or hostile tone. Judges may intervene to remind a questioner that it is for the court/jury to be the decision-maker, not the agent.

16 [2023] SAC Crim 12.
17 2015 SLT 602.
18 *MacDonald (Gavin) v HM Advocate* [2020] HCJAC 21.

- Cross-examination should not be insulting or intimidating to a witness (*Begg v HMA*, above, at para 39).
- Judges can stop questioning that is 'protracted, vexatious and unfeeling' (*Inch v Inch*,[19] at p 998, quoted with approval in *Begg v HMA*, above, at para 40).
- Questions should not be 'fired' at witnesses. Many people require time to think before answering. It might reflect that the questioning is on a difficult topic, rather than raising a credibility issue.
- Repeated questions can denote that questioning is not properly directed or focussed (see above) and also raises an issue as to the length of cross-examination (see below). If there is a genuine misunderstanding over a witness's answer that justifies repeating a question or line of questions, the judge may intervene to clarify. A witness who may be struggling to articulate themselves, for any number of reasons, is likely to become frustrated at the same question being asked repeatedly.
- A judge can set down a time limit for questioning (*Begg v HMA*, above, at para 40).

## PROHIBITION ON ACCUSED REPRESENTING THEMSELVES

**8.81** Accused persons cannot represent themselves in all cases. DA(S)A 2018 amended CP(S)A 1995 at s 288DC to prohibit accused persons in proceedings for an offence under DA(S)A 2018, s 1 or an offence aggravated by ABSH(S)A 2016, s 1(1)(a) from personally conducting their defence. The court must appoint a solicitor where the accused has not engaged one, has dismissed a solicitor, or the solicitor has withdrawn, unless the accused intends to engage another solicitor.

## THE RELUCTANT WITNESS

**8.82** There are a number of situations in which a witness may be referred to their prior statement. If a witness appears not to be co-operating, CP(S)A 1995, s 263(4) allows challenge to the credibility of a witness's evidence where he or she denies having made a statement on any specified occasion on any matter pertinent to the issue at the trial which is different from the evidence given by him or her at the trial where the statement taker subsequently gives evidence of the taking of the statement.[20]

19 (1856) 18 D 997.
20 See also *Jamieson v HM Advocate (No 2)* 1995 SLT 666

**8.83** Practitioners should familiarise themselves with Criminal Courts Practice Note No 1 of 2014,[21] 6 January 2014, 'Reference to prior statements of witnesses'. It stresses that where a statement not lodged as a production needs to be referred to in the course of proceedings, 'a copy should be made available in advance to the presiding judge or sheriff so that he or she can continue to monitor the fairness of the proceedings by reference to the questions asked'.

**8.84** If a practitioner intends to put a witness' statement to them, the court should be advised what provision the practitioner seeks to rely on. In *Asif Rehman and Adel Ishaq v HMA*[22], the Lord Justice Clerk (Carloway) made the following observation:

> 'It is possible to carry out an in-depth analysis of the various situations in which the content of a statement to the police, if admitted or proved, can be used as evidence against (or for) an accused person and those in which it can only be employed to test the maker's credibility and reliability. Tracing the history of the increasing use of statements in criminal trials may be an interesting topic for the lawyer. It was done recently in *A v HM Advocate* 2012 JC 343 (Lord Bonomy at paras [1] to [6]). However, the important feature about the use of this technique in modern times is that often 'the purpose is not clearly identified at the outset and … the examination proceeds in a fairly haphazard way' (*ibid*, para [1]).'

**8.85** Reference should be made to CP(S)A 1995, s 260, which allows a witness to 'adopt' a prior statement or report that he or she has made. For the purposes of s 260, any prior statement made by the witness shall be admissible as evidence of any matter stated in it of which direct oral evidence by him would be admissible if given in the course of those proceedings.

**8.86** Section 260(1) of CP(S)A 1995 provides that a prior statement will not be admissible unless:

> '(a) the statement is contained in a document;
>
> (b) the witness, in the course of giving evidence, indicates that the statement was made by him and that he adopts it as his evidence; and
>
> (c) at the time the statement was made, the person who made it would have been a competent witness in the proceedings.'

**8.87** Per CP(S)A 1995, s 260(5), a prior statement made by a witness shall not, in any proceedings on indictment, be inadmissible by reason only that it is not included in any list of productions lodged by the parties.

21 www.scotcourts.gov.uk/media/ft1jui53/criminal-courts-practice-note-number-1-of-2014.pdf [accessed 22 August 2025].

22 [2013] HCJAC 172, para 49.

**8.88** Section 261A of CP(S)A 1995 states that the court may allow the witness to see and refer to the 'statement' while he or she is giving evidence, provided both parties have had an opportunity to review the statement.

**8.89** In terms of CP(S)A 1995, s 262, a 'statement' is:

> '(a) any representation, however made or expressed, of fact or opinion; and
>
> (b) any part of a statement,
>
> but does not include a statement in a precognition other than a precognition on oath.'

## FAILURE TO ATTEND TRIAL BY A DOMESTIC COMPLAINER

**8.90** It is understood that COPFS policy is that warrants to apprehend complainers in domestic cases will only be sought in exceptional circumstances and only following review by a senior prosecutor. Careful consideration would be given to the circumstances and all relevant factors, including the vulnerability of the individual witness or complainer, and COPFS would look to re-engage with the witness to explore the reasons for the failure to attend and to assess what support can be offered.

*Chapter 9*

# Sentencing

**9.01** As discussed in previous chapters, a range of different offences can involve domestic abuse, and when they do the court must ensure that the sentence imposed reflects that the offence has been committed within the context of that domestic abuse.

**9.02** Section 12 of the Domestic Abuse (Scotland) Act 2018 (DA(S) A 2018)[1] introduced a Schedule which modified certain enactments relating to domestic abuse. Chapter 4 of the Schedule deals with specific matters related to sentencing.

## VICTIM SAFETY AND NON–HARASSMENT

**9.03** In terms of the Criminal Procedure (Scotland) Act 1995 (CP(S) A 1995), the court is required, when sentencing a person convicted of an offence aggravated by domestic abuse to have particular regard to the aim of ensuring the victim of that abuse is not subject to further such offences by the convicted person. In terms of CP(S)A 1995, s210AB;

> '(1) When sentencing a person convicted of an offence listed in subsection (2)(b), the court must have particular regard to the aim of ensuring that the victim is not the subject of a further such offence committed by the convicted person.
>
> (2) For the purpose of subsection (1)—
>
> (a) "victim" means the person against whom the offence was committed,
>
> (b) the list is_
>
> (i) an offence under section 1(1) of the Domestic Abuse (Scotland) Act 2018,
>
> (ii) an offence that is aggravated as described in section 1(1)(a) of the Abusive Behaviour and Sexual Harm (Scotland) Act 2016.'[2]

1 Which came into force on 1 April 2019.
2 CP(S)A 1995, s 210AB.

**9.04** Furthermore, in terms of CP(S)A 1995, s 234AZA there is a duty on the court to consider in every case, without the necessity of an application by the crown, whether to make a non-harassment order against a person convicted of a domestic abuse offence. That section also contains provisions for the making of non-harassment orders for the protection of children.[3]

## SENTENCING GUIDELINES

**9.05** The Scottish Sentencing Council has produced sentencing guidelines, which apply to all offenders sentenced on or after 22 September 2021. These guidelines are also applicable to the sentencing of domestically aggravated offending and provide a framework for the sentencing process. The guidelines set out a sequence of steps, which the courts should follow in order to reach their decision. The guidelines also outline some of the factors, which may be taken into account when selecting a disposal. These guidelines must be read alongside the overarching guideline, which sets out the principles and purposes of sentencing.[4]

**9.06** At the time of writing there are no approved offence specific guidelines in relation to domestic abuse, however the Scottish Sentencing Council have recently announced that it is currently developing a principles-based guideline for domestic abuse, a process which is currently at stage two.[5]

### The principles and purposes of sentencing

**9.07** Throughout the sentencing process the court should ensure that any sentence imposed is fair and proportionate. This is the core principle of sentencing in Scotland.

**9.08** The application of this core principle requires that:

- all relevant factors of a case must be considered including the seriousness of the offence, the impact on the victim and others affected by the case, and the circumstances of the offender;
- sentences should be no more severe than is necessary to achieve the appropriate purposes of sentencing in each case;
- reasons for sentencing decisions must be stated as clearly and openly as circumstances permit;

3 CP(S)A 1995, s 234AZA
4 First Scottish sentencing guideline approved by High Court 30 October 2018.
5 www.scottishsentencingcouncil.org.uk/sentencing-guidelines/guidelines-in-development/domestic-abuse [accessed 22 August 2025].

- sentencing decisions must be made lawfully and sentencers must have regard to any sentencing guidelines which are applicable;
- people should be treated equally, without discrimination; and
- sentencing decisions should treat similar cases in a similar way, assisting consistency and predictability.[6]

## The purposes of sentencing

**9.09** There are a number of purposes of sentencing, which may include the following considerations;

- Protection of the public – sentencing may seek to protect the public from offending behaviour through preventative measures and by deterring offending behaviour.
- Punishment – sentencing may seek to punish the offender as a consequence of their criminal behaviour, normally resulting in some element of loss depending on the sentence chosen.
- Rehabilitation of offenders – sentencing may seek to reduce the risk of reoffending through the effective rehabilitation of offenders, providing people with the opportunity to change and move away from past offending behaviour.
- Giving the offender the opportunity to make amends – sentencing acknowledges the harm caused to victims and communities and may aim to recognise and meet the needs of victims and communities by requiring the offender to repair at least some of the harm caused.
- Expressing disapproval of offending behaviour – sentencing may act as an expression of society's concern, revulsion and disapproval of the offending behaviour under consideration.[7]

## The sentencing process

**9.10** This guideline applies to all offenders who are sentenced on or after 22 September 2021. The guideline provides a framework for the sentencing process. It sets out a sequence of steps which courts should follow in order to reach a sentencing decision, including some of the factors which may be taken into account. It should be read alongside the Overarching Principles and Purposes of Sentencing Guideline.

6 First Scottish sentencing guideline approved by High Court 30 October 2018.

7 Scottish Sentencing Council, Principles and purposes of sentencing: Sentencing guideline (2018).

## The headline sentence

**9.11** The sentencing process requires the court to decide upon the headline sentence. The guideline details several steps which the court should take in arriving at the headline sentence. Steps one to four of the guideline deal with the selection of the headline sentence.

- Step 1 – Assess the seriousness of the offence.
- Step 2 – Select the sentencing range.
- Step 3- –Identify aggravating and mitigating factors.
- Step 4 – Arrive at the headline sentence.

**9.12** It is important to note that the timing of a plea of guilty and any time spent in custody should not be taken into account at this stage. This will be taken into account later in the process. [8]

## Other considerations

**9.13** Steps five to seven cover other issues which will not apply in every case, but where they do apply should be taken into account in arriving at the final sentence. These are:

- Step 5 – Take into account a plea of guilty.
- Step 6– Consider time spent in custody.
- Step 7 – Consider ancillary orders.[9]

## Step 8 – Impose sentence and give reasons

**9.14** At the end of the process set out in steps 1 – 7 the court decides on the sentence to be imposed. The court should be satisfied that the overall sentence, taken together with any ancillary order to be imposed, is fair and proportionate. When imposing the sentence the court should set out the reasons for its decision as clearly and openly as circumstances permit. The court must also state its reasons if it decides not to follow, or departs from, an applicable sentencing guideline.[10]

8 Scottish Sentencing Council, The sentencing process: Sentencing guideline (2021), p 5.
9 Scottish Sentencing Council, The sentencing process: Sentencing guideline (2021), p 4.
10 Scottish Sentencing Council, The sentencing process: Sentencing guideline (2021), p 13.

## THE SERIOUSNESS OF AN OFFENCE

**9.15** In general terms the domestic context of offending behaviour makes that offending more serious because it represents a fundamental violation of the trust and security that normally exists between those in an intimate relationship. In addition, there might well also be a continuing threat to the victim's safety or indeed a threat to their life or the lives of others around them.

**9.16** Domestic abuse can cause lasting damage and trauma to victims and their families, especially children and young people who witness that abuse, or who are aware of it having taken place. Research suggests that domestic abuse is rarely a one-off incident but instead the context is often a background or history of physical, sexual, psychological or emotional abuse or a combination of these in what can amount to coercive control within an intimate relationship As a consequence, domestic abuse offences are regarded as very serious in the criminal justice system.[11]

**9.17** As set out in the Scottish Sentencing Guidelines, the seriousness of a particular offence is determined by two factors, namely the culpability of the offender and the harm caused by the offence. This assessment of seriousness is a key factor, firstly, in deciding the appropriate type of sentence and thereafter in deciding the level of sentence to be imposed. For example, it may well impact on the length of any sentence of imprisonment or restriction of liberty order imposed, or the number of hours of unpaid work ordered in the context of a community payback order.[12]

## CULPABILITY

**9.18** In assessing culpability, relevant factors include: whether the offender intended to cause harm or was reckless as to whether harm was caused; whether there was any prior planning or premeditation; and whether the offender knew, or should have known of the harm which could arise from their actions, even though they may not have intended to cause the resultant harm. [13]

**9.19** The offender's, age and level of maturity at the time of committing the offence should also be considered. Specific sentencing guidelines apply to young persons – that is offenders who were under the age of 25 at the date of their plea of guilty or where a finding of guilt is made against them.[14]

11 England and Wales Sentencing guidelines – domestic abuse: overarching principles (2018).
12 Scottish Sentencing Council, The sentencing process: Sentencing guideline (2021) – step1.
13 Scottish Sentencing Council, The sentencing process: Sentencing guideline (2021), p 6.
14 Scottish Sentencing Council, Sentencing young people guideline (2022).

**9.20** In assessing culpability in relation to a young person, the court must consider the intellectual and emotional maturity of that person at the time the offence was committed and should recognise that young people are generally less able to exercise good judgement and are less able to consider what could happen as the result of their actions. Accordingly, the culpability of a young person will generally be regarded as lower than that of an older person who is to be sentenced for the same or similar offence.

**9.21** In relation to the sentencing of young people, rehabilitation is also a primary consideration, and the court should, when selecting a sentence have appropriate regard to the prospect of the rehabilitation of the young person to reduce the risk of future reoffending. This consideration recognises that the character of a young person is not as fixed as that of an older person and that a young person may have greater capacity to change.[15]

## HARM

**9.22** In relation to harm, an important factor to be taken into account is the impact on the victim. In assessing the level of harm the court should consider any victim impact statement which has been placed before it, to the extent that it considers the information in the statement to be relevant to the offence.[16]

## VICTIM IMPACT STATEMENTS

**9.23** From 1 April 2009, victims of prescribed offences have been entitled to submit a 'victim statement' in solemn criminal courts in Scotland in certain circumstances.

**9.24** In terms of s 14 of The Criminal Justice (Scotland) Act 2003, victim statements may only be submitted by those who have been the victim of a prescribed offence (or, in circumstances where a victim has died, certain qualifying arrangements listed in s 14). The applicable prescribed offences are set out in the Victim Statements (Prescribed Offences) (Scotland) Order 2009. Victim statements may only be made in the High Court or in a sheriff court sitting as a court of solemn jurisdiction.[17]

15 SSC guideline which applies to the sentencing of any young person on or after 26 January 2022.

16 Criminal Justice (Scotland) Act 2003, s 14.

17 Criminal Justice (Scotland) Act 2003, s 14(1) and the Victim Statements (Prescribed Courts) (Scotland) Order 2009 (laid before the Scottish Parliament on 4th February 2009).

**9.25** Victims of prescribed offences should, so far as is reasonably practicable, be given the opportunity to make a victim statement about the way in which the offence has affected or continues to affect them.

**9.26** When moving for sentence, the prosecutor must lay before the court the victim statement, or part of the victim statement, which relates to the offence in question.[18] In determining sentence, the court must have regard to as much of that statement as it considers to be relevant to the offence. The court may also have regard to any information within such a statement concerning harm to the victim caused by the offender's conduct even if this is not specified in the charge, providing it is relevant to the offence.[19]

**9.27** If the accused pleads guilty or is found guilty, a copy of the victim statement must be provided to the accused by the prosecutor.[20] A victim impact statement need not be disclosed by the Crown as part of its general disclosure obligation,[21] but any material information contained in the statement ought to be disclosed.[22]

## OTHER FACTORS RELEVANT IN ASSESSING HARM

**9.28** Other factors which may be relevant in assessing the level of harm, include for example, deliberate degradation or humiliation of a victim, a sustained offence or repeated offences against the same victim, serious physical injury or a serious psychological impact on a victim.

**9.29** As acknowledged in the Scottish Sentencing Council guidelines, the assessment of seriousness can be a complex exercise, particularly where there is an imbalance between the low culpability of conduct which results in a high degree of harm (for example where a single push results in a fall and a fractured skull).

**9.30** The sentencer should also ensure that the factors included in the initial assessment of seriousness are not also considered as aggravating or mitigating factors to avoid double counting[23]

18 Criminal Justice (Scotland) Act 2003, s 14(5).
19 *HM Advocate v GH* [2023] HCJAC 45 at para 19.
20 Criminal Justice (Scotland) Act 2003, s 14(4).
21 Criminal Justice and Licensing (Scotland) Act 2010, s 160(4) and (5).
22 *JB v HM Advocate* [2025] HCJAC 1.
23 Scottish Sentencing Council, The sentencing process: Sentencing guideline (2021), para 22.

## THE SENTENCING RANGE

**9.31** The court must also select the range of sentences within which the appropriate headline sentence for the offence appears to fall, having regard to the seriousness, any applicable sentencing guideline or judgement and any statutory provision relevant to the offence or the offender.

## STATUTORY RESTRICTIONS IN RELATION TO THE IMPOSITION OF CUSTODIAL SENTENCES

**9.32** Section 204 of CP(S)A 1995 states that a person over the age of 21 who has not previously been sentenced to prison or detention may not be sentenced to a period of imprisonment unless the court considers that no other method of dealing with that offender is appropriate.[24]

**9.33** In terms of CP(S)A 1995, s 207(3), a person under 21 years may not be given a custodial sentence unless the court is satisfied that no other method of dealing with him is appropriate. In both cases the court must obtain a report from an officer of the local authority.

**9.34** Section 204(3A) of CP(S)A 1995 provides that a court must not pass a sentence of imprisonment for a term of 12 months or less on a person unless it considers that no other method of dealing with the person is appropriate.

**9.35** If the court does decide to impose a sentence of imprisonment despite these presumptions, it requires to state its reasons for concluding that no other method of dealing with the person is appropriate and record those reasons in the record of proceedings.

## AGGRAVATING AND MITIGATING FACTORS

**9.36** The court must also identify applicable aggravating and mitigating factors. In general terms, aggravating factors are those facts and circumstances, which may make the offence more serious for the purposes of sentencing, whilst mitigating factors may include factors personal to the offender, or pertinent to the offence, which may lead to the imposition of a more lenient sentence. Examples of possible aggravating and mitigating factors can be found in Annex B and C of the sentencing process guideline.[25]

24 Criminal Procedure (Scotland) Act 1995, s 204(2).

25 Scottish Sentencing Council, The sentencing process: Sentencing guideline (2021), pp 15 and 16.

## STATUTORY AGGRAVATIONS

**9.37** The court must also have regard to any statutory aggravations which apply. In the context of domestic abuse, as discussed in **Chapter 6** above, the most common aggravations will be those relating to: the abuse of a partner or ex-partner in terms of s 1 of the Abusive Behaviour and Sexual Harm (Scotland) Act 2016; domestic abuse aggravations in relation to a child in terms of s 1(1) of the Domestic Abuse (Scotland ) Act 2018; and bail aggravations in terms of s 27(3) of the Criminal Procedure (Scotland ) Act 1995.

### Abusive Behaviour and Sexual Harm (Scotland) Act 2016, s 1

**9.38** This aggravation, where it is libelled in an indictment or complaint applies to those offences committed on or after 24 April 2017 where it is admitted or proved that in committing the offence that the perpetrator intended to cause the partner or ex-partner to suffer physical or psychological harm, or in the case only of an offence committed against the partner or ex-partner, the person is reckless as to causing the partner or ex-partner to suffer physical or psychological harm. The court must take that aggravation into account and must state and record on conviction that the offence was so aggravated and where the sentence is different from that which the court would have imposed if the offence was not so aggravated, the extent and reasons for that difference or otherwise the reasons for there being no such difference.

### Domestic Abuse (Scotland) Act 2018, s 1(1)

**9.39** Where, in relation to an offence committed under s 1(1) of the Domestic Abuse (Scotland ) Act 2018 after 1 April 2019, it is specified in the complaint or libelled in the indictment that the offence is aggravated by reason of involving a child under 18 and it is proved that the offence is so aggravated, the court must expressly state on conviction that the offence is so aggravated and record the conviction to show that the offence was so aggravated and it must take that aggravation into account when determining the appropriate sentence as above.

**9.40** An offence is also aggravated if, at any time during the commission of that offence, the accused directed behaviour at a child or makes use of a child in directing behaviour at their partner or former partner. Further the offence is so aggravated if a child sees or hears, or is present during an incident or behaviour that the perpetrator directs towards the complainer as part of the course of behaviour. The offence will be so aggravated if a reasonable person would consider the course of behaviour, or an incident of behaviour that forms part of the course of behaviour, to be likely to adversely affect a child usually residing with the perpetrator or complainer or both.

## Bail aggravations

**9.41** If appropriate the court must have regard to the fact that the principal offence was committed whilst the offender was subject to bail and in terms of CP(S)A 1995, s 27(3) and (5) the maximum sentence of imprisonment permitted can be increased by virtue of the aggravation by six months and the court must give reasons for including any element of the penalty for a bail aggravation.[26]

## AGGRAVATING FACTORS

**9.42** Some specific examples of possible aggravating factors are detailed in the Scottish Sentencing Guidelines, and these include, but are not limited to the following:

- the presence of children during the commission of the offence;
- steps taken by the perpetrator to prevent the victim reporting the offence or seeking assistance;
- the offence was committed whilst the perpetrator was on licence or subject to another order of court;
- any relevant previous convictions which the offender has should be taken into account – particularly where the offender has a history of similar offending. For example, a proven history of violence or threats by the offender in a domestic context;
- the offence was committed whilst under the influence of drugs or alcohol consumed voluntarily;
- the particular vulnerability of the victim. All victims of domestic abuse are vulnerable due to the nature of the abuse, but some victims of domestic abuse may be more vulnerable than others and not all vulnerabilities are immediately apparent;
- the victim is forced to leave their home or steps have been taken to exclude the offender from the home to ensure the victim's safety.
- the impact on children – directly and indirectly;
- using contact arrangements with a child to instigate an offence;

26 Criminal Procedure (Scotland) Act 1995 ss 27(3) and (5).

- a history of disobedience to court orders such as breach of bail, breach of non-harassment, orders, breach of community, payback, orders and restriction of liberty orders; and
- abuse of trust and abuse of power.[27]

## MITIGATING FACTORS

**9.43** Some specific examples of mitigating factors include the following:

- the offender suffers from mental illness or has a disability;
- if there is likely to be a particularly adverse effect of a particular sentence on the offender or their family. For example, the offender is the primary or sole carer of any dependants and a sentence of imprisonment might result in the offender's children being looked after away from home;
- the offender demonstrates genuine remorse;
- the offender demonstrates a willingness to address issues pertinent to the commission of the offence, for example by addressing any drug, alcohol or mental health issues; and
- the offender is of previous good character, with no previous or recent relevant convictions.

## SENTENCING GUIDELINES ENGLAND AND WALES – DOMESTIC ABUSE

**9.44** With regard to an offender's lack of previous convictions, see the sentencing guidelines in England and Wales. These state, that although as a general principle of sentencing a court will take account of an offender's previous good character, in relation to domestically aggravated offending it should be borne in mind that one of the factors that can, in some cases, allow domestic abuse to continue unnoticed for lengthy periods is the ability of the perpetrator to have a public and a private face in respect of offences committed within a domestic context.[28]

## THE EXPRESSED WISHES OF THE VICTIM

**9.45** In cases involving domestic abuse, the court is often made aware of the victim's wishes either directly or indirectly. On some occasions, the victim

27 Scottish Sentencing Council, The sentencing process: Sentencing guideline (2021), Annex B.

28 England and Wales Sentencing guidelines – Domestic abuse: overarching principles (2018),

will write directly to the court, pleading for leniency for the offender, and perhaps advising the court that the victim and offender wish to reconcile. In other cases information about the victim's wishes will be indirect, via COPFS or sometimes via the offender's legal representative, or through an organisation such as ASSIST.[29] (ASSIST supports victims and survivors of domestic abuse in relation to cases going through the criminal courts.)

**9.46** As stated above, there are at present no offence-specific sentencing guidelines available in Scotland in relation to domestic abuse; however, as also mentioned above, at the time of writing the Scottish Sentencing Council is working on a general guideline on domestic abuse.[30] The sentencing guidelines in England and Wales in relation to domestic abuse include guidance regarding how the court should approach an expressed wish by the victim for leniency and is in the following terms:

> 'A sentence imposed for an offence committed within a domestic context should be determined by the seriousness of the offence, not by any expressed wishes of the victim. There are a number of reasons why it may be particularly important that this principal is observed within this context.
>
> - The court is sentencing on behalf of the wider public.
> - No victim is responsible for the sentence imposed.
> - There is a risk that a plea for mercy made by a victim will be induced by threats, made by or by a fear of the offender.
> - The risk of such threats will be increased if it is generally believed that the severity of the sentence may be affected by the wishes of the victim.'

In relation to other factors influencing sentence, the guidance states that the following points of principle should be considered by a court when imposing sentence in offences committed in a domestic context:

> '13. Provocation is no mitigation to an offence within a domestic context, except in rare circumstances.
>
> 14. The offender or the victim may ask the court to consider the interests of any children by imposing a less severe sentence. The court should consider not only the effect on the children if the relationship is disrupted, but also the likely effect of any further incidents of domestic abuse- the court should take great care with such a request as a sentence should primarily be determined by the seriousness of the offence.

29 ASSIST stands for Advocacy|Support|Safety|Information|Services|Together.

30 www.scottishsentencingcouncil.org.uk/sentencing-guidelines/guidelines-in-development/domestic-abuse [accessed 22 August 2025].

15. Offences involving serious violence or where the emotional or psychological harm caused is severe will warrant a custodial sentence in the majority of cases.

16. [...]

17. Passing the custody threshold does not mean that a custodial sentence should be deemed inevitable. Where the custody threshold is only just crossed, the court will consider whether the better option is instead to impose a community order, including a requirement to attend an accredited domestic abuse programme or domestic abuse specific intervention. Such an option will normally only be appropriate, where the court is satisfied that the offender genuinely intends to reform his or her behaviour, and that there is a real prospect of rehabilitation being successful.'[31]

**9.47** It has been acknowledged by the Scottish Courts, in the context of different types of offending, that the English sentencing guidelines might serve as a useful cross-check for sentences in Scotland whilst cautioning against too rigid an application.[32]

**9.48** The Sheriff Appeal Court and the High Court have also considered the issue of the victim's wishes in the context of special conditions of bail [33] and the imposition of non-harassment orders.[34]

## APPLICATION OF THE SCOTTISH SENTENCING GUIDELINES – THE CORRECT APPROACH

**9.49** In the case of *HM Advocate v GH,*[35] the appeal court considered, inter alia, the application of the guidelines and the correct approach to be adopted in relation to the sentencing process and principles and purposes of sentencing guidelines. In this case the crown had appealed against a sentence imposed in respect of domestically aggravated offences on the ground of undue leniency. The appeal was upheld and the sentence increased from 15 months to four years' imprisonment. It was submitted by the Crown that the sheriff had erred in his application of the guidelines which required that he follow the eight-

31 Sentencing Council England and Wales, Sentencing guidelines – Domestic abuse:overarching principles.

32 See *HM Advocate v David Docherty* [2024] HCJAC 36 at para 20 where a crosscheck with the English guidelines would have revealed a 'major disparity' with the sentences imposed.

33 *Procurator Fiscal, Alloa v Ross Porch* [2015} HCJAC 111 – see para 36.

34 *Finlay v Procurator Fiscal, Perth* [2020] SAC (CRIM)1– see para 11.

35 2023 HCJAC 45.

step process contained therein. The appeal court had this to say about the application of the guidelines and the process to be followed by sentencers.

> 'We are satisfied that the sentence in question meets the test set out in *HM Advocate v Bell* 1995 SLT 350 and is unduly lenient. Before setting out the reasons for that conclusion, we should make it clear that we do not accept the suggestion that the Sentencing Process Guideline somehow imposes a requirement on judges to set out in detail the method by which they arrived at the final sentence, or requires them to approach the issue of sentence by approaching the factors in question in a prescribed order. The Guideline itself makes that clear in paras C and D of the introduction thereto:
>
> > C. The sentencing decision may be made swiftly and in many cases the court may appear to consider some or all relevant factors at the same time. Where a court does not expressly take any individual step, that does not in itself amount to a decision not to follow the guideline.
> >
> > D. A court may choose to explain aspects of a sentence it has passed by reference to a specific part of this guideline. It does not have to give full reasons as to how each part of the process has affected the sentence.
>
> When faced with an argument that a sentencing judge has not followed a guideline the court will not approach that matter as if the judge were required to set out a template or tick sheet showing his workings. The guidelines are just that: guidance. They do not impose a rigid framework on the judge. Sentencing remains an essentially holistic exercise and whether a sentence may be described as excessive or unduly lenient will be determined according to the whole approach taken by the trial judge, and it is not to be assumed that simply because a specific step is not recorded, or not mentioned, that it has not been taken into account.'[36]

## THE DISPOSALS AVAILABLE

**9.50** These range from an absolute discharge to imprisonment and include the following:

- admonition;
- financial penalties, such as a fine or a compensation order;
- structured deferred sentences;
- community payback orders;

36 *HM Advocate v GH* 2023 HCJAC 45 at paras [14] and [15].

- restriction of liberty orders and electronic monitoring orders;
- drug treatment and testing orders: and
- imprisonment.

**9.51** These disposals will be discussed in more detail below. However a vital part of the disposal of cases involving domestic abuse is the consideration of the imposition of a non-harassment order.

## NON-HARASSMENT ORDERS

**9.52** In cases involving domestic abuse the court must consider whether or not to make a non-harassment order to protect the victim, irrespective of whether any such motion is made by the crown

**9.53** The terms of CP(S)A 1995, ss 234AZA and 234A govern the imposition of non-harassment orders in domestic abuse cases. Section 234AZA was added to CP(S)A 1995, by the Domestic Abuse (Scotland) Act 2018 and applies in respect of proceedings commenced on or after 1 April 2019, in relation to a person convicted of an offence involving domestic abuse.

## WHAT IS A NON-HARASSMENT ORDER?

**9.54** A non- harassment order is an order requiring that the person to whom it applies must refrain for such period (including an indeterminate period) as may be specified in the order, from such conduct in relation to the victim, as may be specified in the order. In practice the conduct specified often mirrors the terms of special conditions of bail, namely prohibition against any approach, contact or communication or attempted approach, contact or communication by the perpetrator in respect of the victim, often combined with a prohibition against that person entering the victim's home or street.

**9.55** A non-harassment order made by a criminal court may be appealed against as if the order were a sentence. In addition, the person against whom the order is made or the prosecutor in the case in which the order is made can apply to the court which made the order for its revocation or variation. The court can thereafter, if satisfied on a balance of probabilities that it is appropriate to do so, revoke or vary that order, although it cannot increase the period for which the order is to run.

**9.56** Breach of a non-harassment order is a separate offence and an offender will be liable on conviction on indictment to imprisonment for a term not exceeding five years, or a fine up to the statutory maximum or both. On summary conviction, an offender will be liable to imprisonment for a period, not exceeding six months, or to a fine again not exceeding the statutory maximum.

## NON-HARASSMENT ORDERS IN DOMESTIC ABUSE CASES

**9.57** In terms of CP(S)A 1995, s 234AZA, if a person is convicted of an offence under s 1(1) of the Domestic Abuse (Scotland ) Act 2018 or if an offence is aggravated as described in s 1(1)(a) of the Abusive Behaviour and Sexual Harm (Scotland) Act 2016 the court *must*, without an application by the prosecutor, consider the question of whether to make a non- harassment order in the person's case. The court must however do so only after hearing from the prosecutor and the offender.

**9.58** A non-harassment order *must* be made unless the court concludes that there is no need for the victim or the children (if any) to be protected by such an order from harassment or further harassment.[37]

## The complainer's views

**9.59** In the case of *Finlay v PF Perth,* [38]the Sheriff Appeal Court dealt with an appeal against the imposition of a six-month non-harassment order in a case involving domestic abuse. The sentencing sheriff's interpretation of CP(S)A 1995, s 234AZA was that it was weighted in favour of the granting of an order, unless the court was satisfied that it would be unnecessary to do so. In considering the issue, the sheriff had regard to the Crown narration, the appellant's offending history and the terms of the criminal justice social work report. He did not consider that arguable grounds existed to demonstrate why a non-harassment order would be unnecessary. The sheriff recorded in his report that the complainer's views were not before him, but he had in fact 'readily inferred' that she was not supportive of an order being made. Whilst taking those views into account he afforded the aforementioned other factors greater weight. The solicitor advocate for the appellant submitted that a non-harassment order had not been necessary, and that the sheriff had fallen into error in making one, given that the complainer did not want the protection of such a non-harassment order. It had been made clear to the sheriff that both parties wished the relationship to continue, and accordingly, the complainer's views had not been given sufficient weight. It was argued therefore that the court should not 'protect' a person who did not wish to be protected. The Sheriff Appeal Court commented on the unusual wording of CP(S)A 1995, s 234AZA(4) and (5) but considered that:

37 CP(S)A 1995, s 234AZA(4) and (5).

38 [2020] SAC (Crim)1.

'Marrying those provisions together, the court *must* make a non- harassment order unless it concludes that there is no need for the victim to be protected by such an order. In other words, the court *must* make an order, unless it is positively able to conclude that there is no need for the victim to be protected by such an order. If the court on the information before it is not able to so conclude, the order must be made'.[39]

**9.60** As to the victim's views, it was noted that the statutory provision makes no reference whatsoever to the victim's view being sought. Indeed, the only criteria for making an order is that of necessity, which, as noted in the case of *Finlay*, 'trumps the views of the victim'. That said the Sheriff Appeal Court did acknowledge that when considering necessity, the views of the victim may be relevant, for example where a victim said she had only been assaulted once, that it was out of character for the accused, she did not fear the accused and there were other protective factors in place. The Sheriff Appeal Court opined that in these circumstances, the court may well feel able to conclude that there was no necessity for such a person to have the protection of an order. Further, where the court was not able to conclude that there was no need for an order, nonetheless, an order should not be declined simply because the victim did not want one because that would be to misinterpret the provisions of the section, and conflate the questions of appropriateness, which is the criteria for making an order in a non-domestic abuse case, with necessity.

## Provision of information to the court

**9.61** The Sheriff Appeal Court also stated that if a complainer's views are to be taken into account in considering necessity, it is incumbent on parties to furnish the court with information as to what those views are rather than leaving it to be inferred that because an order has not been sought, the victim must not be in favour of one being granted. The absence of information will invariably count against an appellant as a consequence of the manner in which Parliament has legislated.[40]

## Revocation of a non-harassment order

**9.62** It was also observed that if a complainer turns out to be so aggrieved by a non-harassment order that she felt compelled to take some action, it would be open to that complainer to approach the crown and request that the prosecutor applies to have it revoked in terms of CP(S)A 1995, s 234A(6).

39 *Finlay v Procurator Fiscal, Perth* (fn 34 above) at para 11.
40 *Finlay v Procurator Fiscal, Perth* (fn 34 above) at para 13.

The applicable test in that section allows the court to revoke the order if it is satisfied on a balance of probabilities that it is appropriate to do so.[41]

**9.63** The case of *Finlay* was approved in the High Court case of *HMA v RM.* [42] In this case the crown had appealed against the sentences imposed in respect of an accused who was convicted of three charges of rape in respect of three different complainers. Two of the charges were domestically aggravated by virtue of the Abusive Behaviour and Sexual Harm (Scotland) Act 2016. The crown contended that the sentences were unduly lenient and also that it was inappropriate not to make non-harassment orders.

**9.64** The Appeal Court considered inter alia the law relating to non-harassment orders in cases involving domestic abuse.[43]

**9.65** In relation to the first complainer, the Crown had moved for a non-harassment order under CP(S)A 1995, s 234A, and the trial judge had declined to make the order on the basis that he was not satisfied that the complainer's concerns arose from the charge before him for sentence, but rather, that any concerns were related to earlier assaults. The Appeal Court made clear that in considering the question of a non-harassment order the court was not restricted to simply considering the events forming the charge on the indictment but was entitled to have regard to previous convictions (see CP(S)A 1995, s 234A(2A)). The court was satisfied in that case that the complainer spoke to numerous incidents of actual harassment by the respondent causing her alarm and distress and that there was ample basis for considering that a non-harassment order would be appropriate.

**9.66** The court also considered the application of CP(S)A 1995, s 234AZA in relation to the remaining two complainers. The trial judge had declined to make non-harassment orders on the basis that there were no indications that the respondent had contacted the complainers or that they feared he would do so and that the second complainer now lived in England. Further, given that the respondent would be in prison for a lengthy period of time, he did not consider that non-harassment orders would be 'appropriate'.

**9.67** The court confirmed that this was the wrong test and made reference to the case of *Finlay*, approving the correct test as noted by the Sheriff Appeal Court,[44] and further stating;

> 'The fact that the legislation speaks of protecting against harassment or further harassment makes it clear that prior incidents of harassment,

41 CP(S)A 1995, s 234A(6).
42 2023 HCJC 43.
43 *HM Advocate v RM* at paras 49–51.
44 *Finlay v Procurator Fiscal,* Perth (fn 34 above) at para 11.

communication, or contact are not prerequisites for the making of an order. The complainer in charge two had left Scotland but remained in the UK … She retained friends and family in Scotland and would remain contactable through modern means of communication and social media. The third complainer in her victim impact statement referred to panic attacks, even when seeing a car similar to that which the respondent owned or seeing someone with similar features … applying the correct statutory test, [the Appeal Court] were unable to say that there was no need for those complainers to be protected by the imposition of a non-harassment order.' [45]

**9.68** The court thereafter imposed a non-harassment order in respect to each complainer for a period of 15 years.

## CHILDREN

**9.69** In terms of CP(S)A 1995, s 234AZA, if an offence is aggravated as described in s 1(1)(a) of the Abusive Behaviour and Sexual Harm (Scotland) Act 2016 or if a person is convicted of an offence under s 1(1) of the Domestic Abuse (Scotland ) Act 2018 (DA(S)A 2018), the court is able to include certain children within the scope of an NHO. In terms of CP(S)A 1995, s 234AZA(3) (4) and (5), in relation to a child, this is a two-stage process.

**9.70** First, the court must be satisfied that the child falls into one of the prescribed categories and, that it is appropriate for the child to be protected by the order.

**9.71** The prescribed categories are, in any circumstances, a child usually residing with the person or a child residing with the victim or both.[46] Or, in relation to an offence under DA(S)A 2018, s 1(1), where the offence is libelled as aggravated by reason of involving a child and it is proved that the offence is so aggravated as described in DA(S)A 2018, s 5(1), a child to whom the aggravation relates.

**9.72** In terms of DA(S)A 2018, s 5, the offence in question can be aggravated in the following ways:

> '(2) … if, at any time in the commission of the offence—
>
> (a) A directs behaviour at a child, or
>
> (b) A makes use of a child in directing behaviour at B.

45 *HMA v RM* (fn 35 above) at para 51.

46 CP(S)A 1995, s 234AZA(3)(a).

(3) If a child sees or hears, or is present during, an incident of behaviour that A directs at B as part of the course of behaviour.

(4) If a reasonable person would consider the course of behaviour, or an incident of A's behaviour that forms part of the course of behaviour, to be likely to adversely affect a child usually residing with A or B (or both).'

**9.73** Secondly, if the court is satisfied that it is appropriate for the child to be protected by the order the court *must* make an NHO applying to that child as well as the victim, unless it concludes that there is no need for that child to be protected by such an order.[47]

**9.74** It should also be noted that in terms of CP(S)A 1995, s 234AZA(4) the court must consider the question of whether to make an order without an application by the prosecutor and must first give the prosecutor and the person an opportunity to be heard. If the court reaches the conclusion that there is no need for the child to be protected by an NHO it must explain the basis for this.

**9.75** In the case of *GRPW v Her Majesty's Advocate,*[48] the court considered the test to be applied when considering the imposition of an NHO to protect a child. The court agreed that there was a two-stage process to be applied insofar as children are concerned, namely that there is first the issue of appropriateness in terms of CP(S)A 1995, s 234AZA(3), and secondly the statutory question referred to in subsections (4) and (5) in relation to the need for protection.

**9.76** The court had this to say about the appropriateness test:

> 'We agree with counsel and the advocate depute that there is indeed a two-stage process insofar as children are concerned. However, in our opinion the appropriateness 'test' is nothing more than a threshold. It is not for us to try to re-write the words of the statute but one approach which commends itself to us is to consider whether the child is within the orbit of the offending and affected or likely to be affected by it.
>
> Where the child falls within section 234AZA(3)(b), it is difficult to conceive of any circumstances in which an order will not be appropriate. Less straightforward issues could perhaps arise where the child qualifies for consideration only under sub-section (3)(a). That will obviously depend on the circumstances of each case. Where such a child has witnessed, overheard or been a victim of domestic violence, it will only be rarely that the court should not have that child 'in mind' for the purposes of addressing the question posed in section 234AZA(4).

47 DA(S)A 2018, s 5(4) and (5).

48 [2021] HCJA 47.

Thereafter, issues such as the nature of the offence, the persistence of the offending, the offender's record, steps taken to address any issues the offender might have etc., will come into play when the statutory question is being considered, although there may well be some overlap between the two stages. [49]

In the *GRPW* case, the two children in question were residing with their mother ( the victim) and in relation to two of the charges had witnessed or heard at least part of the offending, the court concluded:-

> 'It is fair to proceed on the basis that (the children) were or would have been affected by (the offending) … and were entitled to be considered for protection'. [50]

**9.77** Refusing the appeal against the imposition of three-year non-harassment orders prohibiting the appellant from approaching or contacting the complainer and the two children and from entering their home the court also said:

> 'The statute does not require that the views of those who might be protected by an order should be sought and we do not ourselves think it is necessary in any event. See *Finlay v PF Perth* 2021 SLT (Sh Ct) 133'.[51]

## SPECIFIC DISPOSALS

### Absolute discharge

**9.78** In certain circumstances, a court may, instead of sentencing an offender, make an order discharging him absolutely. [52] A person can be granted an absolute discharge if convicted on indictment or on summary complaint of an offence other than an offence the sentence for which is fixed by law, when the court is of the opinion, having regard to the circumstances, including the nature of the offence and the character of the offender, that it is inexpedient to inflict punishment.

**9.79** There require to be exceptional circumstances before the court orders absolute discharge (see *AS v Procurator Fiscal, Kilmarnock*).[53] This case involved a contravention of s 38 of the Criminal Justice and Licensing (Scotland) Act 2010 in a domestic context. The sheriff concluded that this was not a trivial incident and that this type of offending in the domestic

49 [2021] HCJA 47(para 23).
50 [2021] HCJA 47(para 25).
51 [2021] HCJA 47(para 26).
52 Criminal Procedure (Scotland) Act 1995, s 246(2) and (3).
53 2017 SLT(Sh Ct) 89, para [5]).

context was serious and far from unusual in the Sheriff Court. The sheriff's decision not to grant an absolute discharge was upheld by the Sheriff Appeal Court, applying the criteria in *HMA v Bell.*[54] This decision can however be contrasted with the case of *SB v Procurator Fiscal, Aberdeen,*[55] in which case the Sheriff Appeal Court refused a crown appeal against the sheriff's decision to grant an absolute discharge in respect of a charge of assault aggravated by the terms of s 1 of the Abusive Behaviour and Sexual Harm (Scotland)Act 2016. In this case the appellant pled guilty to assaulting the complainer by seizing her by the throat, causing her breathing to be restricted. Thereafter in the case of *Graham Kane v Procurator Fiscal, Kilmarnock*[56] the Sheriff Appeal Court made it clear that the decision in *SB v PF Aberdeen*[57] above should not be taken as signalling a departure from the high test to be met in reaching the decision not to proceed to conviction and to grant an absolute discharge.[58] In this case the appellant relied principally upon the adverse consequences of a conviction for his employment and future prospects. The Appeal Court observed as follows:

> 'Two general observations require to be made. First, upon tendering a plea of guilty or being found guilty after trial, those in employment do not enjoy any particular privilege or special status not enjoyed by those who are unemployed. The consequences of conviction for an offender in employment may include disciplinary proceedings with a range of disposals from reprimand to dismissal and may have an effect upon future employment prospects. However, those are consequences which ordinarily those who offend require to bear. The effect upon current and future employment may, in appropriate cases, be relevant to the question of whether an admonition ought to be granted but will not, in most cases, on its own, amount to "exceptional circumstances" justifying the granting of an absolute discharge. Second, little weight can be attached to vague submissions that a conviction "may affect" or "could affect" an offender's employment ... The information in relation to the appellant's current employment and his future employment prospects was vague. We consider the Justice was correct to have attached little weight to it. The Justice was also correct to have attached significant weight to the nature and circumstances of the offence ... which could not be described as trivial or minor ... or an ill judged reaction to a provocation or momentary lapse of judgement'.[59]

The appeal against the refusal to grant an absolute discharge was refused.

54 1995 SCCR 244.
55 2023 SAC (crim ) 9.
56 2024 SAC (Crim) 7.
57 Fn 55 above.
58 Fn 56 above at para 19.
59 Fn 56 above at paras 22–24.

## ADMONITION

**9.80** The court may admonish an accused after conviction if it appears to meet the interests of justice in the case.[60] This disposal may be deemed appropriate in very low level/minor offending in the domestic context. In practice, this will often be imposed after a deferral for good behaviour for a suitable period in terms of CP(S)A 1995, s 202. This section provides that sentence may be deferred after conviction for a period and on such conditions as a court may determine. Sentence can be deferred on more than one occasion and almost all such deferred sentences have a condition that the accused be of good behaviour during the period of deferral. When deferring sentence, the court should not give an indication that any particular outcome will follow. The court at the deferred diet retains the same powers of sentence as it had at the time of conviction. If sentence is deferred to enable an offender to demonstrate that they can be of good behaviour and they are of good behaviour, then in practice it is often the case that the court may admonish the accused.

## FINANCIAL PENALTY – FINES AND COMPENSATION ORDERS

**9.81** Fines are not generally imposed in domestic abuse cases, particularly when the complainer and accused are still in a relationship or hope to reconcile, and where there are children of the relationship living in the household. This is on the basis that any financial penalty will likely have an impact on the finances of the household as opposed to just the offender.

**9.82** A compensation order may be appropriate, either as a standalone disposal or as part of a community payback order (referred to as 'a compensation requirement') in certain limited circumstances, perhaps, for example, in relation to a former partner, where there is no prospect of reconciliation and there are no children of the relationship. Fines are governed by CP(S)A 1995, ss 211–226 and compensation orders by CP(S)A 1995, ss 249–252.

## RESTRICTION OF LIBERTY ORDERS

**9.83** A restriction of liberty order (ROLO) in terms of CP(S)A 1995, s 245A can be imposed in appropriate cases as a direct alternative to custody. Following the passing of the Management of Offenders (Scotland) Act 2019, such orders, imposed after 17 May 2022, are combined with an electronic monitoring order (EMO). The purpose of these orders is to enable designated persons to electronically monitor restrictions placed on an individual requiring

60 CP(S)A 1995, s 246(1).

them to remain at or away from a specified place for specified periods of time. The benefit of this disposal is that it contains a significant punitive element while enabling an offender to remain at home and continue in employment or training. The order can be made for a period up to 12 months and for up to 12 hours a day.[61]

**9.84** The accused person must consent to the imposition of a ROLO and an EMO. In the context of offences involving domestic abuse there may be a potential risk to others living within the household associated with that person being restricted to a particular address. For example, if the offender and victim plan to reconcile and continue living together after sentence the address is likely to be deemed unsuitable for restriction and monitoring given that it might exacerbate tensions within that domestic setting.

**9.85** If an offender is assessed as requiring a degree of supervision and/ or support, a restricted movement requirement with an EMO can be imposed as part of a community payback order and supervised by a social worker. The electronic monitoring part of the requirement, is monitored by the service provider, (at the present time G4S) who will report any breaches of curfew or movement to the supervising officer, who would then be bound to report this to the court as a breach of the community pay back order within five working days.[62] Breaches of EMOs can be dealt with at hearings considering breaches of ROLOs.[63]

## STRUCTURED DEFERRED SENTENCE

**9.86** A structured deferred sentence is a flexible form of intervention which provides structured social work support for offenders post-conviction but before sentencing. In practice, a structured deferred sentence can be used for offenders with underlying issues, which might be addressed through social work and/or multi-agency intervention. Suitability for structured deferred sentence is assessed within the Criminal Justice Social Work Report and action plans will be based on risk and needs assessment. At the end of the period of intervention, (typically three–six months), the court can dispose of the matter in any way which would have been available and appropriate at the time of conviction. When the matter calls for review at the end of the period of deferral the supervising officer will provide a detailed report to the court in relation to the offender's conduct, engagement and progress during the period of deferral.

61 CP(S)A 1995, s 245A.

62 CP(S)A 1995, s 227A(2)(j) and Management of Offenders (Scotland ) Act 2019, ss 1 and 3.

63 Management of Offenders (Scotland) Act 2019, s 14.

## COMMUNITY PAYBACK ORDERS

**9.87** The provisions relating to community payback orders (CPO) are contained in CP(S)A 1995, ss 227A–227ZO. They are used extensively at summary level in cases involving domestic abuse.

**9.88** Where a person is convicted of an offence punishable by imprisonment, the court may, instead of imposing a sentence of imprisonment, impose a CPO on the offender.[64]

**9.89** Before a community payback order can be imposed (at level 2) the court must obtain a report from an officer of the local authority. In practice, a criminal justice social worker will prepare the report. A level one order, restricted to the imposition of 20–100 hours of unpaid work, can be imposed without a report. When the court is considering imposing a CPO it must be satisfied that the offence is serious enough to warrant such an order. If imposing two or more requirements, it is important to make sure that these requirements are compatible; and that, so far as practicable, any requirement avoids conflict with the offender's religious beliefs, his employment or education or any voluntary work they do.[65] The report will contain an assessment of the extent of the individual's needs, ability and willingness to successfully complete a CPO. If the offender is already subject to a CPO the court will ask that a review of progress in respect of any extant order be included in the report. The assessment will consider the pattern, nature, seriousness, likelihood and imminence of reoffending to inform decisions about whether a CPO or other community based disposal is appropriate and should consider whether, and in what form intervention is required to address the individual's offending behaviour.

## RISK ASSESSMENT

**9.90** An important part of the foregoing process is the exploration of any risks present (particularly where there is evidence of imminent risk of serious harm) together with any protective factors that could mitigate these risks. In addition to a general risk assessment, a specialist assessment tool, typically, SARA (spousal assault risk assessment) V3 is currently used in Scotland in the preparation of pre-sentencing reports for those convicted of domestically aggravated offending. It can be used to assess both men and women involved in heterosexual, same-sex and transgender relationships. The SARA helps to characterise the risk that a perpetrator poses to their spouse, children, other family members, or any other person involved, in terms of likelihood, imminence, and severity of future offending.

64 CP(S)A 1995, s 227A.
65 CP(S)A 1995, s 227E.

**9.91** In the context of the SARA assessment, the nature and seriousness of the index offence or offences will be considered. The nature and severity of any violence (including sexual violence) inflicted will also be explored. For example, in cases involving domestic abuse, strangulation is considered to be extremely high-risk behaviour which can result in serious harm and even fatality. In addition to physical and sexual abuse, the nature, level and duration of other forms of conduct and courses of conduct will be assessed, such as psychological and economic abuse, intimidation and coercive control. In addition to the index offence before the court, the assessment will include an analysis of previous offending in relation to both the present victim and previous intimate partners in recognition of the fact that domestic abuse is often hidden or unreported. Further, in recognition that the statutory aggravation of domestic abuse was not available prior to 2016, a detailed exploration of the accused's offending history should be carried out. The author of the report will typically check departmental records and where appropriate inquiries will be made with the Police Domestic Abuse Investigation Unit to establish whether there is a history of call outs to the individual's home for domestic incidents. Where available, other agencies, for example domestic abuse court support and advocacy services such as ASSIST[66] may also provide additional information in relation to compliance with statutory orders and other risk factors. The assessment may also, where appropriate, take account of information held on local authority systems, perhaps due to concerns raised about a child or children in the household.

**9.92** If the court decides to impose a CPO, there are a number of requirements available to the court, namely:

- an offender supervision requirement;
- a compensation requirement;
- an unpaid work or other activity requirement;
- a programme requirement;
- a residence requirement;
- a mental health treatment requirement;
- a drug treatment requirement;
- an alcohol treatment requirement;
- a conduct requirement; and
- a restricted movement requirement.

66 ASSIST was established in 2004 and is a specialist Independent domestic abuse advocacy and support service focussed on reducing the risk to and improving the safety of victims of domestic abuse.

## OFFENDER SUPERVISION REQUIREMENT

**9.93** This requirement is imposed regularly in practice. It must be for a specified period (between six months and three years) and during that period the offender must attend appointments with his/her responsible officer for the purpose of promoting rehabilitation.[67]

## COMPENSATION REQUIREMENT

**9.94** Whilst this requirement is less commonly imposed, it can be imposed in favour of the victim for a relevant matter, which means any personal injury, loss, damage or other matter in respect of which a compensation order could be made against the offender. As stated earlier in this chapter, if the offender and victim reconcile or if there are children of the parties, compensation is likely to be thought inappropriate in light of its financial impact on the victim and the wider family.[68]

## UNPAID WORK OR OTHER ACTIVITY REQUIREMENT

**9.95** This requirement requires the offender to undertake a number of hours of unpaid work or other activity in the community. The number of hours is specified by the court imposing the order together with the time allowed for completion of the order. At level one this will be between 20–100 hours with three months to complete. At level two this will be 101–300 hours with six months to complete. The court can specify a longer period for completion and at the time of writing the most common period is 12 months.[69]

## PROGRAMME REQUIREMENT

**9.96** A programme requirement orders that the offender must participate in a specified programme, at a specified place and on a specified number of days. This requirement is used regularly in relation to domestically aggravated offending.[70]

## CALEDONIAN MEN'S PROGRAMME

**9.97** A common programme requirement used in Scotland in the context of domestic offending is the Caledonian Men's Programme. This is a behaviour-

67 CP(S)A 1995, s 227G.
68 CP(S)A 1995, s 227H.
69 CP(S)A 1995, ss 227I–227O.
70 CP(S)A 1995, s 227P.

based programme for men convicted of domestic abuse offences which includes support, safety planning and advocacy services for offenders partners and children. The programme comprises;

- The men's programme, which men attend as a requirement of a CPO. It lasts at least two years and includes six months of 1:1 assessment, engagement and motivation sessions, 25 group- work sessions and post-group maintenance work.
- The women's service, which provides safety planning, information, advice, advocacy and emotional support to female partners and ex-partners. It works with other services, like social work and the police, so that they can give women and their families the support they need.
- The Children's Service, which makes sure that the needs of the children whose parents are involved with the Caledonian System are met, their rights upheld and the impact that domestic abuse has on their lives is reduced.

**9.98** All of these services are based on risk and needs assessment, and are designed to prevent and minimise possible future harm to women and children. At the present time the Caledonian Men's Programme is available in 19 council areas, and similar programmes are available in other council areas, for example the Fergus Programme is available in Angus and the UP2U Programme is available in four other council areas.[71]

**9.99** In practice when the court orders a criminal justice social work report to assist with sentencing it can also ask that an assessment is carried out to determine whether a particular offender is suitable for participation in the Caledonian (or alternative) Programme. This will usually require an adjournment, on cause shown, for six weeks as opposed to the usual four weeks to enable the assessment to be carried out. In most cases, however, the initial CJSW report will include a preliminary assessment of suitability with a recommendation that a full assessment be carried out to determine if an offender is suitable.

## RESIDENCE REQUIREMENT

**9.100** A residence requirement requires that the offender must reside at a specified place if an offender supervision requirement is also imposed.[72]

71 The Community Justice Scotland website provides information regarding availability of programmes.

72 CP(S)A 1995, s 227Q.

## MENTAL HEALTH TREATMENT REQUIREMENT

**9.101** As part of this order the offender is required to submit during a specified period to treatment by, or under the direction of, a registered medical practitioner and/or a registered psychologist with a view to improving the offender's mental condition. A supervision requirement must also be imposed, and the court must be satisfied on the written or oral evidence of an approved practitioner that this treatment is appropriate.[73]

## DRUG TREATMENT REQUIREMENT

**9.102** This order requires the offender to submit during a specified period to treatment by/under the direction of a specified person with a view to reducing or eliminating the offender's dependency on, or propensity to misuse drugs. An offender supervision requirement must also be imposed.[74]

## ALCOHOL TREATMENT REQUIREMENT

**9.103** This order requires that the offender submit during a specified period to treatment by/under the direction of a specified person with a view to reducing or eliminating the offender's dependency on alcohol. Again, an offender supervision requirement must also be imposed in conjunction with this order. [75]

## CONDUCT REQUIREMENT

**9.104** This requires the offender to do, or to refrain from doing, specified things if the court is satisfied that the requirement is necessary with a view to securing or promoting the good behaviour of the offender, or preventing further offending by the offender. It must be for a specified period of not more than three years. In practice, the court regularly imposes a conduct requirement to engage with addiction services or a named programme as and when directed by the offender's supervising officer.[76] It should not however include a requirement to be of good behaviour or not to commit another offence.[77]

73 CP(S)A 1995, ss 227R to 227T.
74 CP(S)A 1995, s 227U.
75 CP(S)A 1995, s 227V.
76 CP(S)A 1995, s 227W.
77 *Kirk v Brown*, 2012 SCCR 558.

## RESTRICTED MOVEMENT REQUIREMENT

**9.105** This requirement restricts the offender's movements as specified in the order and may require the offender either to be, or not to be, in a specified place, or not to be in a specified place, at a specified time or during specified periods. The court must be satisfied that the offender can be monitored by the method specified in the requirement and taken alone or together with any other restricted movement requirement or restriction of liberty order, must not exceed a total of 12 hours in any one day. The requirement must be for a specified period of not less than 14 days and not more than 12 months and a supervision requirement must be imposed. An electronic monitoring order can also be imposed.[78]

## DRUG TREATMENT AND TESTING ORDER

**9.106** A drug treatment and testing order (DTTO) is designed for an offender who is dependent on or who has a propensity to misuse drugs and may be susceptible to treatment. The offender must be 16 or over (although in some schemes the offender must be over 18). A DTTO may be imposed instead of a sentence, where the offender submits to treatment and the order is imposed with a view to reducing or eliminating the dependency or propensity to misuse drugs. The duration of the order must be specified by the court and must be between six months and three years.[79]

## IMPRISONMENT AND DETENTION

**9.107** A person who has not previously been sentenced to imprisonment or detention by a court who is not legally represented cannot be sentenced to imprisonment or detention unless legal aid has been refused as not financially eligible, or having been informed of the right to apply for legal aid, and having had the opportunity, failed to do so.[80]

**9.108** An offender who is either over 21 but not previously sentenced to imprisonment or detention,[81] or under 21[82] may not be given a custodial sentence unless no other method of dealing with them is appropriate. If such a sentence is imposed the court must state, and record in the minute of proceedings, its reasons for so concluding that no other method is appropriate.

78 CP(S)A 1995, ss 227ZE–227ZK.
79 CP(S)A 1995, ss 234(B)–234H.
80 CP(S)A 1995, s 204(1).
81 CP(S)A 1995, s 204 (2).
82 CP(S)A 1995, s 207(2).

**9.109** Further, a court must not pass a sentence of imprisonment for a term of 12 months or less on a person unless the court considers that no other method of dealing with the person is appropriate and must state its reasons as above. [83]

## MAXIMUM CUSTODIAL SENTENCE

**9.110** On indictment, in the High Court there is no maximum custodial sentence at common law but for offences prosecuted in the sheriff court the maximum custodial sentence which can be imposed is one of five years. [84] In relation to statutory offences, the maximum length of any custodial sentence will depend on the relevant statute.

**9.111** For common law offences prosecuted on summary complaint, the maximum custodial sentence is 12 months[85] For statutory offences, if the offence is triable either on indictment or summary complaint, and if the offence is contained in an Act passed before 18 January 2007 it is 12 months.[86] For other statutory offences the maximum custodial sentence will depend on the terms of the relevant statute.

## BAIL AGGRAVATIONS

**9.112** If a bail aggravation is libelled the maximum custodial sentence available to the court is increased by six months.[87] The use of this provision is only for punishment for that aggravation.[88] and the court must give reasons for including or not including the element of the sentence imposed attributable to that aggravation. [89]

## MULTIPLE CHARGES

**9.113** Where there are two or more charges on one complaint/indictment, the maximum custodial sentence is the maximum prescribed for the offence which carries the highest penalty (but the higher penalty applies only to that offence, not the others) and the maximum that may be imposed is the sentence imposed on the charge with the highest penalty.[90]

83 CP(S)A 1995, s 204(3A) and (3B).
84 CP(S)A 1995, s 3(3).
85 CP(S)A 1995, s 5(2).
86 Criminal Proceedings etc (Reform) (Scotland) Act 2007, s 45.
87 CP(S)A 1995, s 27(5).
88 *Penman v Bott* 2007 SCCR 277, 283, paras [14] and [15].
89 CP(S)A 1995, s 27(6) and (6A).
90 *Nicholson v Lees* 1996 JC 173, 1996 SCCR 551, explained in *Fleming v Munro* 1997 SCCR 527 and *Minto v Harrower* 2010 SLT 440 (Five Bench).

## CUMULO, CONSECUTIVE AND CONCURRENT SENTENCES

**9.114** At common law, sentences are deemed to be concurrent unless it is specifically stated by the court that they are to be consecutive. The court must state the date of commencement of a custodial sentence.[91] If this is not done, then the sentence will be deemed to commence from the date on which the sentence is pronounced and will be concurrent to sentences already being served.[92]

**9.115** Where there are a number of complaints or indictment and fairness does not require otherwise, the total sentence imposed may exceed the maximum that can be imposed on any one complaint/indictment. There are no absolute rules that sentences must be concurrent if charges arise out of the same course of conduct. Sentences for charges of breach of bail or failing to attend court should normally be consecutive.

**9.116** A custodial sentence on a charge which would not otherwise attract a competent custodial sentence should normally be made concurrent to a custodial sentence on another charge.[93]

**9.117** In the case of *HM Advocate v RM*,[94] the appeal court considered concurrent, consecutive and cumulo sentences in the context of domestically aggravated offending. At para 46 the court stated:

> 'When dealing with a series of offences on an indictment, it is, of course, a matter of discretion for a sentencing judge to determine what form the sentences should take (*Nicholson v Lees* 1996 JC 173). Nor is there an obligation to impose a cumulo penalty merely because the offences form part of a course of conduct, although that is a classic circumstance where such a sentence may be merited … Indeed, there may be specific reasons not to do so, connected, for example with sentencing limits for certain of the offences (see, for example *DS v HM Advocate* 2017 SCCR 129). Equally, however, when sentencing for a series of offences, the court must be alert to the risk that making the sentences consecutive might result in an excessive sentence; whereas concurrent sentences might not reflect the overall criminality of the behaviour on the indictment. In such cases there is much to be said for the imposition of a cumulo penalty, which does so. This is recognised in *McDade v HM Advocate* 1997 SCCR 52; it is also recognised in England – *R v C* [2007] 2 Cr App R (S) 98; *R v Wilding* [2019] 2 Cr App R (S) 37'.

91 CP(S)A 1995, s 210(1)(b).

92 *Moore v MacPhail* 1986 SCCR 669.

93 *Maxwell v HMA*, [2017] HCJAC 64.

94 *HM Advocate v RM* 2023 HCJAC 43.

**9.118** And at para [47];

> 'In the latter, the court observed that it had
>
> > "encouraged the practice whereby in a serious, multiple-count case the sentencing judge should endeavour to impose one term of imprisonment which reflects the defendant's overall criminality. That makes for clarity and simplicity. We are told that the judge was urged to adopt that course here. We consider that it would have been much better if the judge had done so. It would have avoided the problems which we have identified."
>
> A similar point was made in *Gartshore v HM Advocate* [2023] HCJAC 1, where the sentencing judge had imposed consecutive sentences for a series of interlinked offences clearly forming part of a course of conduct. The court noted:
>
> > "[29] … the charges were essentially part of the one course of conduct, involving the same locus and an overlapping timeframe. The individual charges of course reflect the criminality of each accused but this seems to have been a classic case for the assessment of that criminality in each case as an overall whole, ideally suited for the imposition of a cumulo sentence, as in *McDade v HM Advocate* 1997 SCCR 52. The trial judge by approaching matters the way he did greatly overcomplicated what was in essence a simple scenario, and caused himself difficulties further down the line when he had to adjust the sentences to reflect the totality principle. Starting from that principle and imposing a cumulo sentence reflecting the degree of culpability and criminality of each accused as a whole would have avoided that difficulty.'

The appeal court upheld the crown appeal against the sentence imposed by the trial judge, finding that it met the test of undue leniency.

## PERIODS SPENT IN CUSTODY

**9.119** In passing a custodial sentence, the court must also have regard to any period spent in custody. If the court decides not to backdate the sentence at all, or is not backdating to the earliest date when the offender was remanded in custody then the court must give reasons for that decision. [95]

**9.120** In the case of *HM Advocate v Jake O'Docherty,* the court said at para 6:

> 'It is important to recognise that section 210(1) of the 1995 Act only provides that the court must "have regard" to the relevant remand period, and explain

95 1 CP(S)A 1995, s 210(1).

clearly the effect which it has had, including the reasons for any decision not to backdate. The statute does not provide that it is always necessary to backdate a sentence where possible; that credit must be given for the full period on remand, whether continuous or not; or that any deduction made to reflect a period on remand must be increased by a given proportion according to whether the accused qualifies as a long or short term prisoner, and the early release provisions which apply as a consequence.'[96]

## PERIOD SPENT SUBJECT TO ELECTRONIC MONITORING

**9.121** Section 5 of the Bail and Release from Custody (Scotland) Act 2023 came into force on the first of July 2024 and, inserted a new s 210ZA into CP(S)A 1995. This provision obliges all courts to have regard to the time an offender has been subject to electronically monitored bail prior to sentence. If a person has been subject to this type of bail, and a sentence of imprisonment or detention is determined as appropriate, a proportion of the period of time on bail should, ordinarily be directed as being treated as a period of time spent in custody.

**9.122** Section 210ZA of CP(S)A 1995 only applies when considering prison or detention. For the purposes of the section, 'Qualifying bail' is a bail order which obliges the accused to remain in a place for at least nine hours each day and be subject to electronic monitoring. It does not apply to a curfew without electronic monitoring. The requirement to have regard to the bail period is mandatory. The 'relevant period' is the time to be treated by the Scottish Prison Service as time already served when they calculate the offender's release date. It is not a discount as such on the sentence pronounced or a backdated sentence. The relevant period is equivalent to half the bail period (to the nearest day), less such part as the court considers appropriate to disregard.

**9.123** In practice the court will calculate the relevant period, and it should be recorded that in terms of CP(S)A 1995, s 210ZA the court directed that the relevant period is to be treated as having been served. The case of *Prosecutor Fiscal, Airdrie v Antonio Rea*[97] outlined the correct approach in applying s 210ZA, which is that the custodial sentence should be imposed in the usual way and thereafter the relevant period should be specified, with a direction that the accused is to be treated as having served that part of the sentence which is equal to the relevant period.

96 2022 HCJAC 31 at para 6.
97 [2025] SAC (Crim) 2, para 13.

## MODIFICATION OF SENTENCE TO REFLECT TIMING OF PLEA OF GUILTY (DISCOUNTS)

**9.124** The court must also, in determining sentence, take into account the stage at which an offender indicated his intention to plead guilty and the circumstances in which that undertaking was given, and in passing sentence the sentencer must state whether the sentence is different from that which the court would otherwise have imposed, were it not for the guilty plea.[98] In all cases, in respect of any sentence following upon a guilty plea, consideration must be given to the utilitarian benefits of that plea (ie the benefits to the administration of justice); and the implications of the acceptance of guilt by the accused such as demonstrating true contrition, assisting the authorities or sparing the victim from the potential ordeal of having to give evidence at trial. These considerations however should not be allowed to detract from the need to protect the public.[99]

**9.125** In the case of *Gemmell v HM Advocate,*[100] general guidance was given as to the circumstances in which a discount of sentence may be available in relation to both custodial and non-custodial disposals. The grant of a discount, and how much, are questions for the discretion of the sentencer but the court in *Gemmell* also accepted that the approach by way of a sliding scale set out in *Spence v HM Advocate*[101] was sound. The application of that approach in practice is that generally discounts range from between one-third for a plea at the earliest stage of proceedings to one tenth of the sentence for a plea tendered at or near a trial diet. The amount of any modification of sentence will always be a matter for the sentencer, and will depend on the timing and circumstances of the plea.

## NOTIFICATION REQUIREMENTS

**9.126** A person convicted of either a sexual offence as listed in Sch 3 to the Sexual Offences Act 2003 (SOA 2003) or in circumstances where a specific offence is not listed but where the court has determined, in terms of para 60 of Sch 3 to SOA 2003, that there was a significant sexual aspect to the offender's behaviour in committing that offence, becomes subject to the notification requirements specified in Part 2 of SOA 2003. The period for which that person will be required to comply with the notification requirements is set out in SOA 2003, s 82. Where either an order for lifelong restriction or a sentence of imprisonment for a term of 30 months or more has been imposed, the relevant offender will be liable to the notification requirements for an indefinite period.

98 CP(S)A 1995, s 196(1).
99 *Du Plooy v HMA*, 2003 SLT 1237; 2003 SCCR 640.
100 2012 SCCR 176.
101 2008 JC 174.

Where a sentence of imprisonment of between 6 and 30 months is imposed, the notification period will be for 10 years. Where a sentence of imprisonment for a term of six months or less is imposed, then the period will be for seven years. If a community payback order including an offender supervision requirement is imposed, the period will be for the period specified for the supervision requirement. If any other disposal is ordered, the offender will be subject to the notification requirements for a period of five years. Where the offender is under the age of 18 on the relevant date, then the relevant periods referred to of ten years, seven years and five years will be reduced by one half.[102]

**9.127** One perhaps unforeseen consequence of these provisions is that a person who has been fined or admonished for an offence, (presumably reflecting the less serious nature of the offence), could be subject to the notification requirements for considerably longer than a person subject to a higher tariff disposal, such as a community payback order.

## POST-RELEASE SUPERVISION

### Extended sentences

**9.128** Cases involving domestic abuse on indictment may often be constituted by, or at least include, sexual or violent offences, and as such the court may impose an extended sentence in terms of CP(S)A 1995, s 210A(1) in respect of offences committed after 30 September 1998.The purpose of extended sentences is to protect the public from serious harm from the offender and they seek to do so by extending the period of licence to which the offender will be subjected to by a further determinate period. Prior to doing so, the court must obtain a separate risk assessment.[103] To be imposed, the court must have formed the view that when the offender comes to be released from the determinate sentence which it is minded to pass, that they will still pose a risk of serious harm to the public.[104] It is not enough, however, for these purposes for the court to simply conclude that the offender should be subject to post-release supervision or that such supervision would be in the public interest;[105] there must be a risk of serious harm to the public. To trigger the requirements of CP(S)A 1995, s 210A(1) in relation to a violent crime, the sentence imposed must be a custodial sentence of four years of more and be imposed in circumstances where the period of licence available following the release of the offender would not be adequate for the purpose of protecting the public from serious harm from the offender. In the case of sexual offences, where the offence falls within one of the categories as set out in CP(S)A 1995,

102 Sexual Offences Act 2003, s 82.
103 CP(S)A 1995, s 210A(4).
104 *DS v HM Advocate* [2017] HCJAC 12.
105 *Tonkin v HM Advocate* [2018] HCJAC 17.

s 210A(1), the foregoing provisions are applicable in relation to any period of imprisonment imposed. In the case of sexual offences, any period of post-licence supervision can only be by way of an extended sentence, and such offence cannot be subject to supervised release orders.

**9.129** For the purposes of CP(S)A 1995, s 201A(1), an extended sentence is the aggregate of:

(a) the term of imprisonment (known as 'the custodial term'); and

(b) the further period (known as 'the extension period') for which the offender is to be subject to a licence and which is of such length as the court considers necessary for the purpose of protecting the public from serious harm from the offender.

**9.130** The sentence imposed will outline the total period of the sentence, which will be broken down into the custodial term and the extension period. In the Sheriff Court, a sheriff may pass a maximum extended sentence of ten years, being a custodial term of five years and an extension period of five years.[106] The High Court can grant an extension period of up to ten years.[107] However, the total term of any extended sentence cannot exceed the maximum term of imprisonment provided for in relation to any statutory offence.[108]

## Supervised release orders

**9.131** In other cases, other than sexual offences as set out in CP(S)A 1995, s 210A(10) where an offence appears on Indictment and the offender is sentenced to a period of imprisonment of less than four years, then the court can impose a supervised release order in terms of CP(S)A 1995, s 209(1), where the court concludes that such an order is necessary to protect the public from serious harm from the offender on his release. Again, it is not enough for the supervision to benefit the offender.[109] Prior to doing so the court will require to obtain a report from a relevant officer of a local authority about the offender and his circumstances.[110] The period of a supervised release order can be for a period of up to one half of the custodial sentence imposed, although this period should not exceed twelve months after the date of the offender's release,[111] and no part of the period should be later that the date by which the entire term of the period of imprisonment imposed has elapsed.[112]

106 CP(S)A 1995, s 210A (6).
107 CP(S)A 1995, s 210A (3).
108 CP(S)A 1995, s 210A(5).
109 *Woods and Others v HM Advocate* 2017 SCCR 100; *Doherty v HM Advocate* 2019 SCCR 35.
110 CP(S)A 1995, s 209(2).
111 CP(S)A 1995, s 209(7)(a).
112 CP(S)A 1995, s 209 (7) (b).

**9.132** Whilst subject to a supervised release order, the offender will be supervised by an officer of the local authority,[113] and comply with such requirements as may have been imposed by the court,[114] and any reasonable requirements of that officer.[115] The purpose of the aforementioned requirements are for the purpose of the securing the good conduct of the person or preventing, or lessening the possibility of his committing a further offence, and should not therefore be punitive in effect.

113 CP(S)A 1995, s 209(3)(a).
114 CP(S)A 1995, s 209(3)(b) (i).
115 CP(S)A 1995, s 209(3)(b) (ii).

*Appendix 1*

# Domestic Abuse (Scotland) Act 2018

An Act of the Scottish Parliament to create an offence with respect to the engaging by a person in a course of behaviour which is abusive of the person's partner or ex-partner; and to make rules of criminal procedure for that offence and also for offences subject to the statutory aggravation involving abuse of partners or ex-partners.

## PART 1 OFFENCE AS TO DOMESTIC ABUSE

## Engaging in course of abusive behaviour

### *1 Abusive behaviour towards partner or ex-partner*

(1) A person commits an offence if—

- (a) the person ('A') engages in a course of behaviour which is abusive of A's partner or ex-partner ('B'), and
- (b) both of the further conditions are met.

(2) The further conditions are—

- (a) that a reasonable person would consider the course of behaviour to be likely to cause B to suffer physical or psychological harm,
- (b) that either—
  - (i) A intends by the course of behaviour to cause B to suffer physical or psychological harm, or
  - (ii) A is reckless as to whether the course of behaviour causes B to suffer physical or psychological harm.

(3) In the further conditions, the references to psychological harm include fear, alarm and distress.

### *2 What constitutes abusive behaviour*

(1) Subsections (2) to (4) elaborate on section 1(1) as to A's behaviour.

(2) Behaviour which is abusive of B includes (in particular)—

- (a) behaviour directed at B that is violent, threatening or intimidating,

(b) behaviour directed at B, at a child of B or at another person that either—

(i) has as its purpose (or among its purposes) one or more of the relevant effects set out in subsection (3), or

(ii) would be considered by a reasonable person to be likely to have one or more of the relevant effects set out in subsection (3).

(3) The relevant effects are of—

(a) making B dependent on, or subordinate to, A,

(b) isolating B from friends, relatives or other sources of support,

(c) controlling, regulating or monitoring B's day-to-day activities,

(d) depriving B of, or restricting B's, freedom of action,

(e) frightening, humiliating, degrading or punishing B.

(4) In subsection (2)—

(a) in paragraph (a), the reference to violent behaviour includes sexual violence as well as physical violence,

(b) in paragraph (b), the reference to a child is to a person who is under 18 years of age.

## *3 Extra-territorial jurisdiction*

(1) An offence under section 1(1) can be constituted by a course of behaviour engaged in by A even if the course of behaviour occurs wholly or partly outside the United Kingdom.

(2) If the course of behaviour occurs wholly outside the United Kingdom—

(a) A may be prosecuted, tried and punished for the offence—

(i) in a sheriff court district in which A is apprehended or in custody, or

(ii) in a sheriff court district that is determined by the Lord Advocate,

as if the offence has been committed entirely in that district,

(b) the offence is, for all things incidental to or consequential on trial and punishment, deemed to have been committed entirely in that district.

(3) Subsections (1) and (2) apply only if A, when the course of behaviour occurs—

(a) is habitually resident in Scotland, or

(b) is a UK national.

(4) 'UK national' means someone who is, as referred to in the British Nationality Act 1981—

(a) a British citizen,

(b) a British overseas territories citizen, a British National (Overseas) or a British Overseas citizen, or

(c) a British subject or a British protected person.

## Evidence, aggravation and defence

### *4 Evidence of impact on victim*

(1) The commission of an offence under section 1(1) does not depend on the course of behaviour actually causing B to suffer harm of the sort mentioned in section 1(2).

(2) The operation of section 2(2)(b) does not depend on behaviour directed at someone actually having on B any of the relevant effects set out in section 2(3).

(3) Nothing done by or mentioned in subsection (1) or (2) prevents evidence from being led in proceedings for an offence under section 1(1) about (as the case may be)—

(a) harm actually suffered by B as a result of the course of behaviour, or

(b) effects actually had on B of behaviour directed at someone.

### *5 Aggravation in relation to a child*

(1) This subsection applies where it is, in proceedings for an offence under section 1(1)—

(a) specified in the complaint or libelled in the indictment that the offence is aggravated by reason of involving a child, and

(b) proved that the offence is so aggravated.

(2) The offence is so aggravated if, at any time in the commission of the offence—

(a) A directs behaviour at a child, or

(b) A makes use of a child in directing behaviour at B.

(3) The offence is so aggravated if a child sees or hears, or is present during, an incident of behaviour that A directs at B as part of the course of behaviour.

(4) The offence is so aggravated if a reasonable person would consider the course of behaviour, or an incident of A's behaviour that forms part of the course of behaviour, to be likely to adversely affect a child usually residing with A or B (or both).

(5) For it to be proved that the offence is so aggravated, there does not need to be evidence that a child—

- (a) has ever had any—
  - (i) awareness of A's behaviour, or
  - (ii) understanding of the nature of A's behaviour, or
- (b) has ever been adversely affected by A's behaviour.

(6) Evidence from a single source is sufficient to prove that the offence is so aggravated.

(7) Where subsection (1) applies, the court must—

- (a) state on conviction that the offence is so aggravated,
- (b) record the conviction in a way that shows that the offence is so aggravated,
- (c) take the aggravation into account in determining the appropriate sentence, and
- (d) state—
  - (i) where the sentence imposed in respect of the offence is different from that which the court would have imposed if the offence were not so aggravated, the extent of and the reasons for that difference, or
  - (ii) otherwise, the reasons for there being no such difference.

(8) Each of subsections (2) to (4) operates separately along with subsection (5), but subsections (2) to (4) may be used in combination along with subsection (5).

(9) Nothing in subsections (2) to (5) prevents evidence from being led about—

- (a) a child's observations of, or feelings as to, A's behaviour, or
- (b) a child's situation so far as arising because of A's behaviour.

(10) In subsections (4) and (5), the references to adversely affecting a child include causing the child to suffer fear, alarm or distress.

(11) In this section, the references to a child are to a person who—

- (a) is not A or B, and
- (b) is under 18 years of age.

## *6 Defence on grounds of reasonableness*

(1) In proceedings for an offence under section 1(1), it is a defence for A to show that the course of behaviour was reasonable in the particular circumstances.

(2) That is to be regarded as shown if—

(a) evidence adduced is enough to raise an issue as to whether the course of behaviour is as described in subsection (1), and

(b) the prosecution does not prove beyond reasonable doubt that the course of behaviour is not as described in subsection (1).

# Presumption, alternative and penalty

## *7 Presumption as to the relationship*

(1) In proceedings for an offence under section 1(1), the matter of B being A's partner or ex-partner is to be taken as established—

(a) according to the stating of the matter in the charge of the offence in the complaint or indictment, and

(b) unless the matter is challenged as provided for in subsection (2).

(2) The matter is challenged—

(a) in summary proceedings, by—

(i) preliminary objection before the plea is recorded, or

(ii) later objection as the court allows in special circumstances,

(b) in proceedings on indictment, by giving notice of a preliminary objection in accordance with section 71(2) or 72(6)(b)(i) of the Criminal Procedure (Scotland) Act 1995.

## *8 Alternative available for conviction*

(1) In proceedings for an offence under section 1(1), A may be convicted of an alternative offence if the facts proved against A—

(a) do not amount to the offence under section 1(1), but

(b) do amount to the alternative offence.

(2) An alternative offence as referred to in subsection (1) is one or other of these—

(a) an offence under section 38(1) (threatening or abusive behaviour) of the Criminal Justice and Licensing (Scotland) Act 2010,

(b) an offence under section 39 (offence of stalking) of that Act.

### *9 Penalty for offence under section 1(1)*

A person who commits an offence under section 1(1) is liable—

(a) on summary conviction, to imprisonment for a term not exceeding 12 months or a fine not exceeding the statutory maximum (or both),

(b) on conviction on indictment, to imprisonment for a term not exceeding 14 years or a fine (or both).

## Meaning given to key expressions

### *10 Meaning of references to behaviour*

(1) Subsections (2) to (4) explain what is meant by the references to behaviour in this Part.

(2) Behaviour is behaviour of any kind, including (for example)—

(a) saying or otherwise communicating something as well as doing something,

(b) intentionally failing—

(i) to do something,

(ii) to say or otherwise communicate something.

(3) Behaviour directed at a person is such behaviour however carried out, including (in particular)—

(a) by way of conduct towards property,

(b) through making use of a third party,

as well as behaviour in a personal or direct manner.

(4) A course of behaviour involves behaviour on at least two occasions.

### *11 Meaning of partner and ex-partner*

(1) Subsections (2) and (3) describe who is a person's partner or ex-partner as referred to in this Part.

(2) Someone is a person's partner if they are—

(a) spouses or civil partners of each other,

(b) living together as if spouses of each other, or

(c) in an intimate personal relationship with each other.

(3) Whether someone is a person's ex-partner is to be determined accordingly.

*Appendix 2*

# Abusive Behaviour and Sexual Harm (Scotland) Act 2016

An Act of the Scottish Parliament to make provision about abusive behaviour; and to make provision about sexual harm including provision about directions to be given to juries in sexual offence cases and provision about orders to prevent future sexual harm.

## PART 1 ABUSIVE BEHAVIOUR

### Abusive behaviour towards partner or ex-partner

#### *1 Aggravation of offence where abuse of partner or ex-partner*[1]

(1) This subsection applies where it is—

(a) libelled in an indictment or specified in a complaint that an offence is aggravated by involving abuse of the partner or ex-partner of the person committing it, and

(b) proved that the offence is so aggravated.

(2) An offence is aggravated as described in subsection (1)(a) if in committing the offence—

(a) the person intends to cause the partner or ex-partner to suffer physical or psychological harm, or

(b) in the case only of an offence committed against the partner or ex-partner, the person is reckless as to causing the partner or ex-partner to suffer physical or psychological harm.

(3) It is immaterial for the purposes of subsection (2) that the offence does not in fact cause the partner or ex-partner physical or psychological harm.

(4) Evidence from a single source is sufficient to prove that an offence is aggravated as described in subsection (1)(a).

(5) Where subsection (1) applies, the court must—

(a) state on conviction that the offence is aggravated as described in subsection (1)(a),

1 Repealed by the Domestic Abuse (Scotland) Act 2018, s 12(1), Schedule, para 11(1), (2).

(b) record the conviction in a way that shows that the offence is so aggravated,

(c) take the aggravation into account in determining the appropriate sentence, and

(d) state—

(i) where the sentence imposed in respect of the offence is different from that which the court would have imposed if the offence were not so aggravated, the extent of and the reasons for that difference, or

(ii) otherwise, the reasons for there being no such difference.

(6) For the purposes of this section, a person is a partner of another person if they are—

(a) spouses or civil partners of each other,

(b) living together as if spouses …[1] of each other, or

(c) in an intimate personal relationship with each other,

and the references to a person's ex-partner are to be construed accordingly.

(7) In this section—

'cause' includes contribute to causing (and 'causing' is to be construed accordingly),

'psychological harm' includes fear, alarm or distress.

1 Repealed by the Domestic Abuse (Scotland) Act 2018, s 12(1), Schedule, para 11(1), (2).

## *[1A Presumption as to the relationship*[2]

(1) In proceedings for an offence that is aggravated as described in section 1(1)(a), the matter of a person being another person's partner or ex-partner is to be taken as established—

(a) according to the stating of the matter in the charge of the offence in the complaint or indictment, and

(b) unless the matter is challenged as provided for in subsection (2).

(2) The matter is challenged—

(a) in summary proceedings, by—

(i) preliminary objection before the plea is recorded, or

(ii) later objection as the court allows in special circumstances,

2 Inserted by the Domestic Abuse (Scotland) Act 2018, s 12(1), Schedule, para 11(1), (3).

(b) in proceedings on indictment, by giving notice of a preliminary objection in accordance with section 71(2) or 72(6)(b)(i) of the 1995 Act.][1]

## Disclosure of an intimate photograph or film

### *2 Disclosing, or threatening to disclose, an intimate photograph or film*

(1) A person ('A') commits an offence if—

(a) A discloses, or threatens to disclose, a photograph or film which shows, or appears to show, another person ('B') in an intimate situation,

(b) by doing so, A intends to cause B fear, alarm or distress or A is reckless as to whether B will be caused fear, alarm or distress, and

(c) the photograph or film has not previously been disclosed to the public at large, or any section of the public, by B or with B's consent.

(2) For the purposes of this section, a photograph or film is disclosed if it, or any data or other thing which is capable of being converted into it, is given, shown or made available to a person other than B.

(3) In proceedings for an offence under subsection (1), A has a defence if any of the following facts is established—

(a) B consented to the photograph or film being disclosed,

(b) A reasonably believed that B consented to the photograph or film being disclosed,

(c) A reasonably believed that disclosure of the photograph or film was necessary for the purposes of the prevention, detection, investigation or prosecution of crime, or

(d) A reasonably believed that disclosure of the photograph or film was in the public interest.

(4) For the purposes of subsection (3), consent to the photograph or film being disclosed may be—

(a) consent which is specific to the particular disclosure or (as the case may be) the particular threatened disclosure, or

(b) consent to disclosure generally where that consent covers the particular disclosure or (as the case may be) the particular threatened disclosure.

(5) In proceedings for an offence under subsection (1), A has a defence if the following matter is established—

(a) B was in the intimate situation shown in the photograph or film,

(b) B was not in the intimate situation as a result of a deliberate act of another person to which B did not agree, and

(c) when B was in the intimate situation—

(i) B was in a place to which members of the public had access (whether or not on payment of a fee), and

(ii) members of the public were present.

(6) For the purposes of subsection (3), a fact is established, and for the purposes of subsection (5), the matter is established, if—

(a) sufficient evidence is adduced to raise an issue as to whether that is the case, and

(b) the prosecution does not prove beyond reasonable doubt that it is not the case.

(7) A person who commits an offence under subsection (1) is liable—

(a) on summary conviction, to imprisonment for a term not exceeding 12 months or a fine not exceeding the statutory maximum (or both),

(b) on conviction on indictment, to imprisonment for a term not exceeding 5 years or a fine (or both).

## *3 Interpretation of section 2*

(1) For the purposes of section 2, a person is in an 'intimate situation' if—

(a) the person is engaging or participating in, or present during, an act which—

(i) a reasonable person would consider to be a sexual act, and

(ii) is not of a kind ordinarily done in public, or

(b) the person's genitals, buttocks or breasts are exposed or covered only with underwear.

(2) In section 2—

'film' means a moving image in any form, whether or not the image has been altered in any way, that was originally captured by making a recording, on any medium, from which a moving image may be produced, and includes a copy of the image,

'photograph' means a still image in any form, whether or not the image has been altered in any way, that was originally captured by photography, and includes a copy of the image.

*Appendix 3*

# Bail, etc under the Criminal Procedure (Scotland) Act 1995

An Act to consolidate certain enactments relating to criminal procedure in Scotland.

## PART III BAIL

### *[22A Consideration of bail on first appearance*

(1) On the first occasion on which—

(a) a person accused on petition is brought before the sheriff prior to committal until liberated in due course of law; or

(b) a person charged on complaint with an offence is brought before a judge having jurisdiction to try the offence,

the sheriff or, as the case may be, the judge shall, after giving that person and the prosecutor an opportunity to be heard …[1], either admit or refuse to admit that person to bail.

[(1A) Before determining whether to admit or refuse to admit the person accused or charged to bail, the sheriff or judge must also give an officer of a local authority an opportunity to provide (orally or in writing) information relevant to that determination.][2]

[(2) Admittance to or refusal of bail shall be determined before the end of the day (not being a Saturday or Sunday, or a court holiday prescribed for the court which is to determine the question of bail, unless that court is sitting on that day for the disposal of criminal business) after the day on which the person accused or charged is brought before the sheriff or judge.][3]

(3) If, by [that time][3], the sheriff or judge has not admitted or refused to admit the person accused or charged to bail, then that person shall be forthwith liberated.

(4) This section applies whether or not the person accused or charged is in custody when that person is brought before the sheriff or judge.][4]

1 Repealed by the Criminal Proceedings etc. (Reform) (Scotland) Act 2007, s 6(1)(a).
2 Inserted by the Bail and Release from Custody (Scotland) Act 2023, s 1(1), (2).
3 Substituted by the Criminal Proceedings etc. (Reform) (Scotland) Act 2007, s 6(1)(b), (c).
4 Inserted by the Bail, Judicial Appointments etc. (Scotland) Act 2000, s 1.

## *23 Bail applications.*

(1) Any person accused on petition of a crime ...[1] shall be entitled immediately, on any [(other than the first)][2] occasion on which he is brought before the sheriff prior to his committal until liberated in due course of law, to apply to the sheriff for bail, and the prosecutor shall be entitled to be heard against any such application.

(2) The sheriff shall be entitled in his discretion to refuse such application before the person accused is committed until liberated in due course of law.

(3) Where an accused is admitted to bail without being committed until liberated in due course of law, it shall not be necessary so to commit him, and it shall be lawful to serve him with an indictment or complaint without his having been previously so committed.

(4) Where bail is refused before committal until liberation in due course of law on an application under subsection (1) above, the application for bail may be renewed after such committal.

(5) Any sheriff having jurisdiction to try the offence or to commit the accused until liberated in due course of law may, at his discretion, on the application of any person who has been committed until liberation in due course of law for any crime or offence, ...[1], and having given the prosecutor an opportunity to be heard, admit or refuse to admit the person to bail.

[(6) Any person charged on complaint with an offence shall, on any (other than the first) occasion on which he is brought before a judge having jurisdiction to try the offence, be entitled to apply to the judge for bail and the prosecutor shall be entitled to be heard against any such application.][3]

(7) An application under subsection (5) or (6) above shall be disposed of [before the end of the day (not being a Saturday or Sunday, or a court holiday prescribed for the court which is to determine the question of bail, unless that court is sitting on that day for the disposal of criminal business) after the day of][4] its presentation to the judge, failing which the accused shall be forthwith liberated.

(8) This section applies whether or not the accused is in custody at the time he appears for disposal of his application.

1 Repealed by the Bail, Judicial Appointments etc. (Scotland) Act 2000, s 12, Schedule, para 7(1)(a)(i), (b).
2 Inserted by the Bail, Judicial Appointments etc. (Scotland) Act 2000, s 12, Schedule, para 7(1)(a)(ii).
3 Substituted by the Bail, Judicial Appointments etc. (Scotland) Act 2000, s 12, Schedule, para 7(1)(c).
4 Substituted by the Criminal Proceedings etc. (Reform) (Scotland) Act 2007, s 6(2).

## [23A Bail and liberation where person already in custody

(1) A person may be admitted to bail under section 22A, [23, 65(8C) or 107A(7)(b)][1] of this Act although in custody—

(a) having been refused bail in respect of another crime or offence; or

(b) serving a sentence of imprisonment.

(2) A decision to admit a person to bail by virtue of subsection (1) above does not liberate the person from the custody mentioned in that subsection.

(3) The liberation under section [22A(3), 23(7) or 107A(7)(b)][1] of this Act of a person who may be admitted to bail by virtue of subsection (1) above does not liberate that person from the custody mentioned in that subsection.

(4) In subsection (1) above, 'another crime or offence' means a crime or offence other than that giving rise to the consideration of bail under section 22A, [23, 65(8C) or 107A(7)(b)][1] of this Act.][2]

1 Substituted by the Criminal Justice and Licensing (Scotland) Act 2010, s 203, Sch 7, paras 25, 35.
2 Inserted by the Bail, Judicial Appointments etc. (Scotland) Act 2000, s 2.

## [23B Entitlement to bail and the court's function

[(1) Bail is to be granted to an accused person unless the court determines that there is good reason for refusing bail.

(1A) The court may determine that there is good reason for refusing bail only if it considers that—

(a) at least one of the grounds specified in section 23C(1) applies, and

(b) having regard to the public interest, and having considered the imposition of bail conditions in accordance with subsection (2), it is necessary to refuse bail—

(i) in the interests of public safety, including the protection of the complainer from a risk of harm, or

(ii) to prevent a significant risk of prejudice to the interests of justice.][1]

(2) In determining a question of bail in accordance with subsection (1) above, the court is to consider the extent to which the public interest could, if bail were granted, be safeguarded by the imposition of bail conditions.

(3) …[2]

(4) The court must (without prejudice to any other right of the parties to be heard) give the prosecutor and the accused person an opportunity to make submissions in relation to a question of bail [(including submissions in relation

to any information provided by an officer of a local authority under section 22A(1A) or in response to a request under subsection (6))][3].

(5) The attitude of the prosecutor towards a question of bail (including as to bail conditions) does not restrict the court's exercise of its discretion in determining the question in accordance with subsection (1) above.

(6) For the purpose of so determining a question of bail (including as to bail conditions), the court may request the prosecutor or the accused person's solicitor or counsel [or an officer of a local authority][3] to provide it with information relevant to the question.

[(6A) Where relevant to a question of bail, and without prejudice to the generality of subsection (6), the court may in particular request the prosecutor to provide it with information in relation to the risk of harm to the complainer.][3]

(7) However, whether [the prosecutor, the accused person's solicitor or counsel, or an officer of a local authority][4] gives the court opinion as to any risk of something occurring (or any likelihood of something not occurring) is a matter for that party [or officer][3] to decide.

[(8) For the purposes of subsections (1A)(b)(i) and (6A)—

'complainer' means the person against whom the offence to which the proceedings relate is alleged to have been committed,

'harm' means physical or psychological harm,

'psychological harm' includes fear, alarm and distress.

(9) For the purposes of subsection (1A)(b)(ii), 'prejudice to the interests of justice' means—

(a) the accused person evading justice as a result of the proceedings being delayed or discontinued, or

(b) the course of justice in the proceedings being impeded or prejudiced as a result of—

(i) the destruction, concealment or withholding of evidence,

(ii) the giving of false or misleading evidence, or

(iii) the quality of evidence, or its sufficiency in law, being diminished.

(10) In subsection (9)(b)(iii), the reference to the quality of evidence is to its quality in terms of completeness, accuracy and probative value.][5]][1]

1 Substituted by the Bail and Release from Custody (Scotland) Act 2023, s 2(1), (2)(a).
2 Repealed by the Bail and Release from Custody (Scotland) Act 2023, s 2(1), (2)(b).
3 Inserted by the Bail and Release from Custody (Scotland) Act 2023, s 1(1), (3)(a)-(c), (d)(ii).
4 Substituted by the Bail and Release from Custody (Scotland) Act 2023, s 1(1), (3)(d)(i).
5 Inserted by the Bail and Release from Custody (Scotland) Act 2023, s 2(1), (2)(c).
6 Inserted by the Criminal Proceedings etc. (Reform) (Scotland) Act 2007, s 1.

## *[23C Grounds relevant as to question of bail*

(1) In any proceedings in which a person is accused of an offence, the following are grounds on which it may be determined that there is good reason for refusing bail—

(a) [subject to subsection (1A),][1] any substantial risk that the person might if granted bail—

(i) abscond; or

(ii) fail to appear at a diet of the court as required;

(b) any substantial risk of the person committing further offences if granted bail;

(c) any substantial risk that the person might if granted bail—

(i) interfere with witnesses; or

(ii) otherwise obstruct the course of justice,

in relation to himself or any other person;

(d) any other substantial factor which appears to the court to justify keeping the person in custody.

[(1A) When determining whether there is good reason for refusing bail in summary proceedings, the court may take account of any such risk as is mentioned in subsection (1)(a) only where—

(a) the person has previously failed to appear at a relevant diet, or

(b) the proceedings relate to an offence under section 27(1)(a) or 150(8).][1]

(2) In assessing the grounds specified in subsection (1) above, the court must have regard to all material considerations including (in so far as relevant in the circumstances of the case) the following examples—

(a) the—

(i) nature (including level of seriousness) of the offences before the court;

(ii) probable disposal of the case if the person were convicted of the offences;

(b) whether the person was subject to a bail order when the offences are alleged to have been committed;

(c) whether the offences before the court are alleged to have been committed—

(i) while the person was subject to another court order;

(ii) while the person was on release on licence or parole;

(iii) during a period for which sentence of the person was deferred;

(d) the character and antecedents of the person, in particular—

(i) the nature of any previous convictions of the person (including convictions [by courts outside [Scotland][2]][3]);

(ii) whether the person has previously contravened a bail order or other court order (by committing an offence or otherwise);

(iii) whether the person has previously breached the terms of any release on licence or parole (by committing an offence or otherwise);

(iv) whether the person is serving or recently has served a sentence of imprisonment in connection with a matter referred to in sub-paragraphs (i) to (iii) above;

(e) the associations and community ties of the person.

[(3) In subsection (1A)(a), 'relevant diet' means a diet of the court relating to the offence with which the person is charged—

(a) of which the person has been given due notice, or

(b) at which the person is required by this Act to appear.][1]][4]

1 Inserted by the Bail and Release from Custody (Scotland) Act 2023, s 2(1), (3).
2 Substituted by the Criminal Justice (EU Exit) (Scotland) (Amendment etc.) Regulations 2020, SSI 2020/339, reg 13(1), (2).
3 Substituted by the Criminal Justice and Licensing (Scotland) Act 2010, s 71(1), Sch 4, paras 1, 2.
4 Inserted by the Criminal Proceedings etc. (Reform) (Scotland) Act 2007, s 1.

## *[23D Restriction on bail in certain solemn cases*

...[1]][2]

1 Repealed by the Bail and Release from Custody (Scotland) Act 2023, s 3.
2 Inserted by the Criminal Proceedings etc. (Reform) (Scotland) Act 2007, s 1.

## *24 Bail and bail conditions.*

(1) All crimes and offences ...[1] are bailable.

(2) Nothing in this Act shall affect the right of the Lord Advocate or the High Court to admit to bail any person charged with any crime or offence.

[(2A) Whenever the court grants or refuses bail, it shall state its reasons.

[(2AA) Where the court refuses bail in any proceedings in which a person is accused of an offence, it must—

(a) state in particular—

(i) the grounds on which it determines, in accordance with section 23B(1A), that there is good reason for refusing bail,

(ii) if refusing bail solely on the ground specified in section 23C(1)(a) (substantial risk of absconding or failing to appear), its reasons for considering under section 23B(1A)(b) that it is necessary to do so, and

(iii) its reasons for considering under section 23B(1A)(b) and (2) that either it would not be appropriate to impose on the accused bail conditions subject to a requirement to submit to monitoring in accordance with Part 1 of the Management of Offenders (Scotland) Act 2019 (electronic monitoring) or that doing so would not adequately safeguard the interests of public safety or justice as mentioned in section 23B(1A)(b)(i) or (ii), and

(b) have the grounds mentioned in paragraph (a)(i) entered in the record of the proceedings.][2]

(2B) Where the court—

(a) grants bail to a person accused of [an offence falling within subsection (2C)][3]; and

(b) does so without imposing on the accused further conditions under subsection (4)(b)(i) below,

the court shall also state why it considers in the circumstances of the case that such conditions are unnecessary.][4]

[(2C) An offence falls within this subsection if it is—

(a) a sexual offence (having the meaning given by section 210A(10) and (11)),

(b) an offence under section 1(1) of the Domestic Abuse (Scotland) Act 2018,

(c) an offence that is aggravated as described in section 1(1)(a) of the Abusive Behaviour and Sexual Harm (Scotland) Act 2016,

(d) an offence under section 39 of the Criminal Justice and Licensing (Scotland) Act 2010 (offence of stalking),

(e) an attempt, conspiracy or incitement to commit an offence mentioned in paragraph (b), (c) or (d),

(f) aiding, abetting, counselling or procuring the commission of an offence mentioned in paragraph (b), (c) or (d).][2]

(3) It shall not be lawful to grant bail or release for a pledge or deposit of money, and—

(a) release on bail may be granted only on conditions which subject to subsection (6) below, shall not include a pledge or deposit of money;

(b) liberation may be granted by the police under [section 25 of the Criminal Justice (Scotland) Act 2016][5].

(4) In granting bail the court or, as the case may be, the Lord Advocate shall impose on the accused—

(a) the standard conditions; and

(b) such further conditions as the court or, as the case may be, the Lord Advocate considers necessary to secure—

(i) that the standard conditions are observed; …[6]

(ii) …[6]

(5) The standard conditions referred to in subsection (4) above are conditions that the accused—

(a) appears at the appointed time at every diet relating to the offence with which he is charged of which he is given due notice [or at which he is required by this Act to appear][7];

(b) does not commit an offence while on bail;

(c) does not interfere with witnesses or otherwise obstruct the course of justice whether in relation to himself or any other person; …[8]

[(ca) does not behave in a manner which causes, or is likely to cause, alarm or distress to witnesses;][4]

[(cb) whenever reasonably instructed by a constable to do so—

(i) participates in an identification parade or other identification procedure; and

(ii) allows any print, impression or sample to be taken from the accused;][9]

(d) makes himself available for the purpose of enabling enquiries or a report to be made to assist the court in dealing with him for the offence with which he is charged[; and

(e) where the (or an) offence in respect of which he is admitted to bail is one [listed in subsection (7A)(b)][10], does not seek to obtain, otherwise than by way of a solicitor, any precognition of or statement by the complainer in relation to the subject matter of the offence.][11]

(6) The court or, as the case may be, the Lord Advocate may impose as one of the conditions of release on bail a requirement that the accused or a cautioner on his behalf deposits a sum of money in court, but only where the court or, as the case may be, the Lord Advocate is satisfied that the imposition of such condition is appropriate to the special circumstances of the case.

[(6A) Subsection (6) above does not apply in relation to an accused admitted to bail under section 65(8C) of this Act.][1]

(7) In any enactment, including this Act and any enactment passed after this Act—

(a) any reference to bail shall be construed as a reference to release on conditions in accordance with this Act or to conditions imposed on bail, as the context requires;

(b) any reference to an amount of bail fixed shall be construed as a reference to conditions, including a sum required to be deposited under subsection (6) above;

(c) any reference to finding bail or finding sufficient bail shall be construed as a reference to acceptance of conditions imposed or the finding of a sum required to be deposited under subsection (6) above.

[[(7A) For the purpose of subsection (5)(e)—

(a) 'complainer' means the person against whom the offence is alleged to have been committed,

(b) the list is—

(i) an offence to which section 288C applies (certain sexual offending),

(ii) an offence to which section 288DC applies (domestic abuse cases).][10]][11]

(8) In this section [(other than subsection (2AA))][2] and sections 25 and 27 to 29 of this Act, references to an accused and to appearance at a diet shall include references respectively to an appellant and to appearance at the court on the day fixed for the hearing of an appeal.

1 Repealed by the Bail, Judicial Appointments etc. (Scotland) Act 2000, s 3(1).
2 Inserted by the Bail and Release from Custody (Scotland) Act 2023, s 4(1), (2), (4), (5).
3 Substituted by the Bail and Release from Custody (Scotland) Act 2023, s 4(1), (3).
4 Inserted by the Criminal Proceedings etc. (Reform) (Scotland) Act 2007, s 2(1)(a), (c).
5 Substituted by the Criminal Justice (Scotland) Act 2016 (Consequential and Supplementary Modifications) Regulations 2017, SSI 2017/452, reg 2(1), Schedule, para 12(1), (2).
6 Repealed by the Criminal Justice and Licensing (Scotland) Act 2010, s 58(a).
7 Inserted by the Criminal Procedure (Amendment) (Scotland) Act 2004, s 25, Schedule, paras 1, 5.

8 Repealed by the Sexual Offences (Procedure and Evidence) (Scotland) Act 2002, s 5(1)(a).
9 Inserted by the Criminal Justice and Licensing (Scotland) Act 2010, s 58(b).
10 Substituted by the Domestic Abuse (Scotland) Act 2018, s 12(1), Schedule, para 2.
11 Inserted by the Sexual Offences (Procedure and Evidence) (Scotland) Act 2002, s 5(1)(b), (2).

## *[24A ...[1]*

...[1]][2]

1 Repealed by the Criminal Justice and Licensing (Scotland) Act 2010, s 59.
2 Inserted by the Criminal Procedure (Amendment) (Scotland) Act 2004, s 17.

## *[24B ...[1]*

...[1]][2]

1 Repealed by the Criminal Justice and Licensing (Scotland) Act 2010, s 59.
2 Inserted by the Criminal Procedure (Amendment) (Scotland) Act 2004, s 17.

## *[24C ...[1]*

...[1]][2]

1 Repealed by the Criminal Justice and Licensing (Scotland) Act 2010, s 59.
2 Inserted by the Criminal Procedure (Amendment) (Scotland) Act 2004, s 17.

## *[24D ...[1]*

...[1]][2]

1 Repealed by the Criminal Justice and Licensing (Scotland) Act 2010, s 59.
2 Inserted by the Criminal Procedure (Amendment) (Scotland) Act 2004, s 17.

## *[24E ...[1]*

...[1]][2]

1 Repealed by the Criminal Justice and Licensing (Scotland) Act 2010, s 59.
2 Inserted by the Criminal Procedure (Amendment) (Scotland) Act 2004, s 17.

## [[24F][1] Bail: extradition proceedings

(1) In the application of the provisions of this Part by virtue of section 9(2) or 77(2) of the Extradition Act 2003 (judge's powers at extradition hearing), those provisions apply with the modifications that—

(a) references to the prosecutor are to be read as references to a person acting on behalf of the territory to which extradition is sought;

(b) the right of the Lord Advocate mentioned in section 24(2) of this Act applies to a person subject to extradition proceedings as it applies to a person charged with any crime or offence;

(c) the following do not apply—

[(ai) subsection (1A) of section 23C;][2]

(i) paragraph (b) of section 24(3); and

(ii) subsection (3) of section 30; and

(d) sections 28(1) and 33 apply to a person subject to extradition proceedings as they apply to an accused.

[(1A) In the application of the provisions of this Part by virtue of section 7(7) of the Extradition Act 2003 (identity of person arrested), those provisions apply with the modification that subsection (1A) of section 23C does not apply.][2]

(2) Section 32 of this Act applies in relation to a refusal of bail, the amount of bail or a decision to allow bail or ordain appearance in proceedings under this Part as the Part applies by virtue of the sections of that Act of 2003 mentioned in subsection (1) above.

(3) The Scottish Ministers may, by order, for the purposes of section 9(2) or 77(2) of the Extradition Act 2003 make such amendments to this Part as they consider necessary or expedient.

(4) The order making power in subsection (3) above shall be exercisable by statutory instrument subject to annulment in pursuance of a resolution of the Scottish Parliament.][3]

1 Renumbered by the Criminal Procedure (Amendment) (Scotland) Act 2004 (Incidental, Supplemental and Consequential Provisions) Order 2005, SSI 2005/40, art 4(1), 2).
2 Inserted by the Bail and Release from Custody (Scotland) Act 2023 (Consequential Modifications) Order 2024, SI 2024/1316, art 3.
3 Inserted by the Extradition Act 2003, s 199.

## *25 Bail conditions: supplementary.*

[(A1) When granting bail, the court shall (if the accused is present) explain to the accused in ordinary language—

(a) the effect of the conditions imposed;

(b) the effect of the requirement under subsection (2B) below; and

(c) the consequences which may follow a breachof any of those conditions or that requirement.

(B1) The accused shall (whether or not the accused is present when bail is granted) be given a written explanation in ordinary language of the matters mentioned in paragraphs (a) to (c) of subsection (A1) above.

(C1) Such a written explanation may be contained in the copy of the bail order given to the accused or in another document.][1]

(1) The court shall specify in the order granting bail, a copy of which shall be given to the accused—

- (a) the conditions imposed; and
- [(aa) that breach of a condition imposed is an offence and renders the accused liable to arrest, prosecution and punishment under this Act;][1]
- (b) an address, within the United Kingdom (being the accused's normal place of residence or such other place as the court may, on cause shown, direct) which, subject to subsection (2) below, shall be his proper domicile of citation.

(2) The court may on application in writing by the accused while he is on bail alter the address specified in the order granting bail, and this new address shall, as from such date as the court may direct, become his proper domicile of citation; and the court shall notify the accused of its decision on any application under this subsection.

[(2A) Where an application is made under subsection (2) above—

- (a) the application shall be intimated by the accused immediately and in writing to the Crown Agent [and for that purpose the application shall be taken to be intimated to the Crown Agent if intimation of it is sent to the procurator fiscal for the sheriff court district in which bail was granted][2]; and
- (b) the court shall, before determining the application, give the prosecutor an opportunity to be heard.][3]

[(2B) Where the domicile of citation specified in an order granting bail ceases to be the accused's normal place of residence, the accused must make an application under subsection (2) above within 7 days of that happening.

(2C) A person who without reasonable excuse contravenes subsection (2B) above is guilty of an offence and is liable—

- (a) on conviction in the JP court, to a fine not exceeding level 3 on the standard scale or to imprisonment for a period not exceeding 60 days or to both;
- (b) in any other case, to a fine not exceeding level 3 on the standard scale or to imprisonment for a period not exceeding 12 months or to both.][1]

(3) In this section 'proper domicile of citation' means the address at which the accused may be cited to appear at any diet relating to the offence with which he is charged or an offence charged in the same proceedings as that offence or to which any other intimation or document may be sent; and any citation at or the sending of an intimation or document to the proper domicile of citation shall be presumed to have been duly carried out.

[(4) In this section, references to the court (other than in subsection (2A)) shall, in relation to a person who has been admitted to bail by the Lord Advocate, be read as if they were references to the Lord Advocate.][4]

1 Inserted by the Criminal Proceedings etc. (Reform) (Scotland) Act 2007, s 2(2).
2 Inserted by the Criminal Procedure (Amendment) (Scotland) Act 2004 (Incidental, Supplemental and Consequential Provisions) Order 2005, SSI 2005/40, art 3(1), (4).
3 Inserted by the Criminal Procedure (Amendment) (Scotland) Act 2004, s 18(1), (2).
4 Inserted by the Criminal Procedure (Amendment) (Scotland) Act 2004, s 25, Schedule, paras 1, 6.

## *[25A Failure to accept conditions of bail under section 65(8C): continued detention of accused*

An accused who—

(a) is, by virtue of subsection (4) of section 65 of this Act, entitled to be admitted to bail; but

(b) fails to accept any of the conditions imposed by the court on bail under subsection (8C) of that section,

shall continue to be detained under the committal warrant for so long as he fails to accept any of those conditions.]

1 Inserted by the Criminal Procedure (Amendment) (Scotland) Act 2004, s 25, Schedule, paras 1, 7.

## *26 ...[1]*

...[1]

1 Repealed by the Bail, Judicial Appointments etc. (Scotland) Act 2000, s 3(2)

## *27 Breach of bail conditions: offences.*

(1) Subject to subsection (7) below, an accused who having been granted bail fails without reasonable excuse—

(a) to appear at the time and place appointed for any diet of which he has been given due notice [or at which he is required by this Act to appear][1]; or

(b) to comply with any other condition imposed on bail,

shall, subject to subsection (3) below, be guilty of an offence and liable on conviction to the penalties specified in subsection (2) below.

(2) The penalties mentioned in subsection (1) above are—

(a) a fine not exceeding level 3 on the standard scale; and

(b) imprisonment for a period—

(i) where conviction is in the [JP court][2], not exceeding 60 days; or

(ii) in any other case, not exceeding [12][3] months.

(3) Where, and to the extent that, the failure referred to in subsection (1)(b) above consists in the accused having committed an offence while on bail (in this section referred to as 'the subsequent offence'), he shall not be guilty of an offence under that subsection but, subject to subsection (4) below, the court which sentences him for the subsequent offence shall, in determining the appropriate sentence or disposal for that offence, have regard to—

(a) the fact that the offence was committed by him while on bail and the number of bail orders to which he was subject when the offence was committed;

(b) any previous conviction of the accused of an offence under subsection (1)(b) above; and

(c) the extent to which the sentence or disposal in respect of any previous conviction of the accused differed, by virtue of this subsection, from that which the court would have imposed but for this subsection.

[[(3A) The reference in subsection (3)(b) to any previous conviction of an offence under subsection (1)(b) includes—

(a) any previous conviction by a court in England and Wales or Northern Ireland, and

(b) if the court considers appropriate, any previous conviction by a court in a member State of the European Union,

of an offence that is equivalent to an offence under subsection (1)(b).][4]

(3B) The references in subsection (3)(c) to subsection (3) are to be read, in relation to a previous conviction by a court referred to in subsection (3A), as references to any provision that is equivalent to subsection (3).

(3C) Any issue of equivalence arising in pursuance of subsection (3A) or (3B) is for the court to determine.][5]

(4) The court shall not, under subsection (3) above, have regard to the fact that the subsequent offence was committed while the accused was on bail unless that fact is libelled in the indictment or, as the case may be, specified in the complaint.

[(4A) The fact that the subsequent offence was committed while the accused was on bail shall, unless challenged—

(a) in the case of proceedings on indictment, by giving notice of a preliminary objection [in accordance with section 71(2) or 72(6)(b)(i)][6] of this Act; or

(b) in summary proceedings, by preliminary objection before his plea is recorded,

be held as admitted.][7]

[(4B) In any proceedings in relation to an offence under subsection (1) above or subsection 7 below, the fact that (as the case may be) an accused—

(a) was on bail;

(b) was subject to any particular condition of bail;

(c) failed to appear at a diet; or

(d) was given due notice of a diet,

shall, unless challenged in the manner described in paragraph (a) or (b) of subsection (4A) above, be held as admitted.][8]

(5) Where the maximum penalty in respect of the subsequent offence is specified by or by virtue of any enactment, that maximum penalty shall, for the purposes of the court's determination, by virtue of subsection (3) above, of the appropriate sentence or disposal in respect of that offence, be increased—

(a) where it is a fine, by the amount for the time being equivalent to level 3 on the standard scale; and

(b) where it is a period of imprisonment—

  (i) as respects a conviction in the High Court or the sheriff court, by 6 months; and

  (ii) as respects a conviction in the [JP court][2], by 60 days,

notwithstanding that the maximum penalty as so increased exceeds the penalty which it would otherwise be competent for the court to impose.

(6) Where the sentence or disposal in respect of the subsequent offence is, by virtue of subsection (3) above, different from that which the court would have imposed but for that subsection, the court shall state the extent of and the reasons for that difference.

[(6A) Where, despite the requirement to have regard to the matters specified in paragraphs (a) to (c) of subsection (3) above, the sentence or disposal in respect of the subsequent offence is not different from that which the court would have imposed but for that subsection, the court shall state (as appropriate, by reference to those matters) the reasons for there being no difference.][8]

(7) An accused who having been granted bail in relation to solemn proceedings fails without reasonable excuse to appear at the time and place appointed for any diet of which he has been given due notice (where such diet is in respect of solemn proceedings) shall be guilty of an offence and liable on conviction on indictment to the following penalties—

- (a) a fine; and
- (b) imprisonment for a period not exceeding [5][3] years.

(8) At any time before the trial of an accused under solemn procedure for the original offence, it shall be competent—

- (a) to amend the indictment to include an additional charge of an offence under this section;
- (b) to include in the list of witnesses or productions relating to the original offence, witnesses or productions relating to the offence under this section.

[(8A) At any time before the trial of an accused in summary proceedings for the original offence, it is competent to amend the complaint to include an additional charge of an offence under this section.][9]

(9) [A penalty under subsection (2) or (7) above shall][3] be imposed in addition to any other penalty which it is competent for the court to impose, notwithstanding that the total of penalties imposed may exceed the maximum penalty which it is competent to impose in respect of the original offence.

[(9A) The reference in subsection (9) above to a penalty being imposed in addition to another penalty means, in the case of sentences of imprisonment or detention—

- (a) where the sentences are imposed at the same time (whether or not in relation to the same complaint or indictment), framing the sentences so that they have effect consecutively;
- (b) where the sentences are imposed at different times, framing the sentence imposed later so that (if the earlier sentence has not been served) the later sentence has effect consecutive to the earlier sentence.

(9B) Subsection (9A)(b) above is subject to section 204A of this Act.][8]

(10) A court which finds an accused guilty of an offence under this section may remit the accused for sentence in respect of that offence to any court which is considering the original offence.

(11) In this section 'the original offence' means the offence with which the accused was charged when he was granted bail or an offence charged in the same proceedings as that offence.

1 Inserted by the Criminal Procedure (Amendment) (Scotland) Act 2004, s 25, Schedule, paras 1, 8(a).
2 Substituted by the Criminal Proceedings etc. (Reform) (Scotland) Act 2007, s 80, Schedule, para 26(c).
3 Substituted by the Criminal Proceedings etc. (Reform) (Scotland) Act 2007, s 3(1)(a), (d), (e).
4 Substituted by the Criminal Justice (EU Exit) (Scotland) (Amendment etc.) Regulations 2020, SSI 2020/339, reg 13(1), (4).
5 Inserted by the Criminal Justice and Licensing (Scotland) Act 2010, s 71(1), Sch 4, paras 1, 3.
6 Substituted by the Criminal Procedure (Amendment) (Scotland) Act 2004, s 25, Schedule, paras 1, 8(b).
7 Inserted by the Criminal Procedure and Investigations Act 1996, s 73(1), (2).
8 Inserted by the Criminal Proceedings etc. (Reform) (Scotland) Act 2007, s 3(1)(b), (c), (f).
9 Inserted by the Criminal Justice and Licensing (Scotland) Act 2010, s 62(1).

## *28 Breach of bail conditions: arrest of offender, etc.*

(1) A constable may arrest without warrant an accused who has been released on bail where the constable has reasonable grounds for suspecting that the accused has broken, is breaking, or is likely to break any condition imposed on his bail.

[(1ZA) Where—

(a) a constable who is not in uniform arrests a person under subsection (1), and

(b) the person asks to see the constable's identification,

the constable must show identification to the person as soon as reasonably practicable.][1]

[(1A) Where an accused who has been released on bail is arrested by a constable (otherwise than under subsection (1) above), the accused may be detained in custody under this subsection if the constable has reasonable grounds for suspecting that the accused has breached, or is likely to breach, any condition imposed on his bail.

(1B) Subsection (1A) above—

(a) is without prejudice to any other power to detain the accused;

(b) applies even if release of the accused would be required but for that subsection.][2]

(2) An accused who is arrested under [subsection (1) above, or is detained under subsection (1A) above,][3] shall wherever practicable be brought before

the court to which his application for bail was first made not later than in the course of the first day after his arrest, such day not being, subject to subsection (3) below, a Saturday, a Sunday or a court holiday prescribed for that court under section 8 of this Act.

(3) Nothing in subsection (2) above shall prevent an accused being brought before a court on a Saturday, a Sunday or such a court holiday where the court is, in pursuance of the said section 8, sitting on such day for the disposal of criminal business.

[(3A) If—

(a) a person is in custody only by virtue of subsection (1) or (1A), and

(b) in the opinion of a constable there are no reasonable grounds for suspecting that the person has broken, or is likely to break, a condition imposed on the person's bail,

the person must be released from custody immediately.

(3B) An accused is deemed to be brought before a court under subsection (2) or (3) if the accused appears before it by means of a live television link (by virtue of a determination by the court that the person is to do so by such means).][1]

(4) Where an accused is brought before a court under subsection (2) or (3) above, the court, after hearing the parties, may—

(a) recall the order granting bail;

(b) release the accused under the original order granting bail; or

(c) vary the order granting bail so as to contain such conditions as the court thinks it necessary to impose to secure that the accused complies with the requirements of paragraphs (a) to (d) of section 24(5) of this Act.

[(4A) In the case of an accused released on bail by virtue of section 65(8C) of this Act—

(a) subsection (2) above shall have effect as if the reference to the court to which his application for bail was first made were a reference to the court or judge which admitted him to bail under that section; and

(b) subsection (4) above shall not apply and subsection (4B) below shall apply instead.

(4B) Where an accused referred to in subsection (4A) above is, under subsection (2) or (3) above, brought before the court or judge which admitted him to bail under section 65(8C)—

(a) the court or judge shall give the prosecutor an opportunity to make an application under section 65(5) of this Act; and

(b) if the prosecutor does not make such an application, or if such an application is made but is refused, the court or judge may—

(i) release the accused under the original order granting bail; or

(ii) vary the order granting bail so as to contain such conditions as the court or judge thinks necessary to impose to secure that the accused complies with the requirements of paragraphs (a) to (d) of section 24(5) of this Act.][4]

(5) The same rights of appeal shall be available against any decision of the court under subsection (4) above as were available against the original order of the court relating to bail.

(6) For the purposes of this section and section 27 of this Act, an extract from the minute of proceedings, containing the order granting bail and bearing to be signed by the clerk of court, shall be sufficient evidence of the making of that order and of its terms and of the acceptance by the accused of the conditions imposed under section 24 of this Act.

1 Inserted by the Criminal Justice (Scotland) Act 2016, s 56, Sch 2, paras 26, 29.
2 Inserted by the Criminal Proceedings etc. (Reform) (Scotland) Act 2007, s 3(2)(a).
3 Substituted by the Criminal Proceedings etc. (Reform) (Scotland) Act 2007, s 3(2)(b).
4 Inserted by the Criminal Procedure (Amendment) (Scotland) Act 2004, s 25, Schedule, paras 1, 9.

## *[28A Application of the Criminal Justice (Scotland) Act 2016 to persons arrested and detained under section 28*

(1) Section 7(2) of the Criminal Justice (Scotland) Act 2016 ('the 2016 Act') does not apply to an accused who has been arrested under section 28(1) of this Act.

(2) The following provisions of the 2016 Act apply in relation to a person who is to be brought before a court under section 28(2) or (3) of this Act as they apply in relation to a person who is to be brought before a court in accordance with section 21(2) of the 2016 Act—

(a) section 22,

(b) section 23,

(c) section 24.

(3) In relation to a person who is to be brought before a court under section 28(2) or (3) of this Act, the 2016 Act applies as though—

(a) in section 23(2)—

(i) for paragraph (c) there were substituted—

'(c) that the person is to be brought before the court under section 28 of the 1995 Act in order for the person's bail to be considered.', and

(ii) paragraph (d) were omitted,

(b) in section 24—

(i) in subsection (3)(c), for the words 'after being officially accused' there were substituted 'after being informed that the person is to be brought before a court under section 28(2) or (3) of the 1995 Act', and

(ii) in subsection (4), for paragraph (c) there were substituted—

'(c) that the person is to be brought before the court under section 28 of the 1995 Act in order for the person's bail to be considered.',

(c) in section 43(1), for paragraph (d) there were substituted—

'(d) the court before which the person is to be brought under section 28(2) or (3) of the 1995 Act and the date on which the person is to be brought before that court.'.][1]

1 Inserted by the Criminal Justice (Scotland) Act 2016, s 56, Sch 2, paras 26, 30.

## *29 Bail: monetary conditions.*

(1) Without prejudice to section 27 of this Act, where the accused or a cautioner on his behalf has deposited a sum of money in court under section 24(6) of this Act, then—

(a) if the accused fails to appear at the time and place appointed for any diet of which he has been given due notice, the court may, on the motion of the prosecutor, immediately order forfeiture of the sum deposited;

(b) if the accused fails to comply with any other condition imposed on bail, the court may, on conviction of an offence under section 27(1)(b) of this Act and on the motion of the prosecutor, order forfeiture of the sum deposited.

(2) If the court is satisfied that it is reasonable in all the circumstances to do so, it may recall an order made under subsection (1)(a) above and direct that the money forfeited shall be refunded, and any decision of the court under this subsection shall be final and not subject to review.

(3) A cautioner, who has deposited a sum of money in court under section 24(6) of this Act, shall be entitled, subject to subsection (4) below, to recover the sum deposited at any diet of the court at which the accused appears personally.

(4) Where the accused has been charged with an offence under section 27(1)(b) of this Act, nothing in subsection (3) above shall entitle a cautioner to recover the sum deposited unless and until—

(a) the charge is not proceeded with; or

(b) the accused is acquitted of the charge; or

(c) on the accused's conviction of the offence, the court has determined not to order forfeiture of the sum deposited.

(5) The references in subsections (1)(b) and (4)(c) above to conviction of an offence shall include references to the making of an order in respect of the offence under section 246(3) of this Act.

## *30 Bail review.*

(1) This section applies where a court has refused to admit a person to bail or, where a court has so admitted a person, the person has failed to accept the conditions imposed or that a sum required to be deposited under section 24(6) of this Act has not been so deposited.

[(1A) This section also applies where a person who has accepted the conditions imposed on his bail wants to have any of them removed or varied.][1]

(2) A court shall, on the application of any person mentioned in subsection (1) [or (1A) above, have power to review (in favour of the person) its decision as to bail, or its decision as to the conditions imposed, if—

(a) the circumstances of the person have changed materially; or

(b) the person puts before the court material information which was not available to it when its decision was made.][2]

[[(2A) On receipt of an application under subsection (2), the court must—

(a) intimate the application to the prosecutor, and

(b) before determining the application, give the prosecutor an opportunity to be heard.

(2AA) Despite subsection (2A)(b), the court may grant the application without having heard the prosecutor if the prosecutor consents.][3]

(2B) Subsection (2C) below applies where an application is made under subsection (2) above by a person convicted on indictment pending the 5determination of—

(a) his appeal;

(b) any relevant appeal by the Lord Advocate under section 108 or 108A of this Act; or

(c) the sentence to be imposed on, or other method of dealing with, him.

(2C) Where this subsection applies the application shall be—

(a) intimated by the person making it immediately and in writing to the Crown Agent; and

(b) [determined][3] not less than 7 days after the date of that intimation.][4]

(3) An application under this section, where it relates to the original decision of the court, shall not be made before the fifth day after that decision and, where it relates to a subsequent decision, before the fifteenth day thereafter.

(4) Nothing in this section shall affect any right of a person to appeal against the decision of a court in relation to admitting to bail or to the conditions imposed.

1 Inserted by the Criminal Proceedings etc. (Reform) (Scotland) Act 2007, s 4(1)(a).
2 Substituted by the Criminal Proceedings etc. (Reform) (Scotland) Act 2007, s 4(1)(b).
3 Substituted by the Criminal Justice and Licensing (Scotland) Act 2010, s 57(1), (2).
4 Inserted by the Criminal Procedure (Amendment) (Scotland) Act 2004, s 18(1), (3).

## *31 Bail review on prosecutor's application.*

(1) On an application by the prosecutor at any time after a court has granted bail to a person the court may, where the prosecutor puts before the court material information which was not available to it when it granted bail to that person, review its decision.

(2) On receipt of an application under subsection (1) above the court shall—

(a) intimate the application to the person granted bail;

(b) fix a diet for hearing the application and cite that person to attend the diet; and

(c) where it considers that the interests of justice so require, grant warrant to arrest that person.

[(2ZA) Despite subsection (2)(b), the court may grant the application without fixing a hearing if the person granted bail consents.][1]

[(2A) Subsection (2B) below applies to an application under subsection (1) above where the person granted bail—

(a) was convicted on indictment; and

(b) was granted bail pending the determination of—

(i) his appeal;

(ii) any relevant appeal by the Lord Advocate under section 108 or 108A of this Act; or

(iii) the sentence to be imposed on, or other method of dealing with, him.

(2B) Where this subsection applies, the application shall be heard not more than 7 days after the day on which it is made.][2]

(3) On …[3] an application under subsection (1) above the court may—

(a) withdraw the grant of bail and remand the person in question in custody; or

(b) grant bail, or continue the grant of bail, either on the same or on different conditions.

[(3A) In relation to an accused admitted to bail under section 65(8C) of this Act—

(a) an application may be made under subsection (1) above only in relation to the conditions imposed on bail; and

(b) paragraph (a) of subsection (3) above shall not apply in relation to any such application.][4]

(4) Nothing in the foregoing provisions of this section shall affect any right of appeal against the decision of a court in relation to bail.

1 inserted by the Criminal Justice and Licensing (Scotland) Act 2010, s 57(1), (3)(a).
2 Inserted by the Criminal Procedure (Amendment) (Scotland) Act 2004, s 18(1), (4).
3 Repealed by the Criminal Justice and Licensing (Scotland) Act 2010, s 57(1), (3)(b).
4 Inserted by the Criminal Procedure (Amendment) (Scotland) Act 2004, s 25, Schedule, paras 1, 10.

## *32 Bail appeal.*

(1) [Where, in any case, bail][1] is refused or where the [accused][2] is dissatisfied with the amount of bail fixed, he may appeal to the [appropriate Appeal Court][3] which may, in its discretion order intimation to the Lord Advocate or, as the case may be, the prosecutor.

(2) Where, in any case, …[4] bail is granted, or, in summary proceedings an accused is ordained to appear, the public prosecutor, if dissatisfied—

(a) with the decision allowing bail;

(b) with the amount of bail fixed; or

(c) in summary proceedings, that the accused has been ordained to appear,

may appeal to the [appropriate Appeal Court][3], and the [accused][2] shall not be liberated, subject to subsection (7) below, until the appeal by the prosecutor is disposed of.

[(2A) The public prosecutor may, in relation to an accused admitted to bail under section 65(8C) of this Act, appeal under subsection (2) above only in relation to the conditions imposed on bail.][5]

(3) Written notice of appeal shall be immediately given to the opposite party by a party appealing under this section.

[(3A) A notice of appeal under this section is to be lodged with the clerk of the court from which the appeal is to be taken.

(3B) When an appeal is made under this section, that clerk shall without delay—

(a) send a copy of the notice of appeal to the judge whose decision is the subject of the appeal; and

(b) request the judge to provide a report of the reasons for that decision.

(3C) The judge shall, as soon as is reasonably practicable, provide that clerk with the judge's report of those reasons.

[(3CA) The clerk of the court from which the appeal is to be taken (unless that clerk is the Clerk of Justiciary) must—

(a) send the notice of appeal without delay to the clerk of the appropriate Appeal Court, and

(b) before the end of the day after the day of receipt of the notice of appeal, send the judge's report (if provided by then) to the clerk of the appropriate Appeal Court.][3]

(3F) The [clerk of the appropriate Appeal Court][3] shall, upon receipt of the notice of appeal, without delay fix a diet for the hearing of the appeal.

(3G) The [clerk of the appropriate Appeal Court][3] shall send a copy of the judge's report to—

(a) the accused or his solicitor; and

(b) the Crown Agent.

(3H) [In a case where the Sheriff Appeal Court is the appropriate Appeal Court, if][3] the judge's report is not sent as mentioned in subsection [(3CA)][3] above—

(a) the [appropriate Appeal Court][3] may call for the report to be submitted to it within such period as it may specify; or

(b) if it thinks fit, hear and determine the appeal without the report.

(3I) Subject to subsection (3G) above, the judge's report shall be available only to the [appropriate Appeal Court][3], the parties and, on such conditions as may be prescribed by Act of Adjournal, such other persons or classes of person as may be so prescribed.][6]

(4) An appeal under this section shall be disposed of by the [appropriate Appeal Court][3] or any [judge of the appropriate Appeal Court][3] in court or in chambers after such inquiry and hearing of parties as shall seem just.

(5) Where an [accused][2] in an appeal under this section is under 21 years of age, section 51 of this Act shall apply to the [appropriate Appeal Court][3] or, as the case may be, the [judge of the appropriate Appeal Court][3] when disposing of the appeal as it applies to a court when remanding or committing a person of the [accused's][2] age for trial or sentence.

(6) In the event of the appeal of the public prosecutor under this section being refused, the court may award expenses against him.

(7) When an appeal is taken by the public prosecutor either against the grant of bail or against the amount fixed, the [accused][2] to whom bail has been granted [(other than an accused to whom subsection (7B) below applies)][5] shall, if the bail fixed has been found by him, be liberated after 72 hours from the granting of [bail][2], whether the appeal has been disposed of or not, unless the [appropriate Appeal Court][3] grants an order for his further detention in custody.

[(7B) Where, in relation to an accused admitted to bail under section 65(8C) of this Act, the public prosecutor appeals against the conditions imposed on bail, the accused—

(a) may continue to be detained under the committal warrant for no more than 72 hours from the granting of bail or for such longer period as [the appropriate Appeal Court][3] may allow; and

(b) on expiry of that period, shall, whether the appeal has been disposed of or not, be released on bail subject to the conditions imposed.][5]

(8) In computing the period mentioned in subsection (7) above, Sundays and public holidays, whether general or court holidays, shall be excluded.

(9) When an appeal is taken under this section by the prosecutor in summary proceedings against the fact that the accused has been ordained to appear, subsections (7) and (8) above shall apply as they apply in the case of an appeal against the granting of bail or the amount fixed.

(10) Notice to the governor of the prison of the issue of an order such as is mentioned in subsection (7) above within the time mentioned in that subsection bearing to be sent by the [clerk of the appropriate Appeal Court][3] or the Crown Agent shall be sufficient warrant for the detention of the [accused][2] pending arrival of the order in due course of post.

[(11) In this section—

'appropriate Appeal Court' means—

(a) in the case of an appeal under this section against a bail decision of the High Court or a judge of the High Court, that Court,

(b) in the case of an appeal under this section against a bail decision of the Sheriff Appeal Court, the High Court,

(c) in the case of an appeal under this section against a bail decision of a sheriff (whether in solemn or summary proceedings) or a JP court, the Sheriff Appeal Court,

'judge of the appropriate Appeal Court' means—

(a) in a case where the High Court is the appropriate Appeal Court, judge of that Court,

(b) in a case where the Sheriff Appeal Court is the appropriate Appeal Court, Appeal Sheriff,

'the clerk of the appropriate Appeal Court' means—

(a) in a case where the High Court is the appropriate Appeal Court, the Clerk of Justiciary,

(b) in a case where the Sheriff Appeal Court is the appropriate Appeal Court, the Clerk of that Court.

(12) In a case where the Sheriff Appeal Court is the appropriate Appeal Court, the references in subsections (3G)(b) and (10) to the Crown Agent are to be read as references to the prosecutor.][7]

1 Substituted by the Bail, Judicial Appointments etc. (Scotland) Act 2000, s 4.
2 Substituted by the Bail, Judicial Appointments etc. (Scotland) Act 2000, s 12, Schedule, para 7(2)(a), (c).
3 Substituted by the Courts Reform (Scotland) Act 2014, s 122(1)-(7).
4 Repealed by the Bail, Judicial Appointments etc. (Scotland) Act 2000, s 12, Schedule, para 7(2)(b).
5 Inserted by the Criminal Procedure (Amendment) (Scotland) Act 2004, s 25, Schedule, paras 1, 11.
6 Inserted by the Criminal Proceedings etc. (Reform) (Scotland) Act 2007, s 4(2).
7 Inserted by the Courts Reform (Scotland) Act 2014, s 122(1), (8).

## *[32A Bail after conviction: prosecutor's attitude*

(1) Where—

(a) a person has been convicted in any proceedings of an offence; and

(b) a question of bail (including as to bail conditions) subsequently arises in the proceedings (whether before sentencing or pending appeal or otherwise),

the prosecutor and the convicted person must be given an opportunity to make submissions in relation to the question.

(2) But the attitude of the prosecutor towards the question does not restrict the court's exercise of its discretion in determining the question in accordance with the rules applying in the case.

(3) Despite subsection (1) above, the prosecutor need not be given an opportunity to make submissions in relation to a question of bail arising under section 245J of this Act.

(4) This section is without prejudice to any other right of the parties to be heard.][1]

1 Inserted by the Criminal Proceedings etc. (Reform) (Scotland) Act 2007, s 5.

## *33 Bail: no fees exigible.*

No clerks fees, court fees or other fees or expenses shall be exigible from or awarded against an accused in respect of [a decision on bail under section 22A above, an][1] application for bail or of the appeal of such [a decision or][2] application to the High Court.

1 Substituted by the Bail, Judicial Appointments etc. (Scotland) Act 2000, s 12, Schedule, para 7(3)(a).
2 Inserted by the Bail, Judicial Appointments etc. (Scotland) Act 2000, s 12, Schedule, para 7(3)(b).

*Appendix 4*

# Non-harassment orders under the Criminal Procedure (Scotland) Act 1995

## PART XI SENTENCING

### Non-harassment orders

*234A Non-harassment orders.*

[(1) This section applies where a person is—

(a) convicted of an offence involving misconduct towards another person ('the victim'),

(b) acquitted of such an offence by reason of the special defence set out in section 51A, or

(c) found by a court to be unfit for trial under section 53F in respect of such an offence and the court determines that the person has done the act or made the omission constituting the offence.

(1A) The prosecutor may apply to the court to make (instead of or in addition to dealing with the person in any other way) a non-harassment order against the person.

(1B) A non-harassment order is an order requiring the person to refrain, for such period (including an indeterminate period) as may be specified in the order, from such conduct in relation to the victim as may be specified in the order.][1]

(2) On an application under subsection [(1A)][1] above the court may, if it is satisfied on a balance of probabilities that it is appropriate to do so in order to protect the victim from [harassment (or further harassment)][2], make a non-harassment order.

[(2A) The court may, for the purpose of subsection (2) above, have regard to any information given to it for that purpose by the prosecutor—

(a) about any other offence involving misconduct towards the victim—

(i) of which the [person against whom the order is sought][1] has been convicted, or

(ii) as regards which the [person against whom the order is sought][1] has accepted (or has been deemed to have accepted) a fixed penalty or compensation offer under section 302(1) or 302A(1) or as regards which a work order has been made under section 303ZA(6),

(b) in particular, by way of—

(i) an extract of the conviction along with a copy of the complaint or indictment containing the charge to which the conviction relates, or

(ii) a note of the terms of the charge to which the fixed penalty offer, compensation offer or work order relates.

(2B) But the court may do so only if the court may, under section 101 or 101A (in a solemn case) or section 166 or 166A (in a summary case), have regard to the conviction or the offer or order.

[(2BA) The court may, for the purpose of subsection (2) above, have regard to any information given to it for that purpose by the prosecutor about any other offence involving misconduct towards the victim—

(a) in respect of which the person against whom the order is sought was acquitted by reason of the special defence set out in section 51A, or

(b) in respect of which the person against whom the order is sought was found by a court to be unfit for trial under section 53F and the court determined that the person had done the act or made the omission constituting the offence.][3]

(2C) The court must give the [person against whom the order is sought][1] an opportunity to make representations in response to the application.][4]

[(3) A non-harassment order made by a criminal court may be appealed against—

(a) if the order was made in a case falling within subsection (1)(a) above, as if the order were a sentence,

(b) if the order was made in a case falling within subsection (1)(b) or (c) above, as if the person had been convicted of the offence concerned and the order were a sentence passed on the person for the offence.

(3A) A variation or revocation of a non-harassment order made under subsection (6) below may be appealed against—

(a) if the order was made in a case falling within subsection (1)(a) above, as if the variation or revocation were a sentence,

(b) if the order was made in a case falling within subsection (1)(b) or (c) above, as if the person had been convicted of the offence concerned and the variation or revocation were a sentence passed on the person for the offence.][1]

(4) Any person who is ...[5] in breach of a non-harassment order shall be guilty of an offence and liable—

(a) on conviction on indictment, to imprisonment for a term not exceeding 5 years or to a fine, or to both such imprisonment and such fine; and

(b) on summary conviction, to imprisonment for a period not exceeding 6 months or to a fine not exceeding the statutory maximum, or to both such imprisonment and such fine.

[(4A) ...[6]

(4B) ...[6]][7]

(5) ...[8]

(6) The person against whom a non-harassment order is made, or the prosecutor at whose instance the order is made, may apply to the court which made the order for its revocation or variation and, in relation to any such application the court concerned may, if it is satisfied on a balance of probabilities that it is appropriate to do so, revoke the order or vary it in such manner as it thinks fit, but not so as to increase the period for which the order is to run.

[(7) For the purposes of this section—

'harassment' and 'conduct' are to be construed in accordance with section 8 of the Protection from Harassment Act 1997 (c.40),

'misconduct' includes conduct that causes alarm or distress.][2]][9]

1 Substituted by the Abusive Behaviour and Sexual Harm (Scotland) Act 2016, s 5(1)-(4), (6), (7).
2 Substituted by the Criminal Justice and Licensing (Scotland) Act 2010, s 15(b), (d).
3 Inserted by the Abusive Behaviour and Sexual Harm (Scotland) Act 2016, s 5(1), (5).
4 Inserted by the Criminal Justice and Licensing (Scotland) Act 2010, s 15(c).
5 Repealed by the Criminal Justice (Scotland) Act 2003, s 49(1)(a).
6 Repealed by the Criminal Justice (Scotland) Act 2016, s 56, Sch 2, paras 1, 3(1).
7 Inserted by the Criminal Justice (Scotland) Act 2003, s 49(1)(b).
8 Repealed by the Crime and Punishment (Scotland) Act 1997, s 62, Sch 1, para. 21(1), (30), Sch 3.
9 Inserted by the Protection from Harassment Act 1997, s 11; S.I. 1997/1418, art. 2

## *[234AZA Non-harassment orders: domestic abuse cases*

(1) Section 234A applies subject to this section if an offence referred to in subsection (1) of that section is one listed in subsection (2)(c).

(2) For the purposes of this section—

(a) 'victim' has the same meaning as it has in section 234A,

(b) 'child' has the same meaning as given by section 5(11) of the Domestic Abuse (Scotland) Act 2018,

(c) the list is—

(i) an offence under section 1(1) of the Domestic Abuse (Scotland) Act 2018,

(ii) an offence that is aggravated as described in section 1(1)(a) of the Abusive Behaviour and Sexual Harm (Scotland) Act 2016.

(3) A non-harassment order in the person's case may include provision for the order to apply in favour of any of the following, in addition to the victim—

(a) in any circumstances, a child usually residing with the person or a child usually residing with the victim (or a child usually residing with both the person and the victim),

(b) where the offence is one under section 1(1) of the Domestic Abuse (Scotland) Act 2018, and is aggravated as described in section 5(1)(a) of that Act, a child to whom the aggravation relates,

if the court is satisfied that it is appropriate for the child to be protected by the order.

(4) The court must—

(a) without an application by the prosecutor, consider [the question of][1] whether to make a non-harassment order in the person's case,

(b) after hearing the prosecutor as well as the person, make such an order unless of a negative conclusion on the question,

(c) if of a negative conclusion on the question, explain the basis for this.

(5) Here, a negative conclusion on the question is the conclusion by the court that there is no need for—

(a) the victim, or

(b) the children (if any) in mind by virtue of subsection (3),

to be protected by such an order.

(6) In the operation of section 234A along with subsection (4)—

(a) subsection (1A) of that section is of no effect (and the reference in subsection (2) of that section to an application under subsection (1A) of that section is to be ignored),

(b) further—

(i) the references in subsections (2A), (2BA) and (2C) of that section to the person against whom the order is sought are to be read as being to the person in whose case the making of a non-harassment order is being considered,

(ii) the reference in subsection (2C) of that section to representations in response to the application is to be read as being to representations on the question of whether to make a non-harassment order,

(iii) the reference in subsection (6) of that section to the prosecutor at whose instance the order is made is to be read as being to the prosecutor in the case in which the non-harassment order is made.

(7) For the avoidance of doubt, nothing in this section affects the ability to make a non-harassment order in the case instead of or in addition to dealing with the person in any other way.][2]

1 Inserted by the Management of Offenders (Scotland) Act 2019, s 63(2), Sch 1, para 3.
2 Inserted by the Domestic Abuse (Scotland) Act 2018, s 15.

*Appendix 5*

# Vulnerable witnesses under the Criminal Procedure (Scotland) Act 1995

## PART XII EVIDENCE

### Special measures for child witnesses and other vulnerable witnesses

### *271 Vulnerable witnesses: main definitions*

[(1) For the purposes of this Act, a person who is giving or is to give evidence at, or for the purposes of, a hearing in relevant criminal proceedings is a vulnerable witness if—

(a) the person is under the age of 18 on the date of commencement of the proceedings in which the hearing is being or is to be held,

(b) there is a significant risk that the quality of the evidence to be given by the person will be diminished by reason of—

(i) mental disorder (within the meaning of section 328 of the Mental Health (Care and Treatment) (Scotland) Act 2003), or

(ii) fear or distress in connection with giving evidence at the hearing,

(c) the offence is alleged to have been committed against the person in proceedings for—

(i) an offence listed in any of paragraphs 36 to 59ZL of Schedule 3 to the Sexual Offences Act 2003,

(ii) an offence under section 22 of the Criminal Justice (Scotland) Act 2003 (traffic in prostitution etc.),

(iii) an offence under section 4 of the Asylum and Immigration (Treatment of Claimants, etc.) Act 2004 (trafficking people for exploitation),

[(iiia) an offence of human trafficking (see section 1 of the Human Trafficking and Exploitation (Scotland) Act 2015),][1]

(iv) an offence the commission of which involves domestic abuse, or

(v) an offence of stalking, or

(d) there is considered to be a significant risk of harm to the person by reason only of the fact that the person is giving or is to give evidence in the proceedings.][2]

[(1AA) The Scottish Ministers may by order subject to the affirmative procedure modify subsection (1)(c).][3]

(1A) …[4]

(2) In determining whether a person is a vulnerable witness by virtue of subsection (1)(b) [or (d)][3] above, the court shall take into account—

(a) the nature and circumstances of the alleged offence to which the proceedings relate,

(b) the nature of the evidence which the person is likely to give,

(c) the relationship (if any) between the person and the accused,

(d) the person's age and maturity,

(e) any behaviour towards the person on the part of—

(i) the accused,

(ii) members of the family or associates of the accused,

(iii) any other person who is likely to be an accused or a witness in the proceedings, and

(f) such other matters, including—

(i) the social and cultural background and ethnic origins of the person,

(ii) the person's sexual orientation,

(iii) the domestic and employment circumstances of the person,

(iv) any religious beliefs or political opinions of the person, and

(v) any physical disability or other physical impairment which the person has,

as appear to the court to be relevant.

(3) For the purposes of subsection (1)(a)[, section 271B(1)(b) and sections 271BZA to 271BZC][5], proceedings shall be taken to have [commenced—

(a) where it is relevant to a court's consideration of whether to authorise the use of the special measure of taking evidence by commissioner (on its own or in combination with any other special measure) and the accused has appeared on petition, on the date when the accused appeared on petition, or

(b) in any other case, on the date][5] when the indictment or, as the case may be, complaint is served on the accused.

(4) In subsection (1)(b) above, the reference to the quality of evidence is to its quality in terms of completeness, coherence and accuracy.

[(4A) In determining whether a person is a vulnerable witness under subsection (1)(b) or (d), the court must—

(a) have regard to the best interests of the witness, and

(b) take account of any views expressed by the witness.][3]

(5) In this section and sections 271A to 271M of this Act—

['child witness' means a vulnerable witness referred to in subsection (1)(a),][6]

'court' means the High Court or the sheriff court,

['deemed vulnerable witness' means a vulnerable witness referred to in subsection (1)(c),][6]

['hearing in relevant criminal proceedings' means any hearing in the course of any criminal proceedings in the High Court or the sheriff court.][7]

...[8]

(6) In sections 271A to 271M of this Act, 'special measure' means any of the special measures set out in, or prescribed under, section 271H below.][9]

1 Inserted by the Human Trafficking and Exploitation (Scotland) Act 2015, s 43, Schedule, para 1.
2 Substituted by the Victims and Witnesses (Scotland) Act 2014, s 10(a).
3 Inserted by the Victims and Witnesses (Scotland) Act 2014, s 10(b), (d), (e).
4 Repealed by the Victims and Witnesses (Scotland) Act 2014, s 10(c).
5 Substituted by the Vulnerable Witnesses (Criminal Evidence) (Scotland) Act 2019, s 5(1), (6).
6 Inserted by the Victims and Witnesses (Scotland) Act 2014, s 11(3).
7 Inserted by the Criminal Justice and Licensing (Scotland) Act 2010, s 87(1), (2)(b)(ii).
8 Repealed by the Criminal Justice and Licensing (Scotland) Act 2010, s 87(1), (2)(b)(i).
9 Substituted by the Vulnerable Witnesses (Scotland) Act 2004, s 1(1).

## *[271A [Child and deemed vulnerable witnesses]*[1]

(1) Where a child witness [or a deemed vulnerable witness][2] is to give evidence at or for the purposes of [a hearing in relevant criminal proceedings][3], the ...[4] witness is entitled, subject to—

(a) subsections (2) to (13) below, and

(b) section 271D of this Act,

to the benefit of one or more of the special measures for the purpose of giving evidence.

(2) [Subject to section 271AA, a party][5] citing or intending to cite a child witness [or a deemed vulnerable witness][2] shall, [by the required time][6], lodge with the court a notice (referred to in this Act as a '[vulnerable][1] witness notice')—

(a) specifying the special measure or measures which the party considers to be the most appropriate for the purpose of taking the …[4] witness's evidence, or

(b) if the party considers that the …[4] witness should give evidence without the benefit of any special measure, stating that fact.

(3) A [vulnerable][1] witness notice shall contain or be accompanied by—

(a) a summary of any views expressed for the purposes of section 271E(2)(b) of this Act, and

(b) such other information as may be prescribed by Act of Adjournal.

[(3A) In the case where a vulnerable witness notice under subsection (2)(a) specifies only a standard special [measure—

(a) subsection (3)(a) does not apply, and

(b) subsection (5) has effect as if the words 'not earlier than 7 days and' were omitted][7].][2]

(4) The court may, on cause shown, allow a [vulnerable][1] witness notice to be lodged after [the required time][6].

[(4A) Any party to the proceedings may, not later than 7 days after a vulnerable witness notice has been lodged, lodge with the court a notice (referred to in this section as an 'objection notice') stating—

(a) an objection to any special measure (other than a standard special measure) specified in the vulnerable witness notice that the party considers to be inappropriate, and

(b) the reasons for that objection.

(4B) The court may, on cause shown, allow an objection notice to be lodged after the period referred to in subsection (4A).

(4C) If an objection notice is lodged in accordance with subsection (4A) or (4B)—

(a) subsection (5)(a)(ii) does not apply to the vulnerable witness notice, and

(b) the court must make an order under subsection (5A).][8]

(5) The court shall, not [earlier than 7 days and not later than 14][9] days after a [vulnerable][1] witness notice has been lodged, consider the notice in the absence of the parties and, subject to [sections 271B to 271BZB][10] of this Act—

(a) in the case of a notice under subsection (2)(a) above—

(i) if a standard special measure is specified in the notice, make an order authorising the use of that measure for the purpose of taking the …[4] witness's evidence, and

(ii) if any other special measure is specified in the notice and the court is satisfied on the basis of the notice that it is appropriate to do so, make an order authorising the use of the special measure (in addition to any authorised by virtue of an order under sub-paragraph (i) above) for the purpose of taking the …[4] witness's evidence,

(b) in the case of a notice under subsection (2)(b) above, if—

(i) the summary of views accompanying the notice under subsection (3)(a) above indicates that the …[4] witness has expressed a wish to give evidence without the benefit of any special measure, and

(ii) the court is satisfied on the basis of the notice that it is appropriate to do so,

make an order authorising the giving of evidence by the …[4] witness without the benefit of any special measure, or

(c) if—

(i) paragraph (a)(ii) or (b) above would apply but for the fact that the court is not satisfied as mentioned in that paragraph, or

(ii) in the case of a notice under subsection (2)(b), the summary of views accompanying the notice under subsection (3)(a) above indicates that the …[4] witness has not expressed a wish to give evidence without the benefit of any special measure,

make an order [under subsection (5A) below.][6]

[(5A) That order is an order—

(a) in the case of proceedings in the High Court where the preliminary hearing is yet to be held, appointing the [vulnerable][1] witness notice to be disposed of at that hearing;

(b) in the case of proceedings on indictment in the sheriff court where the first diet is yet to be held, appointing the [vulnerable][1] witness notice to be disposed of at that diet; or

(c) in any other case, appointing a diet to be held before [the hearing at which the evidence is to be given][3] and requiring the parties to attend the diet.][11]

(6) Subsection (7) below applies where—

(a) it appears to the court that a party intends to call a child witness [or a deemed vulnerable witness][2] to give evidence at or for the purposes of [a hearing in relevant criminal proceedings][3],

(b) the party has not lodged a [vulnerable][1] witness notice in respect of the …[4] witness by the time specified in subsection (2) above [or lodged a notice with the clerk of court in accordance with section 271AA by the time specified in that section][12], and

(c) the court has not allowed a [vulnerable][1] witness notice in respect of the …[4] witness to be lodged after that time under subsection (4) above [or under section 271AA(5)][12].

(7) Where this subsection applies, the court shall—

(a) order the party to lodge a [vulnerable][2] witness notice in respect of the …[4] witness by such time as the court may specify, or

[(b) where the court does not so order—

(i) in the case of proceedings on indictment where this subsection applies at or before the preliminary hearing or, as the case may be, the first diet, at that hearing or diet make an order under subsection (9) below; or

(ii) in any other case, make an order appointing a diet to be held before [the hearing at which the evidence is to be given][3] diet and requiring the parties to attend the diet.][6]

(8) On making an order under subsection [(5A)(c) or (7)(b)(ii)][6] above, the court may postpone [the hearing at which the evidence is to be given][3].

[(8A) Subsection (9) below applies to—

(a) a preliminary hearing or first diet, so far as the court is—

(i) by virtue of an order under subsection (5A)(a) or (b) above, disposing of a [vulnerable][1] witness notice at the hearing or diet; or

(ii) by virtue of subsection (7)(b)(i) above, to make an order under subsection (9) …[4] at the hearing or diet; and

(b) a diet appointed under subsection (5A)(c) or (7)(b)(ii) above.][11]

(9) [Subject to section 271B, at][13] a [hearing or diet to which this subsection applies][6], the court, after giving the parties an opportunity to be heard—

(a) in a case where any of the standard special measures has been authorised by an order under subsection (5)(a)(i) above, may make an order authorising the use of such further special measure or measures as it considers appropriate for the purpose of taking the …[4] witness's evidence, and

(b) in any other case, shall make an order—

(i) authorising the use of such special measure or measures as the court considers to be the most appropriate for the purpose of taking the …[4] witness's evidence, or

(ii) that the …[4] witness is to give evidence without the benefit of any special measure.

(10) [Subject to section 271B, the court][13] may make an order under subsection (9)(b)(ii) above only if satisfied—

(a) where the …[4] witness has expressed a wish to give evidence without the benefit of any special measure, that it is appropriate for the …[4] witness so to give evidence, or

(b) in any other case, that—

(i) the use of any special measure for the purpose of taking the evidence of the …[4] witness would give rise to a significant risk of prejudice to the fairness of the trial or otherwise to the interests of justice, and

(ii) that risk significantly outweighs any risk of prejudice to the interests of the …[4] witness if the order is made.

(11) A [hearing or diet to which subsection (9) above applies][6] may—

(a) on the application of the party citing or intending to cite the …[4] witness in respect of whom the diet is to be held, or

(b) of the court's own motion,

be held in chambers.

(12) A diet [appointed under subsection (5A)(c) or (7)(b)(ii) above in any case may be conjoined with any other diet to be held before [the hearing at which the evidence is to be given][3].][6]

(13) A party lodging a [vulnerable][1] witness notice [or an objection notice][8] shall, at the same time, intimate the notice to the other parties to the proceedings.

[(13A) In subsections (2) and (4) above, 'the required time' means—

[(a) any time before a date has been fixed for one of the following—

(i) a preliminary hearing in the High Court,

(ii) a first diet in the sheriff court, or

(iii) a hearing at which the evidence is to be given, or

(b) if a date has been fixed—

(i) for a preliminary hearing in the High Court, no later than 14 clear days before the preliminary hearing,

(ii) for a first diet in the sheriff court in the case of proceedings on indictment, no later than 7 clear days before the first diet, or

(iii) in a case in which the proceedings are not to take place in the High Court or on indictment in the sheriff court, for a hearing at which the evidence is to be given, no later than 14 clear days before that hearing.][14]][11]

(14) In this section [and section 271AA][12], references to a standard special measure are to any of the following special measures—

(a) the use of a live television link in accordance with section 271J of this Act …[15]

(b) the use of a screen in accordance with section 271K of this Act, and

(c) the use of a supporter in accordance with section 271L of this Act …[15]

[(15) The Scottish Ministers may, by order subject to the affirmative procedure—

(a) modify subsection (14),

(b) in consequence of any modification made under paragraph (a)—

(i) prescribe the procedure to be followed when standard special measures are used, and

(ii) so far as is necessary, modify sections 271A to 271M of this Act.][16]][17]

1 Substituted by the Victims and Witnesses (Scotland) Act 2014, s 11(4)(b)(ii), (c), (e)(i), (f), (g)(ii), (iv), (h)(i), (i)(i), (m), (5).
2 Inserted by the Victims and Witnesses (Scotland) Act 2014, s 11(4)(a)(i), (b)(i), (d), (g)(i).
3 Substituted by the Criminal Justice and Licensing (Scotland) Act 2010, s 87(1), (3).
4 Repealed by the Victims and Witnesses (Scotland) Act 2014, s 11(4)(a)(ii), (b)(iii), (e)(ii), (g)(iii), (v), (h)(ii), (i)(ii), (j)-(l).
5 Substituted by the Vulnerable Witnesses (Criminal Evidence) (Scotland) Act 2019, s 6(1), (3)(a).
6 Substituted by the Criminal Procedure (Amendment) (Scotland) Act 2004, s 25, Schedule, paras 1, 43(a)-(c), (e), (f), (h)-(j).
7 Substituted by the Vulnerable Witnesses (Criminal Evidence) (Scotland) Act 2019, s 7.
8 Inserted by the Victims and Witnesses (Scotland) Act 2014, s 13(a), (c).
9 Substituted by the Victims and Witnesses (Scotland) Act 2014, s 13(b).
10 Substituted by the Vulnerable Witnesses (Criminal Evidence) (Scotland) Act 2019, s 10(1), (2).
11 Inserted by the Criminal Procedure (Amendment) (Scotland) Act 2004, s 25, Schedule, paras 1, 43(d), (g), (k).

12 Inserted by the Vulnerable Witnesses (Criminal Evidence) (Scotland) Act 2019, s 6(1), (3) (b)-(d).
13 Substituted by the Vulnerable Witnesses (Criminal Evidence) (Scotland) Act 2019, s 2(1), (3).
14 Substituted by the Vulnerable Witnesses (Criminal Evidence) (Scotland) Act 2019, s 8.
15 Repealed by the Victims and Witnesses (Scotland) Act 2014, s 12(a).
16 Inserted by the Victims and Witnesses (Scotland) Act 2014, s 12(b).
17 Substituted by the Vulnerable Witnesses (Scotland) Act 2004, s 1(1).

## *[271AA Using only standard special measures*

(1) This section applies where—

(a) a child witness or a deemed vulnerable witness is to give evidence at, or for the purposes of, a hearing in relevant criminal proceedings, and

(b) the party citing or intending to cite the witness considers that it is most appropriate for the witness to give evidence with the benefit of—

(i) one or more standard special measures, and

(ii) no other special measure.

(2) The party must, by the required time, lodge with the clerk of court a notice specifying—

(a) the standard special measure or measures that the party considers to be the most appropriate for the purpose of taking the witness's evidence,

(b) whether the witness is a child witness or a deemed vulnerable witness,

(c) if the witness is a child witness, the witness's age, and

(d) such other information as may be prescribed by Act of Adjournal.

(3) The party lodging a notice with the clerk of court under subsection (2) must, at the same time, intimate the notice to the other parties to the proceedings.

(4) If the party lodges a notice with the clerk of court by the required time, the witness is entitled to the benefit of the standard special measure or measures specified in the notice as if the use of that measure or measures were authorised by an order made by the court under section 271A(5)(a).

(5) If the party does not lodge a notice with the clerk of court by the required time, the court may, on cause shown, allow the party to lodge a vulnerable witness notice in accordance with section 271A (despite its being lodged later than the deadline for lodging a vulnerable witness notice).

(6) In this section, the 'required time' means—

(a) any time before a date has been fixed for one of the following—

(i) a preliminary hearing in the High Court,

(ii) a first diet in the sheriff court, or

(iii) a hearing at which the evidence is to be given, or

(b) if a date has been fixed—

(i) for a preliminary hearing in the High Court, no later than 14 clear days before the preliminary hearing,

(ii) for a first diet in the sheriff court in the case of proceedings on indictment, no later than 7 clear days before the first diet, or

(iii) in a case in which the proceedings are not to take place in the High Court or on indictment in the sheriff court, for a hearing at which the evidence is to be given, no later than 14 clear days before that hearing.

(7) This section does not apply in a case to which section 271B or 271BZA applies.][1]

1 Inserted by the Vulnerable Witnesses (Criminal Evidence) (Scotland) Act 2019, s 6(1), (2).

## *[271B Further special provision for child witnesses under the age of 12*

(1) This section applies where a child witness—

(a) is to give evidence at, or for the purposes of, [a hearing in relevant criminal proceedings][1] in respect of any offence specified in subsection (2) below, and

(b) is under the age of 12 on the date of commencement of the proceedings in which [the hearing][1] is being or to be held.

(2) The offences referred to in subsection (1)(a) above are—

(a) murder,

(b) culpable homicide,

(c) …[2]

(d) any offence which involves an assault on, or injury or a threat of injury to, any person (including any offence involving neglect or ill-treatment of, or other cruelty to, a child),

(e) abduction, …[2]

(f) plagium.

[(g) an offence to which section 288C applies (certain sexual offending),

(h) an offence under section 1(1) of the Domestic Abuse (Scotland) Act 2018,

(i) an offence that is aggravated as described in section 1(1)(a) of the Abusive Behaviour and Sexual Harm (Scotland) Act 2016.][3]

[(3) Subsection (4) applies if the child witness expresses a wish to be present in the court-room for the purpose of giving evidence.

(4) The court must make an order under section 271A or, as the case may be, 271D which has the effect of requiring the child witness to be present in the court-room for the purpose of giving evidence unless the court considers that it would not be appropriate for the child witness to be present there for that purpose.

[(4A) Where the court is required to make an order having the effect mentioned in subsection (4), an order made by the court under section 271A(5)(a) may authorise the use of a special measure or measures other than those specified in the vulnerable witness notice if that would result in the order having the effect mentioned in subsection (4).][4]

(5) Subsection (6) applies if the child witness—

(a) does not express a wish to be present in the court-room for the purpose of giving evidence, or

(b) expresses a wish to give evidence in some other way.

(6) The court may not make an order under section 271A or 271D having the effect mentioned in subsection (4) unless the court considers that—

(a) the giving of evidence by the child witness in some way other than by being present in the court-room for that purpose would give rise to a significant risk of prejudice to the fairness of the trial or otherwise to the interests of justice, and

(b) that risk significantly outweighs any risk of prejudice to the interests of the child witness if the order were to be made.][5]

[(7) This section does not apply in a case to which section 271BZA applies.][4]][6]

1 Substituted by the Criminal Justice and Licensing (Scotland) Act 2010, s 87(1), (4)(a), (b).
2 Repealed by the Domestic Abuse (Scotland) Act 2018, s 12(1), Schedule, para 6(1), (2)(a).
3 Inserted by the Domestic Abuse (Scotland) Act 2018, s 12(1), Schedule, para 6(1), (2)(b).
4 Inserted by the Vulnerable Witnesses (Criminal Evidence) (Scotland) Act 2019, s 2(1), (2).
5 Substituted by the Victims and Witnesses (Scotland) Act 2014, s 14(1).
6 Substituted by the Vulnerable Witnesses (Scotland) Act 2004, s 1(1).

## *[271BZA Child witnesses in certain solemn cases: special measures*

(1) This section applies where a child witness, other than the accused, is to give evidence at, or for the purposes of, a hearing in relevant criminal proceedings which are—

(a) solemn proceedings, and

(b) in respect of an offence listed in subsection (2).

(2) The offences are—

(a) murder,

(b) culpable homicide,

(c) assault to the danger of life,

(d) abduction,

(e) plagium,

(f) a sexual offence to which section 288C applies,

[(fa) an offence under any of sections 140 to 142 and 152 to 154 of the Health and Care Act 2022 (offences relating to virginity testing and hymenoplasty);][1]

(g) an offence under section 1(1) of the Domestic Abuse (Scotland) Act 2018,

(h) an offence that is aggravated as described in section 1(1)(a) of the Abusive Behaviour and Sexual Harm (Scotland) Act 2016,

(i) an offence that would have fallen within paragraph (h) if section 1 of the Abusive Behaviour and Sexual Harm (Scotland) Act 2016 had been in force when the offence was allegedly committed,

(j) an offence of human trafficking (see section 1 of the Human Trafficking and Exploitation (Scotland) Act 2015),

(k) an offence under section 4 of the Human Trafficking and Exploitation (Scotland) Act 2015 (slavery, servitude and forced or compulsory labour),

(l) an offence under section 1 of the Prohibition of Female Genital Mutilation (Scotland) Act 2005 (offence of female genital mutilation),

(m) an offence under section 3 of the Prohibition of Female Genital Mutilation (Scotland) Act 2005 (aiding and abetting female genital mutilation),

(n) an attempt to commit an offence mentioned in any of paragraphs (a) to (m).

(3) The court must enable all of the child witness's evidence to be given in advance of the hearing unless the court is satisfied that an exception is justified under subsection (7) or (8).

(4) For the purposes of this section, the court enables all of the child witness's evidence to be given in advance of the hearing if—

(a) the court makes an order under section 271A which satisfies the following requirements—

(i) it authorises the use of one or both of the special measures listed in subsection (5) for the purpose of taking all of the child witness's evidence,

(ii) it does not authorise the use of an incompatible special measure for the purpose of taking any of the child witness's evidence, and

(iii) it does not authorise the giving of any of the child witness's evidence without the benefit of any special measure, and

(b) the court, if it commences a review under section 271D before the hearing has commenced, does not make an order under that section which—

(i) revokes the order made under section 271A, or

(ii) varies it in such a way that it no longer satisfies the requirements set out in paragraph (a)(i), (ii) and (iii).

(5) The special measures mentioned in subsection (4)(a)(i) are—

(a) taking of evidence by a commissioner in accordance with section 271I,

(b) giving evidence in chief in the form of a prior statement in accordance with section 271M.

(6) In this section, 'incompatible special measure' means a special measure which is capable of being used only if the child witness gives evidence at the hearing (whether or not its use would require the child witness to be present in the courtroom).

(7) An exception is justified if—

(a) the giving of all of the child witness's evidence in advance of the hearing would give rise to a significant risk of prejudice to the fairness of the hearing or otherwise to the interests of justice, and

(b) that risk significantly outweighs any risk of prejudice to the interests of the child witness if the child witness were to give evidence at the hearing.

(8) An exception is justified if—

(a) the child witness is aged 12 or over on the date of commencement of the proceedings in which the hearing is being or is to be held,

(b) the child witness expresses a wish to give evidence at the hearing, and

(c) it would be in the child witness's best interests to give evidence at the hearing.

(9) The Scottish Ministers may by regulations—

(a) modify subsection (2),

(b) remove the condition set out in subsection (1)(b) and the list of offences in subsection (2).

(10) Regulations under subsection (9) are subject to the affirmative procedure.][2]

1 Inserted by the Health and Care Act 2022, s 160, Sch 16, paras 4, 6.
2 Inserted by the Vulnerable Witnesses (Criminal Evidence) (Scotland) Act 2019, s 1.

## *[271BZB Child witnesses in certain solemn cases: modifications of section 271A*

(1) In a case to which section 271BZA applies, section 271A applies with the following modifications.

(2) References to a standard special measure are to be read as references to any of the following special measures (and subsection (14) is to be read accordingly)—

(a) taking of evidence by a commissioner in accordance with section 271I,

(b) use of a supporter in accordance with section 271L,

(c) giving evidence in chief in the form of a prior statement in accordance with section 271M.

(3) Section 271A(2) has effect as if—

(a) the words 'Subject to section 271AA,' were omitted,

(b) the words 'or a deemed vulnerable witness' were omitted.

(4) Section 271A has effect as if the following subsection were inserted after subsection (2)—

'(2A) A vulnerable witness notice must—

(a) state that section 271BZA applies, and

(b) explain why the party considers that an exception is justified under section 271BZA(7) or (8) if the notice—

(i) does not specify one or both of the special measures listed in section 271BZA(5) for the purpose of taking all of the child witness's evidence,

(ii) specifies an incompatible special measure (as defined in section 271BZA(6)) for the purpose of taking any of the child witness's evidence, or

(iii) states that the party considers that the child witness should give any of the child witness's evidence without the benefit of any special measure.'.

(5) Section 271A has effect as if the following subsections were inserted after subsection (10)—

'(10A) Subsections (5), (9) and (10) are subject to subsections (10B) to (10F).

(10B) Where the court is considering a notice in accordance with subsection (5) and the notice does not specify one or both of the special measures mentioned in section 271BZA(5) for the purpose of taking all of the child witness's evidence, the court may nonetheless make an order which has the effect of authorising the use of one or both of those special measures for that purpose.

(10C) Unless the court is satisfied that an exception is justified under section 271BZA(7) or (8), an order made by the court under this section—

(a) must authorise the use of one or more of the special measures mentioned in section 271BZA(5) for the purpose of taking all of the child witness's evidence,

(b) must not authorise the use of an incompatible special measure (as defined in section 271BZA(6)) for the purpose of taking any of the child witness's evidence, and

(c) must not authorise the giving of any of the child witness's evidence without the benefit of any special measure.

(10D) Even if the court is satisfied that an exception is justified under section 271BZA(7) or (8), an order made by the court under this section must not have the effect of requiring the child witness to be present in the courtroom to give evidence unless the court is satisfied that subsection (10E) or (10F) applies.

(10E) This subsection applies if—

(a) the giving of evidence by the child witness in some way other than by being present in the courtroom for that purpose would give rise to a significant risk of prejudice to the fairness of the hearing or otherwise to the interests of justice, and

(b) that risk significantly outweighs any risk of prejudice to the interests of the child witness if the child witness were to be present in the courtroom to give evidence.

(10F) This subsection applies if—

(a) the child witness is aged 12 or over on the date of commencement of the proceedings in which the hearing is being held or is to be held,

(b) the child witness expresses a wish to be present in the courtroom to give evidence, and

(c) it would be in the child witness's best interests to be present in the courtroom to give evidence.'.][1]

1 Inserted by the Vulnerable Witnesses (Criminal Evidence) (Scotland) Act 2019, s 1.

## *[271BZC Child witnesses in certain solemn cases: modifications of section 271D*

(1) In a case to which section 271BZA applies, section 271D applies with the following modifications.

(2) Section 271D has effect as if—

(a) subsections (3A) to (3C) were omitted,

(b) subsection (4A) were omitted, and

(c) the following subsections were inserted after subsection (4A)—

'(4B) Subsections (2) to (4) are subject to subsections (4C) to (4H).

(4C) Unless the hearing has already commenced when the court commences its review or the court is satisfied that an exception is justified under section 271BZA(7) or (8), an order made by the court under this section must not—

(a) revoke the earlier order, or

(b) vary it in such a way that it no longer satisfies the requirements set out in section 271BZA(4)(a)(i), (ii) and (iii).

(4D) An order made by the court under this section must have the effect of authorising the use of the special measure of taking of evidence by a commissioner in accordance with section 271I if—

(a) that is requested by any party to the proceedings, and

(b) the earlier order authorises only the special measure of giving evidence in chief in the form of a prior statement in accordance with section 271M.

(4E) However, an order made by the court under this section need not have the effect described in subsection (4D) if—

(a) the hearing has already commenced when the court commences its review, or

(b) the court is satisfied that an exception is justified under section 271BZA(7) or (8).

(4F) Even if the hearing has already commenced when the court commences its review or the court is satisfied that an exception is justified under section 271BZA(7) or (8), an order made under this section must not have the effect of requiring the child witness to be present in the courtroom to give evidence unless the court is satisfied that subsection (4G) or (4H) applies.

(4G) This subsection applies if—

(a) the giving of evidence by the child witness in some way other than by being present in the courtroom for that purpose would give rise to a significant risk of prejudice to the fairness of the hearing or otherwise to the interests of justice, and

(b) that risk significantly outweighs any risk of prejudice to the interests of the child witness if the child witness were to be present in the courtroom to give evidence.

(4H) This subsection applies if—

(a) the child witness is aged 12 or over on the date of commencement of the proceedings in which the hearing is being held or is to be held,

(b) the child witness expresses a wish to be present in the courtroom to give evidence, and

(c) it would be in the child witness's best interests to be present in the courtroom to give evidence.'][1]

1 Inserted by the Vulnerable Witnesses (Criminal Evidence) (Scotland) Act 2019, s 1.

## *[271BA Assessment of witnesses*

(1) This section applies where a party intends to cite a witness other than a child witness or a deemed vulnerable witness to give evidence at, or for the purposes of, a hearing in relevant criminal proceedings.

(2) The party intending to cite the witness must take reasonable steps to carry out an assessment under subsection (3).

(3) An assessment must determine whether the person—

(a) is likely to be a vulnerable witness, and

(b) if so, what special measure or combination of special measures ought to be used for the purpose of taking the person's evidence.

(4) In determining under subsection (3)(a) whether a person is likely to be a vulnerable witness the party must—

(a) take into account the matters mentioned in section 271(2),

(b) have regard to the best interests of the person, and

(c) take account of any views expressed by the person.][1]

1 Inserted by the Victims and Witnesses (Scotland) Act 2014, s 16(1).

## *[271C [Vulnerable witness application][1]*

(1) This section applies where a party citing or intending to cite a person (other than a child witness [or a deemed vulnerable witness][2]) to give evidence at, or for the purposes of, [a hearing in relevant criminal proceedings][3] (such a person being referred to in this section as 'the witness') [and, having carried out an assessment under section 271BA,][2] considers—

(a) that the witness is likely to be a vulnerable witness, and

(b) that a special measure or combination of special measures ought to be used for the purpose of taking the witness's evidence.

(2) Where this section applies, the party citing or intending to cite the witness shall, [by the required time][4], make an application (referred to as a 'vulnerable witness application') to the court for an order authorising the use of one or more of the special measures for the purpose of taking the witness's evidence.

(3) A vulnerable witness application shall—

(a) specify the special measure or measures which the party making the application considers to be the most appropriate for the purpose of taking the evidence of the witness to whom the application relates, and

(b) contain or be accompanied by—

(i) a summary of any views expressed for the purposes of section 271E(2)(b) of this Act, and

(ii) such other information as may be prescribed by Act of Adjournal.

(4) The court may, on cause shown, allow a vulnerable witness application to be made after the [the required time][4].

[4A) Any party to the proceedings may, not later than 7 days after a vulnerable witness application has been lodged, lodge with the court a notice (referred to in this section as 'an objection notice') stating—

(a) an objection to any special measure specified in the vulnerable witness application that the party considers to be inappropriate, and

(b) the reasons for that objection.

(4B) The court may, on cause shown, allow an objection notice to be lodged after the period referred to in subsection (4A).

(4C) If an objection notice is lodged in accordance with subsection (4A) or (4B)—

(a) subsection (5) does not apply to the vulnerable witness application, and

(b) the court must make an order under subsection (5A).][5]

(5) The court shall, not [earlier than 7 days and not later than 14][6] days after a vulnerable witness application is made to it, consider the application in the absence of the parties and—

(a) make an order authorising the use of the special measure or measures specified in the application if satisfied on the basis of the application that—

(i) the witness in respect of whom the application is made is a vulnerable witness,

(ii) the special measures or measures specified in the application are the most appropriate for the purpose of taking the witness's evidence, and

(iii) it is appropriate to do so after having complied with the duty in subsection (8) below, or

(b) if not satisfied as mentioned in paragraph (a) above, [make an order under subsection (5A) below.][4]

[(5A) That order is an order—

(a) in the case of proceedings in the High Court where the preliminary hearing is yet to be held, appointing the vulnerable witness application to be disposed of at that hearing,

(b) in the case of proceedings on indictment in the sheriff court where the first diet is yet to be held, appointing the vulnerable witness application to be disposed of at that diet, or

(c) in any other case, appointing a diet to be held before [the hearing at which the evidence is to be given][3] and requiring the parties to attend the diet.][7]

(6) On making an order under subsection [(5A)(c)][4] above, the court may postpone [the hearing at which the evidence is to be given][3].

[(6A) Subsection (7) below applies to—

(a) a preliminary hearing or first diet so far as the court is, by virtue of an order under subsection (5A)(a) or (b) above disposing of a vulnerable witness application at the hearing or diet, and

(b) a diet appointed under subsection (5A)(c) above.][7]

(7) At a [hearing or diet to which this subsection applies][4], the court may—

(a) after giving the parties an opportunity to be heard, and

(b) if satisfied that the witness in respect of whom the application is made is a vulnerable witness,

make an order authorising the use of such special measure or measures as the court considers to be the most appropriate for the purpose of taking the witness's evidence.

(8) In deciding whether to make an order under subsection (5)(a) or (7) above, the court shall—

(a) have regard to—

 (i) the possible effect on the witness if required to give evidence without the benefit of any special measure, and

 (ii) whether it is likely that the witness would be better able to give evidence with the benefit of a special measure, and

(b) take into account the matters specified in subsection (2)(a) to (f) of section 271 of this Act.

(9) A [hearing or diet to which subsection (7) above applies][4] may—

(a) on the application of the party citing or intending to cite the witness in respect of whom the diet is to be held, or

(b) of the court's own motion,

be held in chambers.

(10) A diet [appointed under subsection (5A)(c) above in any case may be conjoined with any other diet to be held before [the hearing at which the evidence is to be given][3].][4]

(11) A party making a vulnerable witness application [or an objection notice][6] shall, at the same time, intimate the application [or, as the case may be, the notice][6] to the other parties to the proceedings.

[(12) In subsections(2) and (4) above, 'the required time' means—

(a) in the case of proceedings in the High Court, no later than 14 clear days before the preliminary hearing,

(b) in the case of proceedings on indictment in the sheriff court, no later than 7 clear days before the first diet,

(c) in any other case, no later than 14 clear days before [the hearing at which the evidence is to be given][3].][7]][8]

1 Substituted by the Victims and Witnesses (Scotland) Act 2014, s 11(6).
2 Inserted by the Victims and Witnesses (Scotland) Act 2014, s 16(2).
3 Substituted by the Criminal Justice and Licensing (Scotland) Act 2010, s 87(1), (5).
4 Substituted by the Criminal Procedure (Amendment) (Scotland) Act 2004, s 25, Schedule, paras 1, 44(a)-(c), (e), (g)-(i).
5 Inserted by the Victims and Witnesses (Scotland) Act 2014, s 17(a), (c).
6 Substituted by the Victims and Witnesses (Scotland) Act 2014, s 17(b).
7 Inserted by the Criminal Procedure (Amendment) (Scotland) Act 2004, s 25, Schedule, paras 1, 44(d), (f), (j).
8 Substituted by the Vulnerable Witnesses (Scotland) Act 2004, s 1(1).

## *[271D Review of arrangements for vulnerable witnesses*

(1) In any case in which a person who is giving or is to give evidence at or for the purposes of [a hearing in relevant criminal proceedings][1] (referred to in this section as the 'witness') is or appears to the court to be a vulnerable witness, the court may at any stage in the proceedings (whether before or after the commencement of [the hearing][1] or before or after the witness has begun to give evidence)—

(a) on the application of [any party to the proceedings][2], or

(b) of its own motion,

review the current arrangements for taking the witness's evidence and, after giving the parties an opportunity to be heard, make an order under subsection (2) below.

(2) The order which may be made under this subsection is—

(a) where the current arrangements for taking the witness's evidence include the use of a special measure or combination of special measures authorised by an order under section 271A or 271C of this Act or under this subsection (referred to as the 'earlier order'), an order varying or revoking the earlier order, or

(b) where the current arrangements for taking the witness's evidence do not include any special measure, an order authorising the use of such special measure or measures as the court considers most appropriate for the purpose of taking the witness's evidence.

(3) An order under subsection (2)(a) above varying an earlier order may—

(a) add to or substitute for any special measure authorised by the earlier order such other special measure as the court considers most appropriate for the purpose of taking the witness's evidence, or

(b) where the earlier order authorises the use of a combination of special measures for that purpose, delete any of the special measures so authorised.

[(3A) If an earlier order has the effect of enabling all of the witness's evidence to be given in advance of the hearing, the court may not make an order under subsection (2)(a) varying the earlier order in such a way that it no longer has that effect.

(3B) However, the court may vary the earlier order in the way mentioned in subsection (3A) if the hearing has already commenced when the court commences its review or if the court is satisfied—

(a) where the witness has expressed a wish to give evidence at the hearing, that it is appropriate for the witness to do so, or

(b) in any other case, that—

(i) if the court does not vary the earlier order in that way, there would be a significant risk of prejudice to the fairness of the hearing or otherwise to the interests of justice, and

(ii) that risk significantly outweighs any risk of prejudice to the interests of the witness if the court were not to vary the earlier order in that way.

(3C) For the purposes of this section, an order has the effect of enabling all of the witness's evidence to be given in advance of the hearing if—

(a) it authorises the use of one or both of these special measures for the purpose of taking all of the witness's evidence—

(i) taking of evidence by a commissioner in accordance with section 271I,

(ii) giving evidence in chief in the form of a prior statement in accordance with section 271M,

(b) it does not authorise the use of a special measure which is capable of being used only if the witness gives evidence at the hearing (whether or not its use would require the witness to be present in the courtroom), and

(c) it does not authorise the giving of any of the witness's evidence without the benefit of any special measure.][3]

(4) The court may make an order under subsection (2)(a) above revoking an earlier order only if satisfied—

(a) where the witness has expressed a wish to give or, as the case may be, continue to give evidence without the benefit of any special measure, that it is appropriate for the witness so to give evidence, or

(b) in any other case, that—

(i) the use, or continued use, of the special measure or measures authorised by the earlier order for the purpose of taking the witness's evidence would give rise to a significant risk of prejudice to the fairness of [the hearing][1] or otherwise to the interests of justice, and

(ii) that risk significantly outweighs any risk of prejudice to the interests of the witness if the order is made.

[(4A) In a case in which a notice has been provided to the clerk of court in accordance with section 271AA(2), this section is to have effect as if the special measure or measures specified in the notice were authorised by an order under section 271A.][4]

(5) Subsection (8) of section 271C of this Act applies to the making of an order under subsection (2)(b) of this section as it applies to the making of an order under subsection (5)(a) or (7) of that section but as if the references to the witness were to the witness within the meaning of this section.

(6) In this section, 'current arrangements' means the arrangements in place at the time the review under this section is begun.

[(6A) In this section, 'court' includes a commissioner appointed under section 271I(1).][5]

[(7) This section is subject to [sections 271B to 271BZC][6].][7]][8]

1 Substituted by the Criminal Justice and Licensing (Scotland) Act 2010, s 87(1), (6).
2 Substituted by the Victims and Witnesses (Scotland) Act 2014, s 18.
3 Inserted by the Vulnerable Witnesses (Criminal Evidence) (Scotland) Act 2019, s 4.
4 Inserted by the Vulnerable Witnesses (Criminal Evidence) (Scotland) Act 2019, s 6(1), (4).
5 Inserted by the Vulnerable Witnesses (Criminal Evidence) (Scotland) Act 2019, s 5(1), (8).
6 Substituted by the Vulnerable Witnesses (Criminal Evidence) (Scotland) Act 2019, s 10(1), (3).
7 Inserted by the Victims and Witnesses (Scotland) Act 2014, s 14(3).
8 Substituted by the Vulnerable Witnesses (Scotland) Act 2004, s 1(1).

## *[271E Vulnerable witnesses: supplementary provision*

(1) Subsection (2) below applies where—

(a) a party is considering for the purposes of a [vulnerable][1] witness notice[, a notice that is to be lodged with the clerk of court under section 271AA][2] or a vulnerable witness application which of the special measures is or are the most appropriate for the purpose of taking the evidence of the person to whom the notice or application relates, or

(b) the court is making an order under section 271A(5)(a)(ii) or (b) or (9), 271C or 271D of this Act.

(2) The party or, as the case may be, the court shall—

(a) have regard to the best interests of the witness, and

(b) take account of any views expressed by—

(i) the witness (having regard, where the witness is a child witness, to the witness's age and maturity), and

(ii) where the witness is a child witness, the witness's parent (except where the parent is the accused).

(3) For the purposes of subsection (2)(b) above, where the witness is a child witness—

(a) the witness shall be presumed to be of sufficient age and maturity to form a view if aged 12 or older, and

(b) in the event that any views expressed by the witness are inconsistent with any views expressed by the witness's parent, the views of the witness shall be given greater weight.

(4) In this section—

'parent', in relation to a child witness, means any person having parental responsibilities within the meaning of section 1(3) of the Children (Scotland) Act 1995 (c. 36) in relation to the child witness,

'the witness' means—

(a) in the case referred to in subsection (1)(a) above, the person to whom the notice or application relates,

(b) in the case referred to in subsection (1)(b) above, the person to whom the order would relate.][3]

1 Substituted by the Victims and Witnesses (Scotland) Act 2014, s 11(7).
2 Inserted by the Vulnerable Witnesses (Criminal Evidence) (Scotland) Act 2019, s 6(1), (5).
3 Substituted by the Vulnerable Witnesses (Scotland) Act 2004, s 1(1).

## *[271F The accused*

(1) For the purposes of the application of subsection (1) of section 271 of this Act to the accused (where the accused is giving or is to give evidence at or for the purposes of [a hearing in relevant criminal proceedings][1]), subsection (2) of that section shall have effect as if—

(a) for paragraph (c) there were substituted—

'(c) whether the accused is to be legally represented at [the hearing][1] and, if not, the accused's entitlement to be so legally represented,', and

(b) for paragraph (e) there were substituted—

'(e) any behaviour towards the accused on the part of—

(i) any co-accused or any person who is likely to be a co-accused in the proceedings,

(ii) any witness or any person who is likely to be a witness in the proceedings, or

(iii) members of the family or associates of any of the persons mentioned in sub-paragraphs (i) and (ii) above.'.

(2) Where, if the accused were to give evidence at or for the purposes of [the hearing][1], he would be a child witness—

(a) section 271A of this Act shall apply in relation to the accused subject to the following modifications—

(i) references to a [witness][2] shall be read as if they were references to the accused,

(ii) references to the party citing or intending to cite a …[3] witness shall be read as if they were references to the accused, and

(iii) subsection (6) shall have effect as if for paragraph (a) there were substituted—

'(a) it appears to the court that the accused, if he were to give evidence at or for the purposes of [a hearing in relevant criminal proceedings][1], would be a child witness,', and

[(aa) section 271AA applies in relation to the accused with the following modifications—

(i) in subsection (1)(a), the reference to a child witness or a deemed vulnerable witness is to be read as if it were a reference to the accused,

(ii) in subsections (1) to (5), references to the party citing or intending to cite the witness are to be read as if they were references to the accused,

(iii) in subsections (1)(b), (2)(a) and (4), references to the witness are to be read as if they were references to the accused,

(iv) subsection (2) has effect as if for paragraphs (b) and (c) there were substituted—

'(b) that the notice is lodged by the accused and that the accused is a child witness,

(c) the accused's age, and', and][4]

(b) section 271B of this Act shall apply in relation to the accused as if—

(i) for subsection (1) there were substituted—

'(1) This section applies where the accused—

(a) if he were to give evidence at or for the purposes of [a hearing in relevant criminal proceedings][1] would be a child witness, and

(b) is under the age of 12 on the date of commencement of the proceedings.', and

(ii) in subsection (3), references to the child witness were references to the accused.

(3) Subsection (4) below applies where the accused—

(a) considers that, if he were to give evidence at or for the purposes of [a hearing in relevant criminal proceedings][1], he would be a vulnerable witness other than a child witness, and

(b) has not decided to give evidence without the benefit of any special measures.

(4) Where this subsection applies, subsections (2) to (11) of section 271C of this Act shall apply in relation to the accused subject to the following modifications—

(a) references to the witness shall be read as if they were references to the accused,

(b) references to the party citing or intending the cite the witness shall be read as if they were references to the accused, and

(c) in subsection (8)(b), the reference to subsection (2)(a) to (f) of section 271 of this Act shall be read as if it were a reference to that subsection as modified by subsection (1) above.

(5) Section 271D of this Act shall apply in any case where it appears to the court that the accused, if he were to give evidence at or for the purposes of [the hearing][1], would be a vulnerable witness as it applies in the case referred to in subsection (1) of that section but subject to the following modifications—

(a) references to the witness shall be read as if they were references to the accused,

(b) references to the party citing or intending to cite the witness shall be read as if they were references to the accused.

(6) Where the witness within the meaning of section 271E of this Act is the accused, that section shall have effect in relation to the witness as if—

(a) in subsection (1), paragraph (a) were omitted, and

(b) in subsection (2), the words 'The party or, as the case may be,' were omitted.

(7) Section 271M of this Act shall have effect, where the vulnerable witness is the accused, as if the reference in subsection (2) to the party citing the vulnerable witness were a reference to the accused.

(8) The following provisions of this Act shall not apply in relation to a vulnerable witness who is the accused—

(a) section 271H(1)(c) [and (ea)][5],

(b) section 271I(3).][6]

1 Substituted by the Criminal Justice and Licensing (Scotland) Act 2010, s 87(1), (7).
2 Substituted by the Victims and Witnesses (Scotland) Act 2014, s 11(8)(a).
3 Repealed by the Victims and Witnesses (Scotland) Act 2014, s 11(8)(b).
4 Inserted by the Vulnerable Witnesses (Criminal Evidence) (Scotland) Act 2019, s 10(1), (4).
5 Inserted by the Victims and Witnesses (Scotland) Act 2014, s 20(3).
6 Substituted by the Vulnerable Witnesses (Scotland) Act 2004, s 1(1).

## *[271G Saving provision*

Nothing in sections 271A to 271F of this Act affects any power or duty which a court has otherwise than by virtue of those sections to make or authorise any special arrangements for taking the evidence of any person.][1]

1 Substituted by the Vulnerable Witnesses (Scotland) Act 2004, s 1(1).

## *[271H The special measures*

(1) The special measures which may be authorised to be used under section 271A, 271C or 271D of this Act for the purpose of taking the evidence of a vulnerable witness are—

(a) taking of evidence by a commissioner in accordance with section 271I of this Act,

(b) use of a live television link in accordance with section 271J of this Act,

(c) use of a screen in accordance with section 271K of this Act,

(d) use of a supporter in accordance with section 271L of this Act,

(e) giving evidence in chief in the form of a prior statement in accordance with section 271M of this Act, and

[(ea) excluding the public during the taking of the evidence in accordance with section 271HB of this Act,][1]

(f) …[2]

[(1A) The Scottish Ministers may, by order subject to the affirmative procedure—

(a) modify subsection (1),

(b) in consequence of any modification made under paragraph (a)—

(i) prescribe the procedure to be followed when special measures are used, and

(ii) so far as is necessary, modify sections 271A to 271M of this Act.][3]

(2) …[2]

(3) Provision may be made by Act of Adjournal regulating, so far as not regulated by sections 271I to 271M of this Act, the use in any proceedings of any special measure authorised to be used by virtue of section 271A, 271C or 271D of this Act.][4]

1 Inserted by the Victims and Witnesses (Scotland) Act 2014, s 20(1).
2 Repealed by the Victims and Witnesses (Scotland) Act 2014, s 21(a), (c).
3 Inserted by the Victims and Witnesses (Scotland) Act 2014, s 21(b).
4 Substituted by the Vulnerable Witnesses (Scotland) Act 2004, s 1(1).

## *[271HA Temporary additional special measures*

(1) The Scottish Ministers may, by order subject to the affirmative procedure, specify additional measures which for the time being are to be treated as special measures listed in section 271H(1).

(2) An order under subsection (1)

(3) An order under subsection (1) must specify—

(a) the area in which the additional measures may be used,

(b) the period during which the additional measures may be used, and

(c) the procedure to be followed when the additional measures are used.][1]

1 Inserted by the Victims and Witnesses (Scotland) Act 2014, s 19.

## *[271HB Excluding the public while taking evidence*

(1) This section applies where the special measure to be used in respect of a vulnerable witness is excluding the public during the taking of the evidence of the vulnerable witness.

(2) The court may direct that all or any persons other than those mentioned in subsection (3) are excluded from the court during the taking of the evidence.

(3) The persons are—

(a) members or officers of the court,

(b) parties to the case before the court, their counsel or solicitors or persons otherwise directly concerned in the case,

(c) bona fide representatives of news gathering or reporting organisations present for the purpose of the preparation of contemporaneous reports of the proceedings,

(d) such other persons as the court may specially authorise to be present.][1]

1 Inserted by the Victims and Witnesses (Scotland) Act 2014, s 20(2).

## *[271I Taking of evidence by a commissioner*

(1) Where the special measure to be used is taking of evidence by a commissioner, the court shall appoint a commissioner to take the evidence of the vulnerable witness in respect of whom the special measure is to be used.

[(1ZA) A court which appoints a commissioner under subsection (1) must—

(a) fix a date for the proceedings before the commissioner, and

(b) fix a date for a hearing (to be known as a 'ground rules hearing') for the purpose of preparing for the proceedings.

(1ZB) The ground rules hearing is to be presided over by—

(a) a judge of the court which appointed the commissioner if—

(i) the court directs that the ground rules hearing be conjoined with another hearing or diet that is to be held before the date of the proceedings to which the ground rules hearing relates and that hearing or diet is presided over by a judge, or

(ii) it is not reasonably practicable for the ground rules hearing to be presided over by the commissioner appointed to preside over the proceedings to which the ground rules hearing relates, or

(b) in any other case, the commissioner appointed to preside over the proceedings to which the ground rules hearing relates.

(1ZC) In cases where a judge presides over a ground rules hearing in accordance with subsection (1ZB)(a), references to the commissioner in subsection (1ZD) are to be read as references to the judge.

(1ZD) The commissioner presiding over a ground rules hearing must—

(a) ascertain the length of time the parties expect to take for examination-in-chief and cross-examination, including any breaks that may be required,

(b) to the extent that the commissioner considers it appropriate to do so, decide on the form and wording of the questions that are to be asked of the vulnerable witness,

(c) if the commissioner considers it appropriate to do so, authorise the use of a supporter at the proceedings, in accordance with section 271L,

(d) if the commissioner considers that there are steps that could reasonably be taken to enable the vulnerable witness to participate more effectively in the proceedings, direct that those steps be taken,

(e) subject to section 72(8) which applies in relation to the commissioner as it applies in relation to the court, dispose of any application that—

(i) has been made under section 275(1) or 288F(2), and

(ii) has not yet been disposed of by the court,

(f) consider whether the proceedings should take place on the date fixed by the court and postpone the proceedings if the commissioner considers that it is in the interests of justice to do so having regard to all the circumstances, including—

(i) whether the parties are likely to be ready for the proceedings to take place on the date fixed by the court and if not, the reasons for that,

(ii) any views expressed by the parties on whether the proceedings should be postponed, and

(iii) whether postponement is in the interests of the vulnerable witness, and

(g) consider and, if appropriate, make a decision on, any other matter that the commissioner considers could be usefully dealt with before the proceedings take place.][1]

[(1A) Proceedings before a commissioner appointed under subsection (1) above shall, if the court so directed when authorising such proceedings [or it was so directed at the ground rules hearing][1], take place by means of a live television link between the place where the commissioner is taking, and the place from which the witness is giving, evidence.][2]

(2) Proceedings before a commissioner appointed under subsection (1) above shall be recorded by video recorder.

(3) An accused—

(a) shall not, except by leave of the court on special cause shown, be [present—

(i) in the room where such proceedings are taking place; or

(ii) if such proceedings are taking place by means of a live television link, in the same room as the witness][3],

but

(b) is entitled by such means as seem suitable to the court to watch and hear the proceedings.

(4) The recording of the proceedings made in pursuance of subsection (2) above shall be received in evidence without being sworn to by witnesses.

[(4A) It is not necessary (in solemn cases) for an indictment to have been served before—

(a) a party may lodge a vulnerable witness notice which specifies the special measure of taking evidence by commissioner as the special measure or one of the special measures which the party considers to be the most appropriate for the purpose of taking the witness's evidence,

(b) a court may make an order authorising the use of the special measure of taking evidence by commissioner, whether on its own or in combination with any other special measure specified in the same vulnerable witness notice,

(c) a court may appoint a commissioner under subsection (1), or

(d) proceedings may take place before a commissioner appointed under subsection (1).][1]

[(5) Sections—

(a) 274;

(b) 275;

(c) 275B except subsection (2)(b);

(d) 275C;

(e) 288C;

(f) 288E; and

(g) 288F,

of this Act apply in relation to proceedings before a commissioner appointed under subsection (1) above as they apply in relation to a trial.

(6) In the application of those sections in relation to such proceedings—

(a) the commissioner acting in the proceedings is to perform the functions of the court as provided for in those sections;

(b) references—

(i) in those sections, except section 275(3)(c) and (7)(c), to a trial or a trial diet;

(ii) in those sections, except sections 275(3)(e) and 288F(2), (3) and (4), to the court,

shall be read accordingly;

(c) the reference in section 275B(1) to 14 days shall be read as a reference to 7 days.

(7) In a case where it falls to the court to appoint a commissioner under subsection (1) above, the commissioner shall be a person described in subsection (8) below.

(8) The persons are—

(a) where the proceedings before the commissioner are for the purposes of a trial [which the court (when it appoints the commissioner) expects will be][1] in the High Court, a judge of the High Court; or

(b) in any other case, a sheriff.][2]][4]

1 Inserted by the Vulnerable Witnesses (Criminal Evidence) (Scotland) Act 2019, s 5(1)-(5).
2 Inserted by the Criminal Proceedings etc. (Reform) (Scotland) Act 2007, s 35(3)(a), (c).
3 Substituted by the Criminal Proceedings etc. (Reform) (Scotland) Act 2007, s 35(3)(b).
4 Substituted by the Vulnerable Witnesses (Scotland) Act 2004, s 1(1).

## *[271J Live television link*

(1) Where the special measure to be used is a live television link, the court shall make such arrangements as seem to it appropriate for the vulnerable witness in respect of whom the special measure is to be used to give evidence from a place outside the court-room where [the hearing][1] is to take place by means of a live television link between that place and the court-room.

(2) The place from which the vulnerable witness gives evidence by means of the link—

(a) may be another part of the court building in which the court-room is located or any other suitable place outwith that building, and

(b) shall be treated, for the purposes of the proceedings at [the hearing][1], as part of the court-room whilst the witness is giving evidence.

(3) Any proceedings conducted by means of a live television link by virtue of this section shall be treated as taking place in the presence of the accused.

(4) Where—

(a) the live television link is to be used in proceedings in a sheriff court, but

(b) that court lacks accommodation or equipment necessary for the purpose of receiving such a link,

the sheriff may by order transfer the proceedings to any other sheriff court in the same sheriffdom which has such accommodation or equipment available.

(5) An order may be made under subsection (4) above—

(a) at any stage in the proceedings (whether before or after the commencement of [the hearing][1]), or

(b) in relation to any part of the proceedings.][2]

1 Substituted by the Criminal Justice and Licensing (Scotland) Act 2010, s 87(1), (8).
2 Substituted by the Vulnerable Witnesses (Scotland) Act 2004, s 1(1).

## *[271K Screens*

(1) Where the special measure to be used is a screen, the screen shall be used to conceal the accused from the sight of the vulnerable witness in respect of whom the special measure is to be used.

(2) However, the court shall make arrangements to ensure that the accused is able to watch and hear the vulnerable witness giving evidence.

(3) Subsections (4) and (5) of section 271J of this Act apply for the purpose of the use of a screen under this section as they apply for the purpose of the use of a live television link under that section but as if—

(a) references to the live television link were references to the screen, and

(b) the reference to receiving such a link were a reference to the use of a screen.][1]

1 Substituted by the Vulnerable Witnesses (Scotland) Act 2004, s 1(1).

## *[271L Supporters*

(1) Where the special measure to be used is a supporter, another person ('the supporter') nominated by or on behalf of the vulnerable witness in respect of whom the special measure is to be used may be present alongside the witness to support the witness while the witness is giving evidence.

(2) Where the person nominated as the supporter is to give evidence at [that or any other hearing in the proceedings][1], that person may not act as the supporter at any time before giving evidence.

(3) The supporter shall not prompt or otherwise seek to influence the witness in the course of giving evidence.][2]

1 Substituted by the Criminal Justice and Licensing (Scotland) Act 2010, s 87(1), (9).
2 Substituted by the Vulnerable Witnesses (Scotland) Act 2004, s 1(1).

## *[271M Giving evidence in chief in the form of a prior statement*

(1) This section applies where the special measure to be used in respect of a vulnerable witness is giving evidence in chief in the form of a prior statement.

(2) A statement made by the vulnerable witness which is lodged in evidence for the purposes of this section by or on behalf of the party citing the vulnerable witness shall, subject to subsection (3) below, be admissible as the witness's evidence in chief, or as part of the witness's evidence in chief, without the witness being required to adopt or otherwise speak to the statement in giving evidence in court.

(3) Section 260 of this Act shall apply to a statement lodged for the purposes of this section as it applies to a prior statement referred to in that section but as if—

- (a) references to a prior statement were references to the statement lodged for the purposes of this section,
- (b) in subsection (1), the words 'where a witness gives evidence in criminal proceedings' were omitted, and
- (c) in subsection (2), paragraph (b) were omitted.

(4) This section does not affect the admissibility of any statement made by any person which is admissible otherwise than by virtue of this section.

(5) In this section, 'statement' has the meaning given in section 262(1) of this Act.][1]

1 Substituted by the Vulnerable Witnesses (Scotland) Act 2004, s 1(1).

# Index

*References are to paragraph number.*

**D**